Ready Player Two

Ready Player Two

Women Gamers and Designed Identity

SHIRA CHESS

University of Minnesota Press

Minneapolis

London

Portions of this book were published as "A 36-24-36 Cerebrum: Productivity, Gender, and Video Game Advertising," *Critical Studies in Media Communications* 28, no. 3 (2010): 230–52. Portions of chapter 2 were published as "Going with the Flo: *Diner Dash* and Feminism," *Feminist Media Studies* 12, no. 1 (2011): 83–99.

Published by the University of Minnesota Press
111 Third Avenue South, Suite 290
Minneapolis, MN 55401-2520
http://www.upress.umn.edu

Printed in the United States of America on acid-free paper

The University of Minnesota is an equal-opportunity educator and employer.

22 21 20 19 18 17   10 9 8 7 6 5 4 3 2 1

Library of Congress Cataloging-in-Publication Data
Names: Chess, Shira, author.
Title: Ready player two : women gamers and designed identity / Shira Chess.
Description: Minneapolis : University of Minnesota Press, [2017] | Includes bibliographical references and index.
Identifiers: LCCN 2016043311 (print) | ISBN 978-1-5179-0068-7 (hc) |
ISBN 978-1-5179-0069-4 (pb)
Subjects: LCSH: Women video gamers—Psychology. | Video games—Design—
Psychological aspects. | Women—Identity.
Classification: LCC GV1469.34.P79 C44 2017 (print) | DDC 794.8—dc23
LC record available at https://lccn.loc.gov/2016043311

THIS BOOK IS DEDICATED TO MY MOTHER, CAROL CHESS.
FOR REASONS.

CONTENTS

PREFACE

When I began writing this book, I was a different person. This, unto itself, is not entirely unusual—like many of my colleagues have done with their own works, I began various versions of this project while writing my dissertation. Like this book, my dissertation was a study of the design and marketing of video games targeting women audiences. I completed my dissertation in 2009, following the height in popularity of the Nintendo Wii and Nintendo DS—a transformational moment for gendered gaming. Since that time, the video game industry has continued to change dramatically—what began as inklings of new kinds of games later became more developed and complex. For example, the seedlings of "time management games" (best characterized by *Diner Dash* and its successors) turned into the far more complex systems of the invest/express category (described in great detail in this book). As video game companies saw the monetary potential of marketing video games to women—even women who did not necessarily characterize themselves as gamers—new kinds of games developed and became increasingly robust.

But it is not only the games that have changed since 2005 when I began this journey. I, too, am a different person. When I started I was a single woman in my early thirties. I had not yet met my husband and had not yet had children. I was a graduate student, unemployed beyond a meager graduate stipend. And, in this, my writing was a touch self-righteous. I wrote in great detail about how video games designed for and marketed to women tended to treat all women players as though they were mothers—regardless of whether they occupy this identity in the real world. As presumed mothers their play was meant to be necessarily productive, filling holes of time or functioning as a backdrop to emotional labor. While gaming has changed over the past decade, these aspects have not (although, perhaps, they have become more refined and sometimes a bit more difficult to spot).

While the attributes of gendered gaming have gone relatively unchanged, my perspective on these aspects has changed dramatically. As a single woman graduate student in my thirties, it was very easy to look down on games such as those made for the Nintendo Wii system that were so heavily marketed to mothers (ca. 2006) as a method of gaining love and family togetherness through play. I could look cynically at these ploys and suggest that all women had the right to play, and that play should not be for others; rather, play should be selfish and personal. Similarly, I was troubled by Nintendo DS advertisements that suggested women use small snippets of time to play, as opposed to the long spans of time suggested to men in advertisements for games such as those in the *Madden NFL* series. "Why can't we just have women play for the sake of play?" my dissertation seemed to ask.

Ten years, a tenure-track position, a husband, and a child later, this question feels entirely naïve. I would love a video game that my family could play together. The games I play, I play for research. And most of them, I should add, I play in small snippets of time—whatever is allowed by my busy schedule. When I tell people that I study video games I shrug loosely when they inevitably ask, "Oh . . . what do you play for fun?" I play for work. My play is almost 100 percent productive. Sometimes it feels as though my dissertation was predictive of my own path in life.

And given this shift, one that was inevitable to my own life choices, there is a subtler thing happening here that I cannot possibly deny. When I began this project in 2005, the games I wrote about were not really being designed for *me*. They were being designed, as I already noted, for busy mothers who were looking for snippets of relaxation. And because of that, I was never the target market for the games I studied. My position allowed me the ability to see these games from the perspective of an onlooker.

But as a working parent in her early forties, I am now the person for whom these games are actually *made*. To clarify, what I had written in the paragraphs above implies that my perspective on the games has, itself, shifted dramatically in the past ten years. What I am saying now is different: it is not just that I see these games differently, but that all of a sudden these games are *made for me*. I have become a target market within the central position of my study. This, of course, does not make my work autoethnographic—I am not writing about my feelings or myself during the process of play.[1] I have, however, become strangely entangled with my object of study. I play with the keen understanding that I am part of an idealized audience constructed by the video game industry.

The idealization, though, goes beyond my positionality as a working mother. Although this is part of it, as an intersectional feminist it is impossible for me to look at my own subject position in my research without acknowledging that I am white, middle class, heterosexual, able-bodied, and cis-gendered. Throughout this book, this is the subject position that is presumed to be the identity markers for an idealized woman gamer. This is not to say that game companies would not accept other kinds of players—rather, it is to imply that these players will always be necessarily "othered." My body, my position, implies that I am the game player for whom companies are looking.

At varying points in this project, I have found myself relating heavily to Ruth Schwartz Cowan's groundbreaking book *More Work for Mother: The Ironies of Household Technology from the Open Hearth to the Microwave*. In this book, Cowan documents the historical trajectory of how household technologies create a kind of make-work for their market, producing a system where women will always need to be supplying domestic labor. What strikes me the most, though, in my memory of this book is never the historical aspects but rather the personal. In her conclusion, Cowan writes of how she is of two minds. On the one hand she is fully aware of how she is being manipulated by advertising and technologies and through fear of social stigma to complete specific unnecessary domestic chores. On the other hand, she confesses that she finds it difficult to break out of these culturally predicated norms.

In a similar capacity, I have a mixed relationship with the technologies of play. I am aware that specific kinds of playful technologies are created for *me* and *my* lifestyle, but I feel a constant need to resist the rhetoric of those technologies. My privilege gives me more capacity to break these norms than most—the market conditions help support me to play a never-ending number of casual games that have been designed specifically for me. Yet it is difficult to lose myself in the process of play in the way it was intended. When I play, I feel guilty. I often even remind myself that my video game play is part of work, and therefore justified. I am both trapped and freed by the boundaries of my physical body, career choices, and cultural position. As such, this book might be seen as my own treatise toward a complicated relationship with play, vis-à-vis aging, family, and work life.

While the video game industry and my personal life have changed in the past ten years, another unexpected change has taken hold within our larger cultural landscape: GamerGate, a so-called hashtag movement that began under that name in 2014 (although its seeds can be spotted several years earlier). Others, at this point, have begun to write about GamerGate in quite a bit of detail, which is not my goal here. In short, GamerGate is a movement of hate speech wherein young, primarily male gamers have attacked, doxxed (publishing personal information about an individual), and threatened women in and commenting on the video game industry. Most notably, GamerGate targeted indie game designer Zoë Quinn and cultural critic Anita Sarkeesian, bombarding them online with death and rape threats. Within the larger public sphere, GamerGate advocates have insisted that they are not a hate group but rather that their goal concerns "ethics in game journalism." But the troubling actions of the individuals who have associated themselves with the larger group have forever connected the entire movement with a kind of bullying political position.

GamerGate has been a catalyst for change in the way that many people—gamers, nongamers, feminists, journalists, and audiences—think about video games. This project began before GamerGate, but this book was written during its fallout. This book sits under a dust cloud of Gamer-Gate, a topic that has influenced me in a number of ways. For the most part, I have gone primarily unscathed in terms of GamerGate harassment (although not all of my colleagues have been this lucky). My one brief brush with GamerGate conspiracy theorists has been documented,[2] and for the most part I have been able to observe their behaviors with critical distance. Yet, when this project began around 2005, one could say that GamerGate was both unexpected and inevitable, all at once.

On one level, my work and this project would seem to have absolutely nothing to do with GamerGate. GamerGate's culture war seems to be accusing the influx of women gamers on a shift in style and quality within the industry. While most of the accusations seem without merit, the proponents of GamerGate appear to be claiming that the white male gamer should remain central as the primary gaming audience. When GamerGate proponents write about games, they generally focus on console gaming and what is commonly referred to as "hardcore games," with occasional nods to Steam games and indie games as outliers (and what they acknowledge as a large part of the problem). Many people who associate themselves with the GamerGate movement, for example, heavily criticized Zoë

Quinn's Twine game *Depression Quest*, and similar criticisms have been brought against other recent indie games such as *Gone Home*. The culture war is often poised as a distinction between the hardcore and indie game makers and players.

But when I think about the games I have been studying for ten years now, I see other things at play. It is not only indie games that have transformed the video game industry (although, certainly, they have played a large part in this transformation). The theorized woman player who haunts this book is a central character in how GamerGate happened. As the video game industry began to recognize that young white men were not the only consumer audience, game companies funneled money into alternative modes of gaming and payment models. This shift began subtly in the early 2000s and may have formed the roots of what later became GamerGate. In some ways, I might argue that GamerGate is not only responding to the emergence of women players but is also evidence of the fading dominance of what is often considered the primary audience of video games. The rapid growth and changes to the industry have created a level of anxiety that has supported violent hate speech. Yet these very changes have also turned a medium that had formerly been highly targeted to one with far more mass appeal.

It is with these points of context that this book emerges. A book based on social technologies is a complicated thing to write. In the process of revisions, not only does the author change but so do the ephemeral technologies and culture around them. Surely, by the time this book emerges on the market they will change again, although in less volatile ways than GamerGate. The goal of this book is not to highlight the negative aspects that have engendered recent criticism of the video game industry. Rather, it is to shine a light on the positive aspects via an emerging form of video game play that has become a catalyst for change in video game culture, video game audiences, and the video game industry itself. The games, as I discuss throughout this book, are not ideal—they shed light on both positive and negative assumptions about women and leisure, as well as ethnicity, class, sexuality, and other points of diversity. Yet the games also are the harbinger of positive changes and the revelatory new styles of play that will continue to transform what it means to be a player.

Contextualizing Player Two

NOW WE'RE KNITTING WITH POWER?

In the late 1980s the video game industry, and console gaming in particular, was primarily caught up with their mainstay audience—young boys and men. While there were certainly girls and women who played video games at the time, this was not the primary target audience of the industry. The tacit assumption was that those who paid for and played console game systems were primarily male.

Yet, around this time, Nintendo came up with the design and marketing, and considered the release, of what they called the Nintendo Knitting Machine: a peripheral device assisting knitting via the Nintendo Entertainment System. The "game" was never released to wide audiences.[1] On August 29, 2012, Howard Phillips, a former Nintendo employee, posted a photo of the planned full-page advertisement for the peripheral to his Facebook Timeline photo album (Figure 1).[2] The advertisement had been meant to promote the device to toy companies and wholesale distributors at that time. The single-page image, featuring a photo of the peripheral, leads with the headline "NOW YOU'RE KNITTING WITH POWER" and explains:

> You're looking at the Nintendo Knitting Machine.
> It's not a game; not a toy; not something a young girl can outgrow in three or six months or even a year.
> It's a machine that interacts with the powerful Nintendo Entertainment System to actually knit sweaters: and not just one or two patterns but a multitude of different and unique designs.

The Nintendo Knitting Machine is just one more example of the innovative thinking that keeps Nintendo on the cutting edge of video technology. And your customers at the edge of their seats.

Of course we should probably mention that no other video game system offers anything even remotely similar. But why needle the competition?

While the system was apparently demoed for corporations and at toy shows, it never was released to American audiences.[3]

But the advertisement—the best piece of evidence that the Nintendo Knitting Machine was once considered the "cutting edge" of gaming technology—raises several pertinent questions. First, for whom was this system meant? The advertisement mentions "girls," but a more specific demographic (or whether the peripheral would also be marketed to knitting women) is ambiguous. Second, why did Nintendo feel the need to try to appeal to female audiences in the mid-1980s? No other serious attempts were being made to market console systems to women and girls at this time, and yet Nintendo clearly saw that this demographic might be viable enough to design not only software but an entire peripheral for them. Finally, and most important, it becomes necessary to ask, what happened to the Nintendo Knitting Machine? Why did it disappear, and why was it rejected as a model to get girls and women more interested in gaming?[4]

Beyond the video game industry, though, there are other compelling aspects to the advertisement from a media and cultural studies perspective. The headline of the advertisement suggests that the Nintendo Knitting Machine is a tool of empowerment. But in what way is the peripheral actually empowering? Rather than being a gateway for girls or women interested in gaming, the machine repurposes stereotypes of women in terms of their desire to engage with leisure and play.[5] It allows for non-masculine play but manages that play, parsing it into specific forms of femininity. The Nintendo Knitting Machine suggests that domesticity and labor are the only possible entry points for females interested in engaging with the then rapidly changing and playful technologies of the video game industry. The advertisement leads off with a promise of empowerment, but there is nothing empowering about what is being offered. The suggestion that the peripheral—certainly not a game—would offer a perfect solution to the fickle tastes of young girls who would only have a fleeting interest in "games" or "toys" is a selling point of this technology. The system suggests a condescending solution to the complex problem of leisure and diversification. It manages the potential of gender diversity by

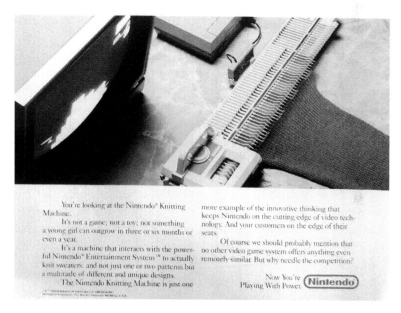

Figure 1. A 1980s advertisement for the Nintendo Knitting Machine raises important questions about the machine's intended demographic. The image was posted on former Nintendo employee Howard Phillips's Facebook page in 2012.

reaffirming common stereotypes about how women and girls are expected to play. And, yet, this absurd example, the Nintendo Knitting Machine, is not alone. While, in recent years, there is an increasing amount of diversity in terms of *whom* video games are being created for, those attempts reflect larger issues regarding gender and leisure, a topic explored at length in this book. At the same time, it is important to not dismiss the Nintendo Knitting Machine in terms of the desire it represents. Clearly certain members of the video game industry recognized and were attempting to respond to the hegemonic masculinity that so deeply guided the ethos of digital play. While the attempt itself was misguided—even comical—the fact that it existed shows promise that change was on the (very distant) horizon.

That change is upon us now. We are entering a new age of digital play—one marked by the sheer volume of games that are being heavily marketed to woman and girl audiences yet remains in flux. Many books have been dedicated to understanding the games that came out of what could be characterized as the first wave of digital games. The games in this era fall into several genres and categories (such as first-person shooters, plat-formers, fighting games, and role-playing games). This book in no way is meant to suggest that female audiences have no interest in these genres. There are well-documented moments that neatly illustrate that many of these games have been loved by a variety of people. Yet it is impossible to disentangle this early video game industry from the masculine forces that drove it.[6] While women and girls indeed *played* these games, they have often been considered outliers, marginalized, pushing their way into a space not originally intended for them.

The second wave of video games can be characterized by a feminine ethos of leisure. This leisure is complicated and messy, and does not always look like play from every angle. It is often demeaned by the video game industry itself, treated as a lesser mode of digital play. And still, it is the harbinger of what is to come. The push and pull of gendered leisure practices are central to this new mode of gaming: like it or not, we are ready for the player I characterize as "Player Two."

The complicated representation of gender and leisure via video games (discussed in detail throughout this book) is by no means surprising. Mass media has long had tumultuous relationships with women's genres, fram-ing women as consumptive of specific styles and themes while simulta-neously mocking those very media objects designed for and marketed to them. For example, the romance—whether in film, television, or book form—is deliberately designed for and marketed to women.[7] Yet, when women show interest or desire in the genre, often they are doing so despite a broad dismissal of the perceived cultural value of those media objects. Melodramas, "chick flicks," romances, and soap operas all are held to be inferior to popular formats that are perceived as more masculine.

This trend has followed through to video games. In recent years, an increasing number of video games have been designed for women and subsequently advertised to them. Currently, females make up approximately 50 percent of the gaming public.[8] Much like the Nintendo Knitting Machine, the games that are deliberately designed for women often repurpose genres, themes, stereotypes, and expectations of feminine styles of play. Additionally, similar to previous forms of media, games designed for women are often overlooked and dismissed as having no importance or value. Yet these games are important. The games discussed in this book are often small—in scope, in budget, and in narrative form—but they are full of meaning. They take on the work of helping us understand the larger issues at play in terms of gender and leisure practices in a more general sense, as well as the larger stories of how they are embedded within the video game industry as a whole.

By analyzing this new mode of feminized digital play, it becomes easier to reconcile the positive and negative baggage it carries. The themes and genres of gendered gaming are not arbitrary. They illustrate strange and compelling patterns and draw a very specific picture of what an idealized woman gamer might look like and how that woman should play. Within this, I am making a strong distinction between the real, lived experiences of women players as opposed to the perception of women players as they are constructed, designed, and managed by the video game industry. I refer to this as "designed identity."

Designed identity is a by-product—an unintended consequence of the repurposing of women's leisure practices into digital play, and the result of industrial forces that idealize specific (lucrative) audiences. Designed identity is a hybrid outcome of industry conventions, textual constructs, and audience placements in the design and structure of video games. It is not exclusive to women—and one can easily argue that the masculine gamer identity of the past is similarly a kind of designed identity. In her book *Coin-Operated Americans: Rebooting Boyhood at the Video Game Arcade*, Carly Kocurek deftly analyzes the construction of the male gamer identity, beginning in the 1970s through analysis of several forms of media. The games and media in this book, however, are almost exclusively intended for women and, in large part, reflect a tenuous relationship between women and leisure. By invoking the notion of designed identity, this book does not emphasize the rich body of literature in identity politics research. The "identities" in question are not real, lived identities, but rather constructed identities suggested within game design, advertising, and narrative. Designed identity allows specific women to be a valid sales point for companies attempting to tap into this emerging demographic, but it also operates as a means of keeping that very demographic in stasis. An unchanging demographic has predictable consumer needs that are easy to satisfy.

The woman player I discuss throughout this book is not a real player so much as a theoretical player—a fictionalized construction of the video game industry. She is a ghost, a shadow. Much as with the theorized player of the Nintendo Knitting Machine, this theoretical woman player is trapped within the stereotypes of expectation. But she is also powerful. She illustrates the influence the consumer can have to reform and change a system that was not initially intended for her. This book explores the content of games and game design to provide a framework for understanding what designed identity tells us about our cultural expectations of women's leisure and relationship to technology. By invoking designed identity, I focus on ways the theoretical woman player is managed through but also plays with gaming technologies: through time, emotions, consumption, and bodies. Ultimately, my goal is not to draw a clearer picture of *actual* women gamers whose experiences and play styles are much broader than the technologies that are built for them, but rather to discuss the larger shifts within and around the video game industry that are both inviting in women audiences yet keeping them at bay.

WHO IS PLAYER TWO?

I refer to this mode of designed identity, this not-quite-real player, as Player Two. If Player One is the—also designed—white, cis-, heterosexual, young, abled, and middle-class male, then Player Two becomes his counterpart as a mode of designed identity. Just as Player One was designed and marketed, bought and sold in terms of a specific, approved identity, so is Player Two. The designed identity of Player Two, like Player One, is a fiction, an amalgamation of many hybridized images of who should play, how they should play, and what that play looks like. Player Two is a ghost, a nonexistent construction, but also one that is rapidly changing the market. On the one hand, the games made for Player Two appear to be limiting and limited—small in scope and absurd in meaning. When compared to the vast and operatically complex games designed for Player One (e.g., those in the *Fallout* or *Metal Gear Solid* series), it might be easy to overlook the importance and value of Player Two games such as *Hungry Babies Mania* or *Kim Kardashian: Hollywood*. These games do not appear to be about life-and-death issues; they represent small stories with small outcomes. And yet these games are important.

Why are these games important? Because they are rapidly changing the video game industry. No matter how many dismissive news articles are written about the *FarmVille* franchise[9] or free-to-play games, and no matter how many industry people ignore the growing popularity of hidden object games such as the *Mystery Case Files* series, their popularity continues to rise. Player Two and her games are inviting in new kinds of players that the industry had not previously served. And while there are still limitations placed on the industry-constructed woman player, that new player has the *potential* to become an important power in redefining what the video game industry looks like.

The book title *Ready Player Two* is meant as a conscious nod toward Earnest Cline's dystopian futuristic novel *Ready Player One*. *Ready Player One* submerges the reader into two worlds simultaneously: a bleak corporate-run real world full of poverty and a robust, all-encompassing game world. This dual-world system is not an unusual trope in science fiction. The story follows a young, white male, Wade, who is attempting to win a massive Easter egg hunt within the virtual world. The hunt's creator—the deceased billionaire James Halliday—has decided, à la Willy Wonka, to will control of the game world and his vast wealth to the winner of the game: the finder of this egg. Halliday is described as the child of a working-class, white family (his whiteness is never explicitly stated, but implied). The book details that "by all accounts, James was a bright boy, but socially inept. He had an extremely difficult time communicating with people around him. Despite his obvious intelligence, he did poorly in school, because most of his attention was focused on computers, comic books, sci-fi and fantasy novels, movies, and above all else, video games."[10] Because of Halliday's own obsession with geek culture from the 1980s, the players of the egg hunt have become obsessed with (and connoisseurs of) films, video games, television shows, and other cultural aspects of the 1980s. The 1980s is treated, as such, as a kind of golden age of gaming. And because the real world in the game—the corporate dystopia—is so bleak, the 1980s stands in contrast, idealized and glorified as a perfect point in history. Halliday is worshipped as a kind of god of this improbable version of the 1980s.

In turn, the novel unavoidably, and simultaneously, glorifies something else: the white masculinity that prevailed during the 1980s. Through constant references to films and sitcoms like *Revenge of the Nerds, Real Genius, Silver Spoons*; white male bands like Rush and Def Leppard; and male computer game programmers, we are reminded as to who "Player One" actually is, and has long since been—a white, heterosexual, cisgendered male. This point is further reinforced when our white male protagonist takes the lead within the competition, a game created by a white man. For sure, the book has strong characters that do not fit into the structural paradigm of glorifying white masculinity. However, like the 1980s media it venerates, the white, heterosexual, cis-gendered males are ultimately the characters that win the game. Yet it is also white males that run the corporate dystopia, suggesting that (perhaps) this rule of white masculinity is a double-edged sword.

In recent years, many have remarked on the privilege of the white geek male, in the popular press[11] and academic writing,[12] as well as specific ramifications of this persona on video game culture.[13] There has long been a sense that this character—the misunderstood white geek male—was an underdog who would use his smarts to gain access to and ultimately reign triumphant against the perceived bullies of his youth. Recent criticisms of this character, though, highlight how the geeky white male perpetuates similar kinds of sexist, heterosexist, and racist undercurrents. This white geeky guy has been idealized (and monetized) in popular culture to the extent that he is now the focal market for the primary video game industry—the console and PC gamer. Culturally and capitalistically, he is Player One.

But there are other players rapidly emerging within the video game market. *Ready Player Two* is meant, in part, as a response to the idealized 1980s youthful white male gamer, as glorified in the designed identity integral to *Ready Player One*. If the novelized version of Player One leads to a dystopian, exclusive society trapped in a classist system, wherein the only release is a game world that glorifies the culture of the (admittedly complicated) 1980s, then Player Two gets to hit the reset button. We are moving beyond the traditional depictions of the popular gamer. Player One no longer gets to define what games and gaming culture look like. We are entering a new phase wherein Player Two, the player highlighted throughout this book, has a distinct voice. And this voice is exactly why these games are so very significant.

VIDEO GAMES AND GENDER: A BRIEF HISTORY

It was not always like this. Video games were not always gendered. There was not always even an attempt at diversity. Over the brief history of video games, much has changed in terms of technology, audience engagement, game mechanics, and play styles. Very early games such as *Pong* (both in the arcade and home versions) were meant primarily for family play.[14] In the late 1970s and early 1980s, arcades were meant to be social places and not necessarily gendered. Early game characters tended to be so pixelated and abstract that it was difficult to make them represent gender in a coherent way (although a few did), and these games were generally meant to appeal to both sexes. Some early games such as *Ms. Pac Man* and *Centipede* were specifically popular with female audiences.[15] The Atari 2600 and the Nintendo Entertainment System—released in 1977 and 1983, respectively—maintained this primarily gender-neutral space, although games such as *Super Mario Bros.*, where the goal was rescuing Princess Peach, perhaps were early predictors of the masculine undertone of video games.[16] The dominance of male protagonists in any form of mass media should not be terribly surprising, though. Much like film and television, video games during this time were primarily dominated by male protagonists, with female protagonists taking secondary roles—if they had any role at all. Carly Kocurek, however, argues that "gender inequalities in video gaming did not develop during the industry's postcrash resurrection or with the rise of home consoles; rather, these historical inequalities emerged through public discourse and public practice that accompanied the rise of video gaming's early commercial success in the coin-op industry."[17] In other words, while the industry had claimed inclusivity in its early days, the underlying masculinity was at play within popular cultural representations for quite some time.

In 1989, the release of the Sega Genesis began to establish video games as a masculine domain, with more mature games such as an uncensored version of *Mortal Kombat* as well as more advanced sports games. At this point home console gaming moved from the domain of being a family system to one primarily marketed to men and boys. In the years that followed, the Super Nintendo Entertainment System (1991) and the PlayStation (1995) maintained this stance of boys and men as the primary target audience. Computer games, too, began to market increasingly to men with multiplayer first-person shooters such as *Doom* and *Quake*.[18] By the 1990s, what could have easily been a relatively gender-neutral form of mass media had become almost exclusively masculine territory.

In the mid-to-late 1990s there began a slow emergence of video games specifically targeting young girls, after research began to illustrate that it might help create more interest in STEM careers. Games such as *Barbie Fashion Designer* were wildly popular but lacked any actual gamelike qualities—they functioned more as software to play with other objects (in this case, Barbie dolls).[19] Famously, Purple Moon was a game company run by the feminist game designer Brenda Laurel, who created games such as *Rockett's New School* and the *Secret Paths* series. Laurel was largely unsuccessful, though, and Purple Moon went out of business in 1999, although her games are fondly remembered as an important outlier pushing the margins.[20] For many years, most of the popular games targeting young girls simply repositioned other popular licensed characters (such as Barbie or Hannah Montana), turning them into video games.

As previously implied, many women did play digital games during this period, but they were often not games specifically designed for women, or even assumed to be gender-neutral. In the 1990s, many women played games that were primarily targeted at male audiences. Gaming leagues such as the PMS Clan and the Frag Dolls helped to form a point of gender resistance and persuade gamers and game companies that certain women did want to play.[21] In recent years, Kishonna Gray's study of women of color playing Xbox Live demonstrates different ways that women have performed resistance in these primarily masculine spaces.[22] The goal of this book, however, is not looking at ways that women and girls have entered this masculine domain, often encountering great resistance. Instead, my focus is on the games that have been made specifically for female audiences. While women often play games that are meant for men (and, vice versa, men often play games that are intended for women), the goal is to try and better understand the games deliberately made for women, to better illustrate what those games might *mean*: about gender constructions, about leisure practices, and about digital play.

As Gray's work illustrates, women are not entirely new to video games—even those that might have been initially intended for masculine audiences. Of note, the rise of massively multiplayer online games (MMOGs) such as *EverQuest* and *World of Warcraft* brought a new kind of diversity to gaming audiences. The anonymity of online play, the flexibilities of play styles, and the ability to select one's own appearance were only a few reasons why the MMOG seemed to appeal to women players. In her ethnographic study of *EverQuest*, T. L. Taylor suggests that it is worth examining the women who play MMOGs precisely because they are not the expected market: "Revisiting the number of women playing the major MMOGs shows that the figures are quite remarkable given they are not the demographic being targeted. In many ways, women play in spite of barriers to entry. Women players are finding fascinating and complicated pleasures in online games."[23] However, even with MMOGs, women players did not become a specific marketing or design focus of the video game industry. They seemed to function as by-product of robust play. While researchers took great pains to study the how and why of an increasingly diverse audience in MMOGs, the games were still understood as a kind of exception. Furthermore, it is worth considering that certain industry practices maintained toxic environments for female players. One recent study, for example, determined that women and girls are less likely to play video games that force players to reveal their identities via voice chat.[24]

Some video game spaces are considered more gender-neutral than others. Computer game series such as *The Sims* and *Myst*, and the popular Nintendo series *Animal Crossing*, all typically boast diverse audiences. Not only do both men and women play these games, but they also often create and modify game worlds in compelling ways. Hanna Wirman, for example, discusses ways that female game modders reskinned *The Sims* to fit into their own desires and cultural contexts.[25] After the shutdown of the game *Uru* (an online sequel to the popular game *Myst*), Celia Pearce documented the diasporic behaviors of diverse players seeking to find a similar experience in other online worlds.[26] Similarly, domestic play has given rise to more inclusive experiences in game worlds. Alison Harvey has demonstrated the use of video games to structure and regulate family play within the domestic sphere, particularly relating to the Nintendo Wii entertainment system.[27]

Given this messy history, it becomes clear that the video game industry has been structured in such a way that the majority of big-budget games (often referred to as AAA titles) have been designed for a predominantly male audience (often referred to as "hardcore gamers").[28] This, of course, is unsurprising—a primarily male workforce has long made up the majority of the industry. In a 2007 poll, only 11 percent of those working in the video game industry were women.[29] In recent years, this number has doubled,[30] but only after years of critics (both inside and outside of gaming culture) pushing for industry change. Still, the realities of how video game companies function—with demanding crunch times and long hours—are often not amenable to a female workforce.[31]

Thus, for a long time the industry ran in cycles that rewarded masculinity and devalued feminine style. In their essay "The Hegemony of Play," Janine Fron, Tracy Fullerton, Jacquelyn Ford Morie, and Celia Pearce elaborate on how the hegemony endemic to the video game industry makes it impenetrable to diverse audiences. While the essay was written at a time before some of these industry changes began, it still breaks down the larger systemic issues at play. They explain:

> The power elite of the game industry is a predominately white, and secondarily Asian, male-dominated corporate and creative elite that represent a select group of large, global publishing companies in conjunction with a handful of massive chain retail distributors. This hegemonic elite determines which technologies will be deployed and which will not; which games will be made and by which designers; which players are important to design for, and which play styles will be supported. The hegemony operates on both monetary and cultural levels. It works in concert with the game developers and self-selected hardcore "gamers," who have systematically developed a rhetoric of play that is exclusionary, if not entirely alienating to "minority" players (who, in numerical terms, actually constitute a majority) such as most women and girls, males of many ages, and people of different racial and cultural backgrounds.[32]

Thus for several decades the video game industry was composed of a majority of male designers and programmers, creating games meant primarily for their own demographic. Games intended specifically for girls or women were, by and large, an anomaly.

This setup, wherein big-budget console gaming made games for a primarily targeted masculine demographic, created a culture of gaming that has been referred to by many as "toxic." Male-dominated gamer culture is often exclusionary. Multiplayer systems and games (e.g., Xbox Live) involve racist, sexist, and heterosexist language that has long alienated new players.[33] Mia Consalvo,[34] Adrienne Shaw,[35] and Amanda Cote[36] have illustrated that gamer culture is problematically constructed in exclusive ways and that the very terminology of "gamer" should be questioned.

This toxicity, in recent years, has culminated in calculated hate speech. As discussed in the preface of this book, GamerGate is a hashtag social movement that uses men's rights activist rhetoric to argue against diversity in both video games and the video game industry. Focusing on specific people in the industry such as game designer Zoë Quinn and cultural critic Anita Sarkeesian, those who associate with the GamerGate movement have illustrated that Player One is not interested in making room for diversity, either in game content or in the larger video game culture. The majority of GamerGate's ire seems to be focused on indie games and games journalism, but critiques have also been directed toward other forms of "casual" gaming, which I discuss below.

HARDCORE AND CASUAL: DEFINING GAMES FOR WOMEN

By the early 2000s women became a marketable demographic for video games. New gaming systems such as the Nintendo Wii and the Nintendo DS Lite were developed and marketed specifically with the potential of Player Two in mind.[37] For example, advertising campaigns appeared in popular women's magazines suggesting that women use the Nintendo Wii to engage better with families through playtime.[38] Wii games tended to focus on family togetherness or on fitness games—such as *Wii Fit*—to engage and involve women audiences. The Nintendo DS Lite, on the other hand, was marketed as a kind of an accessory. In one news article, a Nintendo executive was quoted regarding the intended woman demographic, explaining, "It definitely should be part of every purse . . . you have your cell phone, your iPod, and your DS Lite."[39] Harvey similarly illustrates that Nintendo's paratexts "crystallize a vision of equitable play in the home."[40]

At the same time, beginning in the 2000s, a category of gaming referred to as "casual" games became increasingly popular. Casual games stand in opposition to what are considered "hardcore games"—while "hardcore" games tend to be expensive, difficult to learn and master, and time-consuming, a "casual" game is cheap, easy to learn, and can be played for variable amounts of time. In *A Casual Revolution*, Jesper Juul remarks on the identifiable stereotypes embedded with the expectations of who plays these types of games. He explains that the stereotype of the hardcore player is one "who has preference for science fiction, zombies, and fantasy fictions, has played a large number of video games, will invest large amounts of time and resources toward playing video games, and enjoys difficult games."[41] The casual player stereotype, on the other hand, "is the inverted image of the hardcore player," one who likes "positive and pleasant fictions," has not played many games, and is willing to invest only minimal time.[42] These stereotypes, Juul explains, break down within the realities of who actually plays the games and how they are played. Similarly, Mia Consalvo illustrates that many players of what are considered "casual" games often play in very hardcore ways.[43] Thus, while casual gaming often comes with negative (read: feminine) connotations, the reality is that many games in several different genres can be played with either hardcore or casual styles. Of this negative connotation, John Vanderhoef writes, "When casual games are denigrated as feminine, and therefore 'trivial,' and traditional video games are celebrated for their seriousness and authenticity, both of which are qualities nested in masculinity, a power hierarchy is created that places the masculine in the superior position and the feminine in the inferior position, the result of which is the reproduction and perpetuation of gender inequalities."[44] In other words, there are serious politics to the maligned reputation of the casual market.

Casual games thrived, beginning in the mid-to-late 2000s. Time management games such as *Diner Dash* and its successors tasked players with waiting on customers. Hidden object games such as those in the *Mystery Case Files* series employed a combination of adventure game puzzles and seek-and-find-style hidden object scenes, where players were tasked with finding a series of random things on a page. By 2009, with the increasing popularity of social networking sites such as Facebook, social games like Zynga's *FarmVille* promoted nonsimultaneous group play across networks—both mobile and computer-based. This style of gaming has gradually turned into what the video game industry now refers to as the invest/express model, discussed in more detail later in this book. Finally, following the popularity of *Bejeweled*, the match-3 style of game was quickly cloned with a slew of game mechanics that varied only slightly.[45]

The rise of the smartphone has also shifted audiences significantly. Predicted by Nintendo's DS Lite campaign (suggesting that all women should carry a DS as a purse accessory), smartphones mean that an increased number of people carry gaming systems at all times. These games, still generally considered "casual," often involve networked play—similar to Facebook games—but a larger range of mechanics. Within this market, casual games such as *Candy Crush Saga, Angry Birds, Words with Friends*, and *Kim Kardashian: Hollywood* all have seen successes with diverse audiences. Several of these games are being built with an intended female audience.

Yet this begins to broach a larger question: what does a woman's game *look like*? How do we characterize the games made for Player Two? In popular books, film, and television this question is easily answered after decades of stylistic tropes that help to set our expectations for certain feminized genres, such as romance novels, soap operas, and chick flicks. Women's games, however, are more elusive to define. Taken both separately and cumulatively, games designed for women audiences very specifically tap into expectations of feminine style. The games discussed above often evoke themes of personal beauty, the care of self and others, domesticity, bodily management, and shopping. They suggest the designed identity of the woman player, the expectations of how women *should* play, rather than the realities of how they *do* play. These thematic elements become core to *Ready Player Two*. While the games might be played by a variety of players, the presumption of feminine style keeps the games, themselves, marginalized. As with previous genres that are "women's" genres—the chick flick or melodrama, the soap opera, or the romance novel—there is a tone of disdain under the label "casual game." In her book *Loving with a Vengeance*, for example, Tania Modleski remarks that genres meant for men tend to get taken more seriously than do genres intended for women audiences. Just as in these other categories, it is easy to dismiss feminized gaming, or games created specifically for female audiences, as being unimportant. Their topics and themes are often small, and their scope does not carry the weight of a hardcore, AAA video game. Yet these games are changing the market dramatically and rapidly, forming a new kind of industry and a new kind of player.

The threat of this change has not gone unnoticed. The anti-casual rhetoric among industry figures has been circulating for some time now. For example, in 2007 Michael Kato, an editor of the magazine *Game Informer*, editorialized, "You've probably been hearing about the casual gaming revolution for a while now. You've read about how much money cell phone gaming rakes in, and how middle-aged women in the suburbs love playing games on their PCs when they aren't watching *Oprah*. We've seen companies flat out declare that it's a priority to capture as many of these non-traditional gamers as possible. But is this really what the industry needs?"[46] The presumed answer to Kato's rhetorical question was, indeed, no—the video game industry should not make way for the casual games that had already begun to arrive at this point. But this statement itself expresses the industry derision that often surfaces at the mention of casual gaming. "Casual," the terminology as well as the technology, has politics. The term itself implies a group of dilettantes who do not require the dedication or the skills to necessarily be *real* gamers. Similarly, the GamerGate movement suggests that the advent of casual gaming (in some part) has created a giant, industry-wide rift.

In these ways, the space of "women's games" remains both stereotyped and marginalized. When I refer to "women's games" I am referring not to games that women play, but rather to games that in their design, marketing, or style appear to be intended for late teen or adult female audiences. Just as audiences for a "chick flick" might be broader than what was intended, a variety of people play within the casual market. At the same time, it is important to note that designed identity helps to construct a clear picture of what women's leisure is expected to look like. Further, it is important to acknowledge here that the binaries set forth by game design and marketing tend to place players into male/female categories, rather than less binary approaches. This is all to say, the realities of who plays (and how they play) are very often at odds with actual players. This book is meant to interrogate not *how* these games are played, but rather what kind of meaning we can derive from the games themselves.

FEMINIST GAME STUDIES AND INTERSECTIONALITY

But what is the best possible way to study "women's games"? Feminist game studies is a field of research that first emerged in the mid-to-late 1990s, simultaneously with the development of early games for girls. The initiatives of this research have often combined both industry and academe, with the goal of trying to influence more women and girls to have interests in both the video game industry and their consumer products. The field of study itself suggests that the playful is political—that there are politics to how women and girls spend their leisure time in light of how it ultimately results in careers and cultural interests.[47] In this way, those involved in feminist game studies have taken several paths: studying game characters,[48] examining game-play mechanics,[49] performing ethnographic and qualitative interview research on women and girls who both play and don't play,[50] studying the role of masculinity in game culture,[51] and using intersectional approaches to consider larger issues of diversity.[52] Scholars have studied the video game industry itself in terms of responses to perceived feminine threats[53] and have begun to study the impact and meaning of some of the new kinds of games as they have emerged.[54] The field has grown increasingly robust, and the combinations of industry activism and academic research have helped create the recent influx of female video game players.

Early research in feminist game studies focused primarily on girls, as opposed to women. This emphasis was largely a pragmatic one: research shows that playing video games at a young age makes children more interested in STEM-related careers.[55] Because there was a low percentage of girls and women participating in these fields, many feminist scholars and game designers hoped that a move toward getting girls more involved in gaming might shift those statistics. In response, many began to study what makes girls play[56] and how girls vary from boys in their game play,[57] and many made specific attempts to design games for girls.[58] Others used game design as an end unto itself, with the premise that teaching girls game design might help them better relate to the format.[59] In some ways, we can see this early research as being successful. The work done in the late 1990s and early 2000s clearly affected the industry enough to have caused some subtle but traceable shifts.

As the field of research developed, so did the approaches and the audience demographics. Additionally, as already alluded to, the games themselves continued to change. Increasingly, scholars are expanding research to include both young girls and adult women. Some research noted the flaw of conflating research on women and girls. T. L. Taylor, for example, argued in her book *Play between Worlds* that in this early research "little was done to disentangle the experience of play across age and life cycle. Research on girls thus often was extrapolated to apply to women."[60] By the late aughts, this problem was being dealt with in a large number of studies specifically on women gamers. Pam Royse and colleagues studied women's pleasure in playing in light of their self-acknowledged "level of play,"[61] while others discussed how industry dynamics created difficult environments for women to become game developers, which often resulted in fewer women making—and subsequently playing—video games.[62] The argument here is that a lack of women game designers entices fewer girls to play, resulting in fewer women becoming interested in careers as game designers, and so on. As the field progressed, several researchers have performed ethnographic and qualitative studies of players using feminism to get at larger issues about who plays, how they play, and why they play.[63] Genesis Downey, alternatively, performed auto-ethnographic research on her game play with her daughter, situating the study within what she refers to as her "girl gamer space" or "femme cave," as a mode of self-identifying as a "gamer."[64] Jenson and de Castell neatly sum up the pitfalls and difficulties in the historical trajectory of past research in feminist game studies, suggesting that "in the future, the very real need for research on gender and gameplay that more carefully reports on, documents, and troubles identities of player, producers, and consumers of digital games, especially in relation to gender, cannot be underestimated. In particular, this work would begin from the more nuanced theories of gender and identities that have been developed through postmodern, poststructural, feminist, postfeminist, queer theory, and theories of race and identity and then approach questions around gender and gameplay with a view to reporting on and accounting for those kinds of difference."[65] In turn, *Ready Player Two* is an attempt to trouble the expectations of designed identity by looking more closely at game objects, specifically those made for othered audiences.

Another discussion that has become an essential part of feminist game studies is how the previously mentioned "toxic gamer culture" often creates a barrier to entry for women gamers. Others have analyzed not only games but also the experiences of masculine gamer culture.[66] For example, in her analysis of toxic gamer culture Mia Consalvo puts out a specific call for further research to combat these issues: "Scholars need to research the practices and beliefs of game developers and marketers through both promotional materials and game content to see how both work to shape resulting gamer attitudes and responses."[67] Adrienne Shaw's work has broken down the idea that "gamer" might be a fixed identity, illustrating that many players do not want that identifier and do not wish to perform the identity of gamer, because of the behaviors associated with that identity.[68] Amanda Cote illustrates ways that harassment affects women's experiences of play.[69]

Research has been done on characters and character design, with a frequent focus on avatar bodies and how they might be both empowering and alienating to women players. Nina Huntemann provides an overview of the problem: "The sexualization of women's bodies in video games has paralleled advances in game technology. As the graphics capabilities of computers and video game consoles have improved, game designers have increased the visual detail of backgrounds, objects, and characters."[70] Much focus is placed on the heroic yet buxom and hyper-sexualized Lara Croft from the *Tomb Raider* game series. For example, Anne-Marie Schleiner demonstrates Croft as a potential space for feminist hacking through software patches.[71] Helen W. Kennedy considers ways that "the act of playing *Tomb Raider* as Lara disrupts the relationship between spectator and 'spectacle.'"[72] Media critic Anita Sarkeesian has produced a web series titled *Tropes vs. Women in Video Games* that analyzes how specific female game characters in hardcore gaming might ultimately be alienating to female players. In chapter 5 of this book I will revisit some of this research in my own interrogation of gaming bodies in games designed for women audiences.

Defining women in strict categories creates additional difficulty. Increasingly, feminist scholars have used intersectional approaches when studying video games and game players. Intersectionality is the theoretical premise that when trying to understand systems of oppression (gender, ethnicity, sexuality, class, etc.) the different factors should be seen interdependently rather than independently. Given this, many scholars have begun to consider how issues of sexuality, ethnicity, social class, and other factors play into and exacerbate problems that have already been documented in terms of gender within the video game industry. Scholars such as Gabriela Richard[73] and Kishonna Gray[74] have used intersectional approaches to understanding women's placement in the video game industry and gaming culture.

GENDER AND LEISURE PRACTICES

Commonly, studies on women and games focus on the industry and technology itself—how the industry is structured in a way that is often alienating to diverse audiences. But another factor, slightly less commonly discussed, is the complicated relationship between adult women and leisure activities. Feminist leisure studies is a field that has been growing since the late 1980s, particularly in its examination of the reticence of adult, middle-class women in Western cultures toward leisure activities. Within this research, it has been remarked on that leisure—particularly leisure at home—is a difficult thing to map, often because women have more responsibilities in domestic spaces than men do. While many men find the home a place for relaxation and leisure separate from work, many women are unable to have the same kinds of unconditional leisure that men have in these spaces.[75] Thus there is often a conflation of work activities and leisure activities: practices may have embedded practicality that negates the importance of leisure and play.[76] While the lived experiences of women might all be distinct, there is often a presumption in products marketed to women that they all share this same anxiety about the nature of their leisure activities.

Additionally, these studies often illustrate that *time* is specifically a key factor for women's leisure. Rosemary Deem conducted a study showing that women did not feel they had the right to leisure time given the overriding concerns of maintaining households and work responsibilities. This ultimately affects the quality and type of leisure practices women engage in: "No wonder then that much of women's household leisure consists of needlework, knitting, cooking, reading, TV watching, writing letters, day dreaming and snatching quick naps. All of these activities can be fitted into a fragmented time schedule, don't require large blocks of time, are cheap or free, require little space or equipment and can quickly be disposed of or stopped when work obligations intervene."[77] In this way, issues of women and play have been inextricably linked to issues of time: what a woman considers play or leisure is not necessarily defined only by the activities she enjoys, but also by the activities that fit neatly and cheaply into her fragmented schedule. Leisure, of course, is defined by both personal preferences as well as cultural expectations.

For many women, it becomes difficult to see the home as a site for anything but labor, making leisure unlikely, perhaps even impossible, in domestic spaces. In *The Second Shift*, Arlie Russell Hochschild refers to this as a "leisure gap"[78] and suggests that this gap creates longer-term patterns of inequality: "It sets up a cycle that works like this: because men put more of their 'male' identity in work, their work time is worth more than female work time—to the man and to the family. The greater worth of male work time makes his leisure more valuable, because it is his leisure that enables him to refuel his energy, strengthen his ambition, and move ahead at work. By doing less at home, he can work longer hours, prove his loyalty to his company, and get promoted faster."[79] While the focus in this passage is men's work and leisure, Hochschild asserts that a parallel cycle with less leisure occurs for women. Thus the task of maintaining dual roles leaves little time for leisure, and it is unsurprising that play is often nonexistent in the everyday lives of some women. While these studies do not necessarily compare women's lifestyle choices (e.g., stay-at-home vs. working women), it would seem that, in either case, leisure and play are lacking in many women's lives. It follows, then, that within game design there becomes a presumption built by these conventions—video games intended for women audiences necessarily advocate play in impossible ways, wherein leisure time is required yet assumed to be an impossible standard.

In "One Size Doesn't Fit All: The Meanings of Women's Leisure," Karla A. Henderson warns of the dangers of ascribing singular meanings to various patterns in women's leisure practices. She explains, "The leisure research on women's leisure and gender in the past six years points to 'different sizes' related to leisure and the imperative for social change including both structural and personal changes."[80] Henderson suggests several conclusions and implications of the past research, including (1) contextual rather than biological reasons for leisure differences between men and women, (2) the conclusion that "the more roles undertaken by a woman, the more likely that individual is to have less personal leisure,"[81] (3) that definitions of leisure, itself, vary between women, (4) that leisure constraints are more obvious for women in more marginalized race and class groups, and (5) that leisure may serve as a space for resistance. By Henderson's account, it would seem there is no single cause or effect to the problematic relationship between women and leisure.

Mapping the larger themes of leisure studies back to video games, there are certainly parallels between how women spend leisure time and how that leisure time might relate back to video games. In studies of gender and video games, women have reported that they "don't have time" to play or that they seem like a "waste of time."[82] This suggests that the leisure gap extends to video game spaces. One study of 276 undergraduate students found that the availability of leisure time and the likelihood of video game playtime was completely linked to gendered expectations—wherein female participants had less leisure time and therefore played in shorter snippets of time. While the study only looked at undergraduate students (and not women across entire life cycles) the authors concluded that "looking across the study results, time stress and the perception of limited leisure time is linked to gender, even during college before adult gender roles are fully enacted. Shorter chunks of leisure time, more time spent on homework, less game play and shorter game play sessions, even beyond actual time limitations, characterize the female undergraduates within this study."[83] As noted above, this is significant. College students theoretically have more free time than women do who have careers and families. Yet even at this young age their perception of leisure time, as well as the performance of this leisure, was framed by gendered expectations. This ultimately parses into their personal interests and desire to play video games. It is not surprising, then, that the game-play style of casual gaming would be so heavily designed for and marketed to women audiences, and that the theme of "time" would be so commonly employed, a topic discussed at length in chapter 2.

It is important to acknowledge the contradictory and often tautological elements to leisure studies as they relate to women audiences. While on the one hand women often report that they do not have leisure—or time—for gaming, Henderson's study illustrates that the "one size fits all" model of understanding women audiences and their relationship to real-world time is not necessarily useful. Yet the presence of that stereotype and expectation likely influences both actual women and their perceptions of time. Additionally, I argue, it also influences designer expectations of women's time in game creation. This puts the video games discussed throughout this book in the unique position of being able to comment on the current cultural expectations of how women practice leisure.[84]

VIDEO GAMES AS PRESCRIPTIVE TECHNOLOGIES

So far, I have approached video games (and digital leisure) as though they exist in a technological vacuum. But the development, structure, and infrastructure of the video game industry is complex, messy, and by no means insulated from other equally complicated cultures. As such, my goal is to situate how gaming is part of a broader sociological infrastructure, unable to be disentangled from the messiness of its situational politics that are both embedded in and exceed the complexities of the video game industry. The problem, as I frame it, is not simply one of taste, of industry dynamics, or of biology. Instead, there are broader institutions and philosophies at play: feminism, leisure industries and practices, the way technology frames cultural behaviors, and the already tense relationship between women and technology.

Methodologically, this calls for nuance and a bit of messiness. In the word "messy" I am invoking the work of John Law, who suggests that singular methods and theoretical frameworks are no longer practical or effective in looking at the sociological and technological networked infrastructures. Law explains, "Pains and pleasures, hopes and horrors, intuitions and apprehensions, losses and redemptions, mundanities and visions, angels and demons, things that slip and slide, or appear and disappear, change shape or don't have much form at all, unpredictabilities, these are just a few of the phenomena that are hardly caught by social science methods."[85] Instead, he suggests an increased assemblage of methods. While the results are often messy, the assemblage paints a larger picture than what traditional social science methods are able to offer. Although this book is not based in sociological frameworks—my analysis is far more text-based than human-based—my methods of approaching these technological "objects" try to get at how they attempt to define human behaviors. This study is less interested in the humans themselves than in how technologies attempt to construct and manage the messy realities of leisure performance, particularly with respect to gender construction. Designed identity hybridizes industry conventions, texts, and audiences into game designs, prescribing specific modes of play based on stereotypes—gendered or otherwise.

At the same time, perhaps, it is less useful to make such harsh distinctions between technologies and the humans that create and use them. Bruno Latour's work on actor–network theory (ANT) helps to establish the fuzziness of these distinctions while considering how larger networks help shape and define the frameworks in which they exist. Instead of separating out humans from their technologies, ANT conceives them all as "actors." Latour explains, "To conceive humanity and technology as polar is to wish away humanity: we are sociotechnical animals, and each human interaction is sociotechnical."[86] In other words, we do not exist in opposition to the technological objects that we produce or the industrial practices that allow for that production. Those objects define social structure as much as humans do. Within the same theoretical backdrop, Latour, Law, and others who employ ANT as a theoretical model suggest that all actors—human and nonhuman—are situated in response to a larger network infrastructure.

In light of the ANT perspective suggested by Latour and Law, this book studies video games, but from the perspective that the textual/gamic analysis draws from both sociological and critical/cultural frameworks. Many before me have used similar theoretical frameworks to analyze games and game culture. Notably, T. L. Taylor has proposed that game scholars consider studying video games as products of assemblage:

> Games, and their play, are constituted by the interrelations between (to name just a few) technological systems and software (including the imagined player embedded in them), the material world (including our bodies at the keyboard), the online space of the game (if any), game genre, and its histories, the social worlds that infuse the game and situate us outside of it, the emergent practices of communities, our interior lives, personal

histories, and aesthetic experience, institutional structures that shape the game and our activity as players, legal structures, and indeed the broader culture around us with its conceptual frames and tropes.[87]

Taylor's scope suggests a broad consideration of games and game culture when thinking about the material objects of gaming. Similarly, Casey O'Donnell uses actor–network theory to analyze the industry-level constraints structured into video games.[88]

Those who use the ANT framework often maintain their focus on the industry and human actors. In this way, *Ready Player Two* pushes at the assemblage approach to consider how the games themselves suggest and structure specific styles of play. My interest is not settled on the woman player as she is theorized by the video game industry, because *that* player does not exist. This is not to propose that there are no women playing video games—of course, as already noted, almost half of all video game players are women. Instead, I argue that it is the conception of the woman player deliberately formed by game design that does not exist. The woman player, as conceived of by game designers, is a ghost. Because studying ghosts is methodologically impractical, this book focuses on the games themselves—and the designed identities implied by those games—to consider how this ghost of femininity is formed vis-à-vis expectations of women's work and leisure, as well as relationships to time, bodies, consumption, and emotions.

Even as we are unable to remove ourselves from our technologies, it becomes apparent that just as we form them, they help to form us in prescriptive ways. In many respects, the recent flood of games aimed at women audiences can be seen as prescriptive technologies encouraging women to play in very specific ways through the designed identities they form. For this, it is useful to consider Norbert Elias, who wrote about civilizing processes and technologies. In the essay "The Rise of the Fork," Elias explains that behaviors (such as the use of a fork) are often enculturated into a society through shame, ritual, and institutions. He explains that individuals subsume these rituals, which are culturally mediated, at least initially. According to Elias, "The social standard to which the individual was first made to conform by external restraint is finally reproduced less smoothly within him, through a self-restraint which may operate even against his conscious wishes."[89] Just as the fork became part of human life as an actor within the larger paradigm of institutional networks forming behavior—while also being formed *by* human behavior—so, too, are our technologies of play. Video games are created with specific audiences in mind, managing and policing those audiences.

TECHNOLOGY MANAGING WOMEN

While we are all both complicit with our technologies and managed by our technologies, women have a very specifically complex situation in this respect. In popular culture, women often have the reputation of being particularly incapable concerning technology. Depictions of women in relation to technology often result in simplistic stereotypes and tasteless jokes about women's supposed incompetence in driving or programming a VCR.[90] In "The Gender–Technology Relation: Contemporary Theory and Research," Rosalind Gill and Keith Grint discuss the implications of these problematic stereotypes: "The cultural association between masculinity and technology in Western societies is hard to exaggerate. It operates not only with the popular assumption—from which much sexist humor about women's 'technical incompetence' has been generated—but also as an academic 'truth.'"[91] Gill and Grint suggest that the problem is deeper than just passing jokes; these are assumptions made by both men and women in everyday practices. Breaking these stereotypes is difficult and often feeds into cultural understandings of who is involved in digital play. Thus, along with assumptions about who is able to work with technology, there are expectations about who plays with it and how that play should occur.

Additionally, from a historical perspective, there is a complicated relationship between technologies that are specifically designed for women, and the realities of how those technologies function in lived experience. In *More Work for Mother: The Ironies of Household Technology from the Open Hearth to the Microwave*, Ruth Schwartz Cowan discusses how domestic technologies have served the interests of men but not women, ultimately making "more work for mother" while relieving men and children of their chores and tasks:

> The changes that occurred in household technology during the twentieth century had two principal effects. The first was to separate the work of men and children from the work of women, continuing a process that had begun in the previous century; and the second was markedly to increase the productivity of the average housewife. This conclusion can be put more succinctly by saying that, in the second phase of industrialization, American households and American housewives shifted not from production to

consumption but from the production of one type of commodity to the production of another in even greater quantities.[92]

Thus, according to Cowan, production in household technologies engendered more production. It becomes important to review technologies not just in terms of their perceived reputation of production, but also in terms of the realities they help to construct. In Cowan's account, by analyzing the technological objects meant for women, we can see the realities of how prescriptive technologies might maintain a system of oppression.

Since the 1980s there have been several studies regarding the relationship between gender and technology in general.[93] Often feminist researchers found an inherently masculine undertone to science and technology, which often gave them pause about the nature of this technology. According to Judy Wajcman in *Feminism Confronts Technology*, "A key issue here is whether the problem lies in men's domination of technology, or whether the technology is in some sense inherently patriarchal."[94] Different feminist scholars have subsequently approached this question in various ways. Studies of gender and technology often focus on how masculinity is embedded in technologies and technological practices, and how this helps to give men more "expertise" as owners of technology. According to Wajcman, "It is not simply a question of acquiring skills, because these skills are embedded in a culture of masculinity that is largely coterminous with the culture of technology. Both at school and in the workplace this culture is incompatible with femininity. Therefore, to enter this world, to learn its language, women have to forsake their femininity."[95] One of the agendas of those who study gender and technology is to alleviate patriarchal influences on technology, determine ways to create more opportunities, and remove stereotypes. To some extent this has occurred within the video game industry—with an increase of women players, it would seem that the playing field had begun to level. Yet it remains important to consider the nature of the games that are specifically designed for these audiences.

In her book *Technofeminism*, Wajcman describes what she calls technofeminist theory as a means to continue changing the relationship between women and technology: "An emerging technofeminism conceives of a mutually shaping relationship between gender and technology, in which technology is both a source and a consequence of gender relations. In other words, gender relations can be thought of as materialized in technology, and masculinity and femininity in turn acquire their meaning and character through their enrollment and embeddedness in working machines."[96] Wajcman's technofeminism allows for the relationship between women and technology to be constantly in flux, in response to shifting cultural values and technological developments. This outlook toward technology is overwhelmingly positive and forward thinking: the idea is that emerging technologies can help to push women into more STEM careers.

While the aforementioned studies often use theory to highlight how technology can or cannot help women in workplaces or domestic spaces, few have discussed the benefits of technological play, outside of previously mentioned feminist video game studies. This seems contradictory and problematic: if technology is used only for work and not for leisure, it seems impossible for women to ever gain any real expertise. Playing with technology would help women increase their comfort levels, potentially making them more at ease when using it at home and work. Two ethnographic studies help to shed more light on these very issues. Eileen Green suggests a greater focus on technology and leisure practices, but also warns that with women there is often a "blurring of work and leisure activities."[97] Similarly, in *At Home with Computers*, Elaine Lally discusses ways that domestic computing technologies often blur work/home lives, contributing to the complicated relationship between women and technology. Thus, even as a play space, computers are not necessarily parsed as playful technologies for many women.[98] While Lally's study predates smartphone technologies, one can assume that the slippage might follow there as well.

IDENTITY, VIDEO GAMES, AND A "GLASS CEILING"

With all of these factors in mind—a rapidly shifting game industry, the emergence of feminist game studies, the complexities of women and leisure as well as women and technologies—the realities of women as a gaming audience becomes muddled. It would be easy to look at the thousands of video games targeting women audiences (primarily in the casual category) and suggest that video games are no longer meant solely for Player One, and that Player Two has her own special playing field. But things are not so simple. Many factors have changed, and are still changing. But there is nuance to that change, and that nuance is worth exploration. The expectations of what Player Two's games look like are limiting and create the potential of what might be seen as a kind of a "glass ceiling"—a limitation that prevents further progress toward play. Yet this book attempts to resist this assessment—these games are not meant to be understood in a negative context.

Yet the games for Player Two that have emerged over the last decade and a half are, to some extent, games for an imagined audience, a designed identity. This is not to say that women do not play games, or even that women do not play *these* games. Rather, I argue throughout this book that the kind of woman that is constructed and imagined through these games is fictional, and that the identities designed by these games prescribe specific kinds of play and players. This nonexistent feminized player is almost necessarily white, middle class, and heterosexual. She plays in ways that often presume a desire for domesticity, for consumer goods, and for Western conceptions of beauty. Many of the games designed for Player Two ignore the potential of intersectional politics and the lived realities of women's leisure. Her construction is as fictional as the game narratives created for her.

ORGANIZATION OF THIS BOOK

Ready Player Two is framed in terms of video game technologies that are intended for women audiences, and how those games play with leisure in terms of designed identity. In doing this, I have broken down play into several categories: playing with identity, playing with time, playing with emotions, playing with consumption, and playing with bodies. While several chapters discuss the same games, the point is not to rehash what is being played, but to unpack what is being evoked *during* that play.

In chapter 1, "Playing with Identity," I weave together several sources to find a baseline of what Player Two's games actually look like. Starting with the concept of designed identity, I use a combination of game design textbooks and interviews with designers to conceptualize the identifiable attributes of games designed for this perceived audience. I begin this chapter by discussing scholarship about the power and potential of game design as texts. Next, I use interviews and other sources to create a rubric and set of guidelines for determining specific characteristics and structural considerations when thinking about Player Two's games.

Chapter 2, "Playing with Time," proposes ways that time management is structured into video games designed for Player Two, and how these designs suggest specific identity markers. I begin the chapter by discussing how scheduling and time management are complicated issues for women. In this way, I establish that time becomes a more salient issue for female audiences than male ones. Next, I analyze several games in both the time management and invest/express genres of casual gaming. In these games, I consider how time is constructed and managed both inside and outside the game world. I conclude the chapter by discussing how the narrative pacing of the games and the titles suggest a form of mania and hysteria—afflictions that are often used in "diagnosing" women. In this, I establish that women's playtime often comes to be seen as a form of mania, rather than as an acceptable form of leisure.

In chapter 3, "Playing with Emotions," I use concepts of emotional labor and affective labor to better explore Player Two's situated identity in game design. Women, as I illustrate, are often expected to perform emotional labor both in career and at home. In turn, these elements often slip into game design. Here, designed identity is about the perceived performance of emotional labor. To illustrate emotional and affective labor in game design, I draw on several genres, including time management games, hidden object games, puzzle games, caregiving games, and social network games. Within my analysis, I suggest that games designed for women often highlight the expectation that women will play out roles of emotional labor in games, complicating their experiences of play.

In the fourth chapter, "Playing with Consumption," I discuss how in-game consumption practices relate back to the designed identity of Player Two. As with the previous chapters, I suggest that consumption plays off specific gendered stereotypes via expectations of women as consumers and shoppers. In turn, by studying games that forefront shopping as a thematic element, I analyze how these games manage the expectations of women's consumption. Additionally, I discuss the economic politics of free-to-play games and then focus on the game *Kim Kardashian: Hollywood*. My ultimate argument in this chapter is that, in many ways, the shopping play that occurs in game worlds has leaked into purchasing mechanics, via gendered expectations of consumerism and consumption. Finally, I end the chapter by highlighting food as consumptive practice in video games.

In chapter 5, "Playing with Bodies" I discuss how video games designed for Player Two code the management of bodies into their game texts. Body management, of course, is a necessary part of all video game play. We are unable to properly play a video game without managing our movements, our space, and other body-centric parameters. While the chapter begins with this conceit, my analysis ranges from exergaming to the construction of bodies in women's games, and how these bodies ultimately suggest physical markers (white, middle class, heterosexual, cis-gendered) that reinforce the expectation of *who* the idealized woman player is.

In my conclusion, I focus on how industry shifts and debates have continued to problematize the designed identity of Player Two. As the medium grows up it becomes important to consider how expectations of gender, class, sexuality, and ethnicity all create the potential to structure play in ways that both foreground, and simultaneously limit, new audiences.

READY PLAYER TWO

Player Two is ready. But Player Two is not without glitches. She is trapped in a stereotype and stuck in distinct modes of play, which characterize her leisure time in very specific ways. This book is meant to be an exploration of Player Two's games, an attempt to use those game designs and marketing concepts to tease out and understand the presumptions underlying what we expect out of women's leisure, as well as our expectations of their bodily limitations.

The video game industry might be designing Player Two as a white, cis-gendered, heterosexual, middle-class woman (who is almost necessarily a mother), but that is not the only possible Player Two. This book demonstrates the multitude of ways that this occurs in the designed identity within both game design and marketing. But a by-product of Player Two is that she gets to remap what the video game industry looks like in very concrete ways. As the industry reshapes and reforms, there are endless opportunities for the new, emerging player to help rethink what digital play can and will look like.

In this, I would like to argue that perhaps Player Two embodies two distinct roles: on the one hand, there is the designed identity of Player Two, the white, cis-gendered, heterosexual, middle-class mother for whom video games are designed. But there is also another Player Two—a hopeful Player Two that this book is really about. She characterizes all the other players. She lacks the identity markers of Player One and is not necessarily female. It is finally her turn to redesign a flawed industry that in its several decades of existence has resulted in both beautiful products as well as an astounding amount of hate speech.

It is time to press the START button.

1   *Playing with Identity*

DESIGNED IDENTITY REVISITED

Central to this book is an imaginary player. Let's call her "Jennifer." Jennifer is white, in her thirties, middle class, and lives in Wisconsin. She is a busy mother who doesn't have a lot of time to play video games but likes to fill in extra gaps of time in her everyday life. She doesn't want something too complicated, or violent, but she also doesn't want something boring. Jennifer has complex tastes. While she is not real, I did not invent her. "Jennifer" is a player type referenced by Storm8 chief creative officer Tim LeTourneau as the targeted audience for the company's popular game *Restaurant Story 2*.[1] Jennifer is both real and imaginary. She is a fictional identity built off the lived experiences of many players, yet she helps to illustrate the way that women players can be designed.[2]

In the introduction of this book, I proposed a definition for my term *designed identity*: designed identity is a hybrid outcome of industry conventions, textual constructs, and audience placements in the design and structure of video games. In this way, designed identity is always an ideological construction—it is not something that is planned or motivated in clear-cut ways. It is a result of larger social structures and expectations. These expectations, in turn, seep into game texts.

Designed identity is not a term meant to issue blame to game designers, artists, creators, advertisers, or others involved in the video game industry. It seems important to state this simply and clearly because blame is surely tempting. The targets of this blame would likely fall to the most obvious suspect: the creators. Given this, it is worth noting that nowhere in my definition is there anything explicit or implicit about game designers, marketers, artists, or creators. The three major factors contributing to designed identity are (1) industry conventions, (2) textual constructs, and (3) audience placements. While each of these elements is a result of a series of individual decisions and choices, they speak to larger cultural issues that ultimately manifest in game design and advertising. Designed identity functions ideologically—it is about idealizing an assumed audience and reformatting that audience in an understandable and digestible way.

The analyses throughout this book are meant to operationalize designed identity, specifically in terms of video games that are designed for the player I characterize as Player Two. Player Two is not a real audience, but rather a perceived one, a counterpart to the designed identity necessitated by market-driven game design. That is not to imply that games designed for primarily masculine audiences—or even gender-neutral audiences—do not evoke different kinds of designed identity. In many ways, the work that Carly Kocurek[3] has done on the identity of the masculine gamer is a similar mode of designed identity. Given this, the terminology is not meant to apply solely to feminine genres, although media meant to appeal to women provides an excellent example of this mode of conceptual design. Just as I explain how designed identity can be applied to *Diner Dash* or *Kim Kardashian: Hollywood*, other researchers should be able to similarly apply it to design decisions in *Call of Duty* or *Halo*. One of the goals of this book is to introduce a conceptual framework that can later be applied to other games and audiences to better understand our current media landscape.

Similarly, designed identity is not only about video games. While video games are the medium of focus for this particular work, my aim is to suggest a framework that is transferrable between media. The three major factors of designed identity—industry conventions, textual constructs, and audience placements—are always at play, and it is through this that we can get a sense of the larger ideologies driving a market. Designed identity is a concept that applies neatly to video games but could just as easily be applied to television, film, books, or other industry constructed modes of mediation. As narrowcasting becomes an increasingly prevalent mode of appealing to niche audiences, it follows that studying how those niche audiences are, themselves, *designed* is potentially useful.

Additionally, while I discuss both video games as well as advertisements throughout this book (although more of the former than the latter), it is worth being explicit that those who create video games are rarely those who advertise them. Several of the designers who offer insights throughout this chapter are explicit that they are not the ones that chose the paratexts (i.e., advertising, affiliated artwork, or other modes of marketing materials). Designers and advertisers are, generally speaking, kept isolated. But rather than representing a flaw of the concept of designed identity, this offers further argument in support of the project. Because game designers and advertisers often come from divergent parts of the industry, the similar themes in games and paratexts show evidence that there are larger ideological constructions at play. No one person, no one corporation, and no one advertiser is solely responsible for the images, designs, and texts that make up designed identity. The hybrid outcome of the term implies that it is built off social constructs that exceed one person, one game, one industry, or—sometimes—even one culture. The examples of designed identity offered throughout this book are powerful not because they are constructions of blame that can be issued to individuals, but because they speak to larger trends.

The goal of this chapter is to map some of those trends, specifically as they apply to the designed identity of the theorized woman player, Player Two. Throughout the rest of this book I discuss several games in detail, using them to consider specific aspects of the idealized woman player. But the question is, how do we know who the intended audience for a game is? Similarly, how do we track the patterns and backdrop with which to analyze the games featured in subsequent chapters? It becomes essential to break down the minutiae of gender inclusivity (and gender exclusivity) in game design and elaborate on the specific factors that help establish a continuum in order to decide whether a specific game is intended for female audiences.

Figuring out for *whom* a video game is designed is a difficult business. That is not to say there aren't intended demographics for games, or that sometimes a game doesn't exceed its intended demographics. But demographics information—either intended or actual—is not often released by video game companies or advertising agencies. Furthermore, actual demographics seem to be besides the point: I am less interested in who *actually* plays a game and more interested in the assumptions that were made about a specific demographic when that game was being designed and advertised. Additionally, this book reaches across several different gaming genres: some seem to be intended exclusively for women, some seem to be attempting to be more fluid in terms of the intended players, and some are part of a larger genre of games that (depending on specific stylistic decisions) is meant to appeal to a variety of different audiences, depending on aesthetic decisions. For example, match-3 games sometimes seem to attempt more inclusivity in their style and approach and other times seem to be exclusively targeting women or girls. This necessitates a larger organizational rubric that helps to determine the extent to which games seem to be designed for women, in order to examine the specifics of their designed identity.

To create this organizational rubric, this chapter relies on several interviews with game designers. For this initiative, I performed e-mail and Skype interviews with seven video game designers and professionals, who reported back their understanding of specific themes, genres, play styles, and aesthetic elements that make up industry assumptions of how one designs a game for women. Designers offered insights on their own experience with industry conventions and expectations. As part of my process of selecting interview subjects, I primarily interviewed individuals who reported that they had experience working on games intended for female audiences. Because of nondisclosure agreements, I have kept the majority of these interviews anonymous in my reporting and do not reveal the names of designers or the companies they have worked for unless there were specific reasons and clear consent.[4] My goal with these interviews was to help establish that the video game industry *is* increasingly trying to appeal to women and that there are specific game types and styles assumed to be the ideal design for that audience.

WHAT IS AT PLAY AND WHAT IS AT STAKE?

In Mary Flanagan and Helen Nissenbaum's *Values at Play in Digital Games*, the authors argue that all technology—digital games included—have sets of values, and that by tapping into those values we can design more conscientiously. They explain, "If we accept that technology can embody value, the practical turn allows designers and producers to consider ethical and political concerns alongside more typical engineering ideals. System design is typically guided by goals such as reliability, efficiency, resilience, modularity, performance, safety, and cost. We suggest adding items like fairness, equality, and sustainability to the list."[5] Those who design technology to meet those values, they argue, are considered "conscientious designers"—those who specifically try to embed ethical values into design. While their theoretical framework is broad enough to apply to any kind of technological design, their book specifically focuses on digital games as a core space where values can be neatly embedded into designed spaces.

There is a kind of optimism to Flanagan and Nissenbaum's argument. By cataloging many games and discussing the values that—when broken down to the core elements of game play—help to situate that game as an ethical (or not so ethical) system, Flanagan and Nissenbaum empower game designers to create play spaces that better represent a utopian ideal. The idealism necessary to buy into their argument is both appealing yet somewhat positivist. It seems to suggest that designers have an immense amount of control and can use their powers for good. Conscientious designers are able to recognize their own ideological baggage, yet push beyond it, within the capitalist system that employs them.

While the notion of a conscientious designer is useful for thinking about indie games (those designed by small teams not meant for mass consumption), it becomes a bit less useful at a larger, industrial scale. The video game industry sits at the juncture of aesthetics and commerce. As Casey O'Donnell argues, it is not simply a "software industry," but a delicate balance of art and consumer market.[6] Given that, it seems essential to recognize both sides of this configuration. While game designers often have lofty or artistic ideals, there is also the political economy to consider in terms of decision-making processes. While a game designer might want to be a conscientious designer, the reality is that because games are like all products of mass media industries, he or she is often unable to do so. The zeitgeist of a time period and cultural situation more often reflects ideological underpinnings that may not be quite so conscientious—of course game designers understand their role in the market and their ability to lose their jobs. Flanagan and Nissenbaum, by putting the onus on game designers, ignore the corporate realities of the industry and market—the problem falls back to those very designers, and their failure to meet these standards becomes a means of issuing blame.

Certainly, Ian Bogost's notion of "procedural rhetoric" offers a similar way of considering how specific aspects of game play might have meaning worthy of analysis. He describes procedural rhetoric as "a technique for making arguments with computational systems and for unpacking computational arguments others have created."[7] Using this as his core mode of interpretation, Bogost analyzes several games, paying attention to how specific game mechanics and game-play elements help to rein-force particular ideologies. Thus he pulls apart meaning in both popular games (such as *Animal Crossing*) and political games, demonstrating how specific messages and ideas can come through in ways unique to the medium, by specifically looking at smaller components, rather than the entire game. This methodology, Bogost argues, is useful for analyzing any technological object.

However, procedural rhetoric is not without criticism. In his book *Wordplay and the Discourse of Video Games*, Christopher A. Paul questions one of the core aspects of procedural rhetoric. Paul points out, "Procedures in games are not conceived in a vacuum, which means that it is important to look both at and beyond them."[8] Instead, he suggests his own rhetorical strategy, "wordplay," which is meant to "fill the gap" between game procedures and institutional elements. Paul explains that "wordplay is predicated on identifying ways in which video games persuade, create identifications, and circulate meanings. This process of investigating video games leads to paying more attention to three crucial elements of video games: words, design, and play."[9] In other words, while Paul uses a similar rhetorical strategy to better illustrate the constraints of a difficult medium of study, his research pushes toward trying to understand not only small portions of the game but also its use. Additionally, Paul's work does not place judgment on the game creators—it remains agnostic about the why and how, only looking at the cultural meanings that can come from play.

Thus the goal of studying game design is not to pull apart the elements to analyze them distinctly, but to create a better understanding of the institutional and larger cultural constructions that often affect design. It is inadvisable to be guided solely by procedural rhetoric or values at play; rather, it is best to use an amalgamation. As Paul astutely notes, games are not constructed in a vacuum—we cannot examine games without considering that they were made within an economic system. As such, Flanagan and Nissenbaum's suggestion for conscientious design is useful, but only to an extent. It assumes a great deal of agency on the part of the game designer, who is most commonly situated in a larger industrial context. While that designer certainly has some weight in making choices about the meaning of games, it seems unlikely that he or she would somehow be capable of breaking out of the complex ecosystem of the game industry to suggest more ethical underpinnings to game design. Furthermore, the notion of what is ethical varies from person to person, and culture to culture. It stands, then, that blaming individuals for not having the proper degree of "values" in their design is deeply unfair.

Like all popular art, game design is affected by the culture and time in which it is constructed. Thirty years ago, there were almost no video games exclusively designed for women and girls. However, as games for these audiences began to filter into the market, certain assumptions, trends, themes, and styles became commonplace within design. Often these assumptions, trends, and themes reflected (and continue to reflect) deeper ideological constraints, particularly as they apply to gender. It seems essential, though, to also consider these elements from an intersectional perspective. While thirty or even fifteen years ago the issue of how to get more females to play video games might have been a concern of industry economics, from our current perspective we can pull back even further and ask more in-depth questions. By asking the right questions, we can shed light on deeper constraints of diversity and access that might get baked into game design, such as ethnicity, social class, ability, and sexuality. We are now at a pivotal moment wherein there are enough games being marketed to women that we can ask larger questions about what is at play in gendered game design, while simultaneously interrogating what *is not* at play in the same designs. The goal of this chapter is to systematize how we can analyze a specific kind of game, without simply blaming those who produce those games.

GENDER-INCLUSIVE GAME DESIGN: THEN AND NOW

Before Sheri Graner Ray's *Gender Inclusive Game Design: Expanding the Market* there was no clear-cut discussion about how the video game market, at that time, was alienating to potential female players, and there was minimal discussion about specific methods of appealing to those players. Ray's book begins with a simple premise: "But what if the player is female?"[10] Her goal in the book is reaching beyond "traditional" markets in ways that don't just use pink boxes to appeal to women and girls, but to consider specific aspects of game design that begin to enable more inclusivity. Specifically, Ray suggests a change in conflict-resolution styles, stimulus response, learning and communication styles, reward systems, and avatar selection. Breaking this down, via Ray's suggestions, games with a gender-inclusive appeal should focus on:

- Indirect competition as opposed to direct competition for nonconfrontational conflict resolution. Ray argues that "when faced with conflict, females will choose negotiation, diplomacy, and compromise over direct confrontation."[11]
- A shift of stimulus response away from visual stimulation and toward an increased amount of emotional and tactile stimuli.
- A change in spatial targeting in games. Ray asserts that "males excel in targeting moving objects in uncluttered fields, while women excel in targeting non-moving objects in cluttered fields,"[12] by using an increased number of "hot spots" to enable this differentiation in play style.
- Involving less "risk" within the interface, ultimately making it more intuitive and easier to navigate.
- More friendly styles of communicating to the player (between game and player).
- Less drastic response to failure or errors. In other words, building a game system where players do not have to start over if they fail or "die" in the game. Ray suggests more forgiving game design.
- An increase in games that involve cooperative play.
- More ability for players to select their own avatars, with more variation in character types that are not hypersexualized.

Ray's book was not academic, but rather a game design textbook. The book was popular; according to Ray in a 2015 interview[13] it went through two printings.[14]

Gender Inclusive Game Design was not without its critics. T. L. Taylor, for example, explains in a book review that Ray's "arguments too often link these issues back to a notion of gender difference rooted in contested data and theories. We have long had stories (often dubbed scientific) that try and isolate spatial skills, competition, aggression, cognition, risk or care taking, emotionality, and relational modes of being, within either biology or fairly tenuous notions of bio-social evolutionary theory."[15] In other words, her research often relied heavily on biological determinism and evolutionary theory in ways that suggest inherent biological differences between male/female play, rather than a focus on enculturated styles of play in a masculine/feminine sense (or dealing with it as a continuum of play styles).

However, it is important to contextualize that her book, being early to the market, was the first to broach any of these issues. Biological determinism notwithstanding, Ray's book was an important first step toward broadening a consumer market that had become far too pocketed and insular. Disregarding the question of "gender" or biology, many of her suggestions could map to a larger call for more generally inclusive game design—finding ways to help make games appeal to a broader audience that were not necessarily raised on a diet of hardcore console games. Her book created a solid reminder to game designers that there are multiple kinds of audiences and multiple kinds of play.

The book enjoyed a good deal of popularity, and according to Ray it was used as a textbook in several game design programs.[16] While it is difficult to gauge the exact amount of influence the book has had, it is worth noting two important factors: (1) since Ray's book, there have been no subsequent books entirely dedicated to game design for female audiences; and (2) in the developer interviews I discuss later in the chapter, it becomes clear that many of the premises of Ray's argument have since been integrated into the growing number of video games specifically targeting women.

Yet, despite the growth of games created (theoretically) for women, in our 2015 interview Ray suggests that there are still difficulties regarding how women are viewed by the video game industry: "We have a problem where the game industry does not see women as a market. They see women as a genre. We only have to make this one game for all women. So if you are a middle-aged woman and you want to play a game, you get pointed to *FarmVille*, or *Words with Friends*, or some of those social games that we—and I say we as the industry—have decided this is the game for women."[17] In other words, while there has been growth in terms of more gender-inclusive game design—because the games she references here surely meet the criteria suggested by her book—there is still a problem with how the industry deals with that perceived demographic. Alternatively, she suggests, men are treated "as a market, with lots and lots of different kinds of games."

One problem with viewing females as a genre, according to Ray, is that it leaves no ability to unpack specific segments of that market—particularly when dealing with factors like age. She explains that "the industry doesn't disentangle. They put women as one genre, all ages as female. They consider females as one genre: fashion, and shopping, and makeup, *Farm-Ville*, and social games. That's all female. It's very difficult to disentangle because the industry doesn't disentangle. They lump all women into these categories regardless of age, race, religion, income." Age gets lost in the construction of the female "genre" (as opposed to market segment). This means that, in terms of analysis, while there might be a strong sense that a game is made with a specific (and female) audience in mind, it is difficult to understand whether some games are made for adult females versus teen girls. A good example of this market confusion can be seen in fashion games, which in many ways appear to be meant for tweens but also have aspects that might be intended for adult women. It is impossible to know the specifics of for whom a game was developed, even if it is clear that it was developed for a female audience in general. As discussed earlier in this chapter, game companies are well-known for being tight-lipped about actual and intended demographics. Yet, by considering Ray's work as a foundational industry text and also looking at actual experiences discussed by game designers, it becomes evident that there is some attempt to get at this female demographic of potential video game players—even if that demographic is misunderstood or if there is a conflation of other points of diversification (such as age, ethnicity, income, etc.).

While no other authors have tackled gender as a topic for game design books to the extent that Ray has, a few have approached it either as a small section in a larger game design book or else as essays. Notably, in *Fundamentals of Game Design*, Ernest Adams offers an appendix section on "Reaching Adult Women." Adams warns game designers not to appeal to "stereotypically feminine interests such as fashion or shopping"[18] and instead to make attempts at gender inclusivity through the omission of (1) hypersexualized characters, (2), monotony in play, (3) "play without a meaningful goal," and (4) single-player games.[19] Adding some additional generalities, Adams revisits some of the topics Ray discusses in her book: different learning styles, risk aversion, socialization, resolution styles, and the ability to customize. Thus Adams's advice is relatively analogous to Ray's work regarding gender inclusivity, just with significantly less detail. Similarly, in her essay, "Are Boy Games Even Necessary?" Nicole Lazzaro suggests that game designers need to move further toward gender inclusivity in design, rather than targeting specific demographics.

Yet the video game industry is still an industry. As with any media industry, demographics become an embedded mode of understanding how to design for and find a dedicated audience and fan base. In the following sections, I use interviews with game designers to synthesize some common industry understandings of what makes effective and enjoyable game play for female audiences.

CONVERSATIONS WITH GAME DESIGNERS: FINDING PATTERNS IN GENDERED PLAY

Within all of these discussions about the gendered nature of digital play, there is a tumultuous contradiction: there are those who deny that there are games created for women audiences, but others in the industry who confirm that the video game industry specifically caters to this demographic. This mode of simultaneous admission and denial can—to some extent—be seen in the game design texts discussed above. Women are both portrayed as an untapped market and a misrepresented market. In this, many suggest that digital games can be made to appeal to *all* audiences, and that the only true mode of appealing to diverse audiences is a more far-reaching sense of "inclusivity." Yet others seem to be suggesting that because the majority of digital games are inherently made with a masculine audience in mind, "gender inclusivity" really implies a binary understanding of gender: if men like some things, women clearly like other things. And in this, the only way to balance the market is by making games specifically for feminine audiences.

This contradiction sparked a wide variety of responses with the game designers I interviewed. The interviewees throughout this chapter (also referenced lightly through the rest of this book) have all worked (in part or exclusively) on video games and for game companies that appear to be targeting women. Some developers confirmed that the games they made were for women outright, while others were less comfortable with the assertion.[20] The very fact that this debate exists, though, provides ample evidence that—at least to some extent—games are necessarily designed for women. Yet even those who denied that some games are made for women tacitly admitted just as much, almost in the same breath. Sheri Graner Ray synthesized the reason for the problem's contradictory nature. She explains that companies "can't come out and say they're making games for women because the industry assumes you're going to fail, but on some level they know who they're making them for. They know who their market is and they're making games for women."[21]

Thus there seems to be an underlying conflict in terms of how developers understand their audiences. As one game designer explains, "I don't think they [the games] are intended for 'just women.' That would be an unnecessary and unwise limitation of the buying demographic. You build a game for other reasons, and then you find out who your largest demographic is. You study them and learn what they loved and hated about the game." In many ways this understanding of a targeted audience makes sense. Obviously audience boundaries will always exceed demographic information: people other than an intended demographic will always be interested in a game. Yet, just as men might go to a romantic comedy and find it enjoyable, they are not necessarily the core intended audience. As one game designer explained in an interview, "Most statistical analysis at game companies today only looks at broad patterns based on easily identifiable, concrete factors (like gender)." As such, there seems to be a need to keep statistics and demographics in mind when designing new games, but also a desire to not be too essentializing about what those statistics might actually mean.

As discussed in the introduction, while about half of all game players identify as female only 22 percent of the industry does. In part, the long-time resistance of the industry to female audiences is what has likely kept many women from becoming game designers. In turn, many (though certainly not all) of the game designers making games for women are male, maintaining the image that the industry, itself, is dominantly masculine. One game designer explains, "There is currently still a stereotype that men are inherently more 'core' gamers than women are, but that is slowly shifting with every new generation that is raised with and around games." So part of the problem is that the industry itself is still in flux—it is not yet built around the expectation that women are gamers. As such, regardless of what women actually play (or, for that matter, what men actually play), there is a set of expectations about how one goes about appealing to female audiences in somewhat concrete ways. Even if game designers resist this premise, their responses reveal that there are distinct games that are *othered* from what is considered the typical "hardcore" audience.

THE FIVE DESIGN CATEGORIES

The problem, of course, is in how one determines which games are meant "for women" or, more generally, "for females." How can we know whether a game's design was intended for Player Two? In some ways, this would seem to be a simple exercise: past stereotypes and logics of the media industries make it hard to look at a game like *Kim Kardashian: Hollywood* as anything other than a game for females. Yet, in order to suggest that *KK:H* is meant for this theorized feminine audience, it seems important to go beyond instinct. Interviews with game designers, then, have helped to solidify a specific rubric: a method of distinguishing factors that might help to define what could be considered feminine styles of gaming. Rather than using the rubrics from this list as definite and immovable factors, though, it is useful to consider them on a continuum. Later in the chapter I break down the most effective way of applying these categories. The following five attributes, then, are not meant to be understood as absolute directives, but as a starting point for better understanding the factors that help to unpack gaming perceived to be for women.

Thematic Attributes

The game designers I interviewed were largely in agreement that thematic elements matter, more than most other factors, including game genre. In this way, the specific themes used in a game space are constantly relevant to the expectation of who would ultimately be the likely audience for a game. Among game designers, the most commonly discussed themes included fairy tales, supernatural, mystery, bucolic, animals, cooking, and fashion. Many agreed that these themes were specifically distinct from those used for other kinds of gaming. None of these categories is particularly surprising when compared to other modes of popular media—all are marketed to women in films, books, television, and other mediated spaces. At the same time, some of the themes do follow back to specific genres. For example, mystery stories and supernatural stories work well with hidden object games, whereas cooking, bucolic themes, and fashion tend to fit better with time management or invest/express games. These types of games tend to be more centered on narrative. As one designer explains, "Women like mature story lines with human relationships at the center." Theme, in these ways, can be seen as one of the greatest factors in appealing to Player Two.

Yet theme is also problematic in that using it to appeal to women audiences can specifically alienate male audiences, according to several game designers. For example, slots games—which tend to be fairly repetitive in style—use themes to cater to different kinds of audiences. As one game designer noted, "Picking themes that pander to women is a good idea if you have a great deal of slots games to offer, but you risk alienating the other 45 percent of your male audience if it's too feminine." The designer went on to offer an example, in which his company created a slots game that used a pet theme. The new theme created a surge of new women that installed the game, but then, correspondingly, men did not like the new theme and the company was unable to retain enough audience.

When game designers are male, this thematic disconnect means that those creating the game need to potentially write outside their own tastes and interests. One female game designer explains: "In my work with mainly young male developers, I've had to teach them how to create game narratives for primarily older female audiences, and that has often been different from what they would like to play themselves. In terms of story, this has often come down to theme. They might want to create games about war, zombies, dragons, and the like, but older women tend to be turned off by those themes, looking instead for Gothic settings, the supernatural, or a classic mystery." Yet basing design entirely on stereotypes is not always fruitful. The same designer further explains that women audiences tend not to be interested in romance, which "always surprises some people."[22] So there is a desire to stick to some specific themes that bring in women without alienating them (or potentially alienating other audiences, as with the slots example above).

Finally, some game designers explained that games about getting families together or some physical activity tend to be popular with women. Here we can see the ways that theme integrates with other aspects of game play (such as alternative controllers) as well as an expectation that women want both social and family-centric play. One developer explains, "Women would be much more likely to play *Dance Central* because it's a game where your body is the controller, the music is Top 40 and pop, and you can dance together with your friends." Similarly, one designer discusses the feminine interest in fitness games or "games with family appeal."

Game-Play Attributes

Beyond just theme, specific elements of game play are often used with the intention of appealing to Player Two. Unsurprisingly, many of the game-play assumptions made by game designers reflect suggestions based on Ray's *Gender Inclusive Game Design*. Some of the game-play elements discussed by game designers include:

- increased use of social elements;
- fewer constraints on time;

- less in-game risk;
- simple mechanics; and
- emphasis on creative expression.

While some designers mentioned other aspects, the factors listed above were most frequently referenced as necessary components in making games that appeal to women.

The expectation of women as "social players" was one of the most commonly referenced attributes by the game designers I interviewed. One designer explained that games that have higher percentages of women players "tend to focus on collaborative social personal expression." Similarly, another designer elaborates on social gaming by explaining, "Collaborative social is a big one. As a very general rule, women tend to prefer to socialize with other players in ways that reinforce the ideas of 'togetherness,' as opposed to the 'apartness' of many player vs. player games." Thus the social elements of digital games that drive women audiences should not be situations where players interact with other players in a competitive sense, but rather should focus on more collaborative play that spurs a feeling of togetherness. As one game designer explains, "Women respond very strongly to social games; games that drive real social interaction between themselves and their friends." Thus the expectation of "social" needs, in some way, to be embedded in their real-world friendships, relationships, and experiences—not as a space where random people play with other random people. In turn, games designed for women audiences often focus distinctly on noncompetitive communities. This style of game play contextualizes many of the games discussed throughout this book—games like earlier versions of *FarmVille* (on Facebook) tend to rely more heavily on social interaction, while games like *Kim Kardashian: Hollywood* give players an opportunity to play socially but don't necessarily push that kind of interaction. Other games, such as *Words with Friends*, require far more social interaction—either with friends or strangers—but are more competitive than cooperative, suggesting that it might be more gender-neutral in intended audience.

Another aspect that designers discuss in their interviews is how time factors as an important and distinct element when designing games for women. In particular, game-play elements should not force players to play too quickly or for too long. One designer explains, "Non-time-limited tends to be popular; in general, a lot of women tend to play social/mobile games as a way to relax, escape, or decompress from the stresses of their lives outside of games. Putting in mechanics that deliberately create stress or introduce the possibility of failure tend to not be as popular with players who are playing these games to avoid that sort of situation." This certainly reinforces claims made in *Gender Inclusive Game Design* but also helps to contextualize some of the games I discuss in more detail in chapter 2, where I focus on how games manage women's time. Additionally, it reinforces research on gender and leisure from the introduction, suggesting that women tend toward leisure that can be done in small snippets of time. So, on the one hand, games need to use time in a way that creates a stress-free environment. On the other hand, according to game designers, it should be playable in five- to fifteen-minute bursts. According to one designer, this makes it "accessible for both a mom demographic as well as people at work." This kind of game play, wherein time is pocketed but does not push players toward a stressful countdown, characterizes most of the games discussed throughout this book. *Diner Dash, Kim Kardashian: Hollywood, FarmVille* (and the rest of the Zynga *Ville* series), and hidden object games, as well as puzzle games and more gender-neutral games like *Words with Friends*, are all constructed with small activities that are not necessarily time-based but are capable of taking up large or short periods of time.

Game design intended for women often also attempts to reduce the perception of in-game "risk." One game designer explains that when creating a game for female audiences, there is a tendency to focus on low-stakes competition, "where a loss in one session doesn't carry over to successive sessions the way it might in games in the mid- or hardcore gaming categories." Once again, this nicely reinforces Ray's points in *Gender Inclusive Game Design*. This plays out in games such as *Restaurant Story, Diner Dash, Kim Kardashian: Hollywood,* or *FarmVille* that have no specific repercussions to not doing things properly on the first try. A loss in many of the games intended for women audiences doesn't have negative ramifications in game play—it just prevents them from moving forward to the next level, the opposite of what happens in many console or computer games labeled as "hardcore." This minor shift, while a recommendation for female audiences, is in some ways just good form in game design. A forgiving game makes play less stressful, in general, to all non-experienced game players.

Risk also relates back to interface. As previously noted by Sheri Graner Ray, by creating an easy-to-understand interface, play becomes more attractive to novice players. These players are not necessarily women, although women often fall into this category. The most common simplification of a game interface is a "point-and-click" style, often used in casual computer games. The equivalent to point-and-click on mobile devices, according to designers, are swipes, taps, and zooms. While this simplification of the complex mechanics offered by console games might seem condescending to audiences, one designer notes that the players in question "aren't interested in a lot of complexity in the physical component of the game. They're much more interested in feeling as if their minds are challenged." Thus an accessible interface design is necessary to bring in new audiences, regardless of gender.

Some designers acknowledged that games meant to appeal to women audiences have some degree of "creative expression." As one designer explains, in designing a title for women, he would "focus heavily on building a game with mechanics of skill and creative expression, so that players have the ability to get a strong sense of intrinsic reward through repeated play and that players can talk to one another about unique experiences they have when playing the game." While the idea of creative expression might seem counterintuitive to a gaming environment (wherein actions are generally predetermined), it makes sense when considering that in many games discussed in this book there are several design options *earned* as the player progresses through the game. For instance, in *Kim Kardashian: Hollywood*, the player is given an increasing amount of clothing and hair options with which to personalize his or her avatar while playing. *Restaurant Story 2* and recent versions of *Diner Dash* also give various design options—not always based on clothing fashion, but often on the décor of one's restaurant.

Visual Attributes

Unsurprisingly, many game designers I interviewed remarked on the importance of maintaining an aesthetic style to appeal to women. One explains, "Art and presentation of a theme are extremely critical for nailing the appeal of your audience." Yet, despite stereotypes, this visual design does not necessarily map to "pink." While "pink games" was often the nomenclature used for describing games for girl audiences, most game designers recognize a certain degree of sophistication in their female audiences and a lack of desire for pink. One designer explains, "I've definitely pushed the team to not make the game 'girly'; to avoid plastering the UI [user interface] with pink, which seems to be the temptation any time video game people make games with women in mind." Therefore, while there is a certain degree of stereotype associated with "pink," and certainly pink games are built with an intended gender appeal, most of the game designers I spoke to want to push further than this.

Instead of pink, the key word to describe the visual design for games for women seems to be "lush." As one game designer explains, "We make sure the game is visually lush, with a bright but sophisticated color palette. It can't appear to be targeted toward girls, so anything overtly pink or feminine wouldn't sell." In addition to saturated colors, another game designer noted that there is often a surplus of rounded shapes, shiny elements, and soft shadows. These visual attributes might be buttons, gameplay elements, or menu layouts. The optical overload of *Candy Crush Saga* (Figure 2) and *Candy Crush Soda Saga* are perfect examples of a "lush" aesthetic, although the label of visual lushness can certainly be applied to other game interfaces. While the colors for hidden object games don't tend toward brightness, they make up for this lack of color intensity with a surplus of overwhelming visual data and the "shiny elements" and "soft shadows" mentioned above.

This being the case, several match-3 games seem to fall neatly into this category of both visually lush and full of rounded, almost cartoonish elements. One game designer noted that while game mechanics might be identical, aesthetics vary wildly when considering gender in audience building. The designer explains that while *Candy Crush Saga*'s visual lushness is clearly meant for women, one can find masculine counterparts with games like *Marvel Puzzle Quest*, which has similar mechanics but a different visual skin and a slightly different rule sets.

Character Attributes

In *Gender Inclusive Game Design* Sheri Graner Ray notes that character flexibility—allowing the player to build and play a variety of character types—is key to not alienating female audiences. Industry professionals have noted this for some time, and the game designers I interviewed reinforced this understanding: avatars should be customizable when possible and never sexualized. One developer explains, "In general, women want avatars and NPCs [non-player characters] that they can relate to, customize, and [that] generally don't over-sexualize their character." More specifically, another designer remarks that women tend to have more interest in games "where players aren't forced to play a specific male character."

Figure 2. A screenshot of the mobile game *Candy Crush Saga*, developed by Midasplayer AB and published by King.com. The game provides an illustration of the use of "lush" aesthetics (e.g., bright, vibrant colors and rounded edges).

Thus, much like Sheri Graner Ray implies in her foundational text, diversity of player-playable characters is key to achieving a broad audience base.

In appealing to women, it is important not only to have female characters but also to keep those characters from being overtly sexualized. One designer explains, "Un-sexualized female characters work well for both sexes, but the opposite works well as well." Additionally, the same designer explains that style and fashion also factor into the appearance: "Characters that look fancy or follow the current fashion also catch the player's attention. It's not necessarily sexualized (though a lot of fashion seems to point toward that), just showing that the character values his or her appearance." This accounts for a game like *Kim Kardashian: Hollywood*, where characters might have hourglass figures, but only for the purpose of complementing trendy fashion. Finally, game designers suggest that one mode of bypassing sexualization and bodies is to make avatars or non-player characters animal rather than human. Using cute animal styles feeds into the aesthetic concerns of the above section (by suggesting lush styles and cartoonish curves) while remaining gender-inclusive by all accounts.

Finally, once again highlighting the importance of theme, there seems to be a sense from game designers that story factors into character types. One game designer references hidden object games, explaining that in that kind of title, "Players overwhelmingly like their detectives and private investigators. Beyond that, they like some fantasy characters, and they especially like animals as a helper character. They don't tend to appreciate characters that belittle or heckle them, although some of the family games I've worked on included a bit of good-natured ribbing." Here it seems notable to point out that because many women are novice video game players, the avatars and non-player characters need to avoid appearing threatening or condescending.

Excluded Attributes

The final rubric discussed by game designers is a question of not what is *included* in the digital games, but what is *excluded*. This category is a bit more difficult track with specifics, particularly because so much of it is based on thirty-plus years of development within the AAA gaming industry, as well as controversies in game culture. In short, there is a perception that violent content, as well as spaces that might incur harassment, are not appealing to female audiences.

While Sheri Graner Ray specifically explains in *Gender Inclusive Game Design* that violence is acceptable for women players, she remarks that game violence must be clearly contextualized. This is more or less echoed by the interviewed game designers, with comments suggesting that "games that feature violent men in violent stories where women are treated without respect clearly appeal very little to women." Thus there is a sense that a little violence is acceptable, but an excessive amount of violence—particularly performed by men and directed toward women—is not likely to be accepted by female audiences. This seems generally unsurprising but is worth adding to the set of rubrics. It implies that a game like *Angry Birds*, with its violent subtext but cute animals and lack of gore, is more likely to be accepted by women than a game like *Grand Theft Auto IV*, with more realistic violence performed by humans.

Additionally, games that involve a specific amount of learned acumen—particularly that which would have been accumulated by a lifetime of gaming—are less likely to be desirable to women players. One designer notes that "skill-based games" are thought to be less appealing to women. Finally, games that create a space where players can easily be harassed in real time by other players (particularly by voice) are perceived to not be appealing to women players.

APPLYING THE ATTRIBUTES TO GAMES IN THIS BOOK AND BEYOND

The rubrics listed in the previous section should not be used separately when considering whether a game is intended for female audiences. Instead, the factors should be considered cumulatively. Additionally, while I have five major attributes listed above, it makes more sense to break them down to several smaller aspects. This breakdown comes down to ten distinct categories:

1. *Thematic congruence*: Whether the game maps thematically to topics for women (as outlined in "Thematic Attributes" section).
2. *Collaborative/social*: Whether the game has opportunities for experiences to play with friends or strangers in a noncompetitive way (as outlined in the "Game-Play Attributes" section).

3. *Time positive*: Whether the game structures play so that the player does not need to play for long periods of time and can pick it up again easily (as outlined in the "Game-Play Attributes" section).

4. *Low risk*: Whether failure dramatically affects the player's overall experience (outlined in the "Game-Play Attributes" section).

5. *Creative expression*: Whether there are opportunities to design spaces or characters to show individual expression and style (outlined in the "Game-Play Attributes" section).

6. *Lush aesthetics*: Whether the game has bright, intense colors; rounded edges; and visual surplus (outlined in the "Visual Attributes" section).

7. *Non-sexualized characters*: Whether all or the majority of characters in the game are non-sexualized, which may include animal characters (as outlined in the "Character Attributes" section).

8. *Avatar choice*: Whether the player is given the opportunity to select and/or design his or her own avatar (as outlined in the "Character Attributes" section).

9. *Low violence*: Whether the game has minimal violent content (as outlined in the "Excluded Attributes" section).

10. *Low harassment potential*: Whether the game is structured in a way that players cannot easily be harassed by strangers (as outlined in the "Excluded Attributes" section).

Given this list, it seems that rather than using a specific yes-or-no binary as to whether a game has been designed for perceived woman audiences, it might be more useful to think of this question on a continuum. Cumulatively, several of these factors together help to show a specific design plan that clearly is intended to accommodate women. That is not to say that men would not be interested in playing these games, but that the design tactics clearly demonstrate a woman in mind as at least some part of a target audience. Figure 3 shows these elements in a chart, with several games and check marks indicating which games have which factors. The final column of Figure 3 gives a "score" to each game, depending on the number of factors that apply to that particular game. Figure 4 shows these games on a continuum chart, per their scores. Games with a score below a 5 are on the left side of the chart, indicating that they are more likely intended for masculine audiences, whereas games on the right side of the chart—with a score of 6 or above—indicates that there is a higher likelihood they were intended for Player Two.

Here are a few examples of how specific games play out on this chart:

- *Grand Theft Auto IV* is a game that uses the crime underworld as its primary theme (not a theme listed above) and features complex game-play elements (as opposed to point-and-click), relatively high stakes in terms of failure and interface, sexualized non-player characters, dark shadows and deep aesthetics, and violent content. This version of the game has online play, making it ripe for harassment of female players. It is therefore safe to surmise that *GTV IV* was not designed with a female audience at its core. *GTA IV* has a score of 0.

- *Angry Birds* is a game that uses an animal-centric war as its primary theme with simplified game-play elements, relatively low stakes in failure and interface, animal characters, lush aesthetics, and moderately violent content (violence is portrayed without blood). Thematically, it does not really

	Thematic	Collaborative/social	Time positive	Low risk	Creative expression	Lush aesthetics	Nonsexualized	Avatar selection	Low violence	Low harassment	Total
Grand Theft Auto IV											0
Tomb Raider										✔	1
Angry Birds			✔	✔	✔	✔				✔	5
World of Warcraft		✔	✔	✔		✔		✔			5
Wii Fit			✔	✔		✔	✔	✔	✔	✔	6
Candy Crush Saga	✔		✔	✔		✔	✔		✔	✔	7
Clash of Clans		✔	✔	✔	✔	✔	✔			✔	7
Mystery Case Files	✔		✔	✔		✔	✔		✔	✔	7
Diner Dash	✔		✔	✔	✔	✔	✔		✔	✔	8
Kim Kardashian: Hollywood	✔	✔	✔	✔	✔	✔		✔	✔	✔	9
Restaurant Story 2	✔	✔	✔	✔	✔	✔	✔		✔	✔	9
FarmVille	✔	✔	✔	✔	✔	✔	✔		✔	✔	9

Figure 3. A chart of ten game attributes, breaking down specific in-game aspects that distinguish games that are designed for an intended female audience, per game designer interviews.

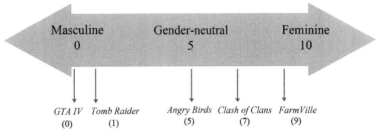

Figure 4. A continuum of masculine/feminine games, after being broken down from the ten attributes. The left side of the continuum illustrates an intended masculine audience, and the right side an intended feminine audience. The center of the chart shows games that are gender-neutral in style.

fit into the spectrum of what is described in category 1. We can say that *Angry Birds* is meant to appeal to appeal to diverse audiences and is relatively gender-neutral, since it hits many of the items listed above. *Angry Birds* has a score of 5.

- *Candy Crush Saga* is a match-3 game that involves matching specific candies in certain patterns. Its theme is an abstraction of food and is relatively low stakes in terms of failure and interface, cherubic characters, lush aesthetics, and no violent content. While *Candy Crush* probably appeals to a wide audience of both men and women, we can assert that it was designed with some aspects of an implied female audience. *Candy Crush Saga* has a score of 7.

- *Kim Kardashian: Hollywood* is a casual role-playing game that uses celebrity and fashion as its primary theme, with low stakes in failure and interface, somewhat sexy characters—but within the context of fashion and avatars that can be changed by players throughout game play—lush aesthetics, and no violence or potential for harassment. *KKH* was clearly designed with a female audience in mind. *KKH* has a score of 9.

Initially this charting appears almost ideal—it helps to begin to distinguish masculine games from gender-neutral and feminine games. However, Figures 3 and 4 are imperfect when dealing with masculine-intended casuals. A good example of this problem can be seen with the game *Clash of Clans*, a casual, free-to-play mobile game where players create armies and troops meant to attack other players, with thematic elements that are typically deemed more masculine. However, the play style itself is structured as casual with check marks for elements like collaborative social, time positive, and creative expression.[23] Thus a game like *Clash of Clans* scores rather high on the chart with a 7. In this way, it becomes apparent that several of the factors listed as attributes are not mapping only theorized masculine/feminine play expectations—they are also mapping whether a game is casual. This confusion, of course, makes sense given what John Vanderhoef refers to as the "feminization of casual."[24]

With this in mind, it seems important to weigh certain factors in the chart more heavily than others. For example, in my interviews, designers suggested that the thematic elements are particularly important when considering how to design a game for a female audience. Thus I argue that Figure 4 does a good job of mapping initially, but then a second chart (Figure 5) helps distribute the games with a score of 5 or higher specifically by whether they fit themes commonly expected in games for women. The games I focus on throughout this book are those that appear on the right side of this final chart: games that score higher than a 5 and maintain thematic relevance, suggesting that they are designed specifically for an intended female audience.

Given all these assessments, there are several categories of video games that most commonly meet these goals and seem to be intended for women audiences. As one game designer explains, certain categories of mobile/social "tend to attract a higher percentage of women players: in

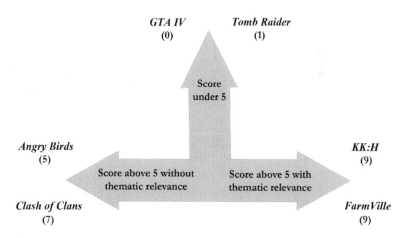

Figure 5. The continuum of game attributes factoring thematic elements. While Figure 4 illustrated a full continuum of all the games, this chart balances out thematic elements. The top of the chart shows games that score below a 5. The bottom left shows games that score 5 or higher but do not have the thematic elements assumed for women audiences. The bottom right shows games with a 5 or higher that do have thematic elements assumed to be directed toward female audiences.

particular, casual puzzle, invest/express, and hidden object games usually tend to see a gender distribution of somewhere between 60/40 to 75/25 in favor of women. These games usually have a few traits in common—they tend to focus on collaborative social, personal expression, and they are generally not time pressured." At the same time, they bear the thematic expectations of "women's genres." Some of the game categories specifically listed by developers that have a tendency to attract more female audiences include:

- hidden object games (e.g., *Mystery Case Files*);
- time management games (e.g., *Diner Dash*);
- invest/express games (e.g., *Farmville*);
- match-3 games (e.g., *Candy Crush Saga*);
- social games (e.g., *Words with Friends*); and
- fashion games (e.g., *Kim Kardashian: Hollywood*)

Additionally, as noted above, Wii games and exergames are also considered popular with women, even if they were not always designed specifically *for* women. The categories provide a clear set of materials worth studying throughout the remainder of this book. Just as the creation of more feminized games has continued to shift the video game industry, studying the outputs of these products will continue to shift the scholarship of how we understand play and leisure in gendered constructs.

As noted already throughout this book, designed identity is about how the individual choices made in game design cumulatively build a shadow gamer. The choices listed above are primarily logical decisions, given the past history of the video game industry's attempts to court gendered audiences. Simplified interfaces, tested themes that are popular with women, visually distinct aesthetics, and more mutable in-game characters all support Sheri Graner Ray's argument about gender inclusivity in game design. At the same time, they also demonstrate variations on how these aspects might be implemented.

The focus throughout this book, however, is not limited to studying this set of rubrics; rather, I explore how designed identity constructs players. While designed identity can be applied to several categories (and in some ways, several forms of media), the focus here is specifically on women audiences. The goal is to use the rubrics of this chapter to isolate and consider which games are specifically meant for women, and subsequently to see what can be learned about how leisure is designed for this audience.

DESPERATELY SEEKING JENNIFER

I began this chapter with a discussion of "Jennifer," the idealized player of *Restaurant Story 2*. Jennifer, of course, is both real and imaginary—she is an amalgam of player types, expectations, and presumptions. She is Player Two. She is also not the only draft of Player Two. One designer interviewed for this study told a story about a game company that had a poster on its wall of a "middle-aged white woman dressed like an insurance agent." When asked why the woman was there, the game designer was told, "So we always remember who our player is." Other designers echoed this sentiment. One designer clearly stated that there is an industry impression that invest/express games (discussed in more detail in the next chapter) were built "for a middle-aged woman, somewhere in the Midwest."

Building player types is not new. It is a practice started by the Wizards of the Coast in their original creation of the card game *Magic: The Gathering*.[25] In many ways the practice makes sense in this sector of the video game industry where teams comprised mostly of men create games for women. In this way, character types can help game designers create outside their own selves and design play that has a degree of empathy toward other kinds of gamers. It would seem that this would be a good practice. However, while other media industries have toyed with player personas, it is not necessarily a widely used practice elsewhere.[26] There is no expectation that there is a "Melissa" for whom the sitcom *Friends* was created. While most film directors are men, to my knowledge there is no "Cynthia" that they are instructed to keep in mind when making a romantic comedy. The creation of this kind of archetype seems to be distinct to the video game industry. In this way, "Jennifer" stands alone as not only a representation of women, but as a representation of the anomalies created within and by the video game industry.

Jennifer is not a representation of what is wrong with the video game industry—she merely illustrates the changes that are happening (both good and bad). In this way Jennifer is both important and problematic. She offers hope. As one game designer explains, "The game market has changed so that women can see themselves in the games they play; they are no longer expected to like what the men in *their* fantasies like, because they can choose to play games designed with women in mind." Jennifer is a result of that shift, but also an illusive character that cannot be captured by a simple player type.

Jennifer is complex; she is multifaceted; she has nuance. Jennifer is the daughter of the conflicts between second-wave feminism and leisure practices—she wants to play but has neither the time nor the resources to do so. While there is an implication that Jennifer is white, middle class, cis-gendered, heterosexual, abled, and maternal, she is not necessarily any of those things, and she is simultaneously all of them. Jennifer is the ghost inside this book, desperately trying to push at the edges of the video game industry to get a just little more play.

2 *Playing with Time*

DO SOMETHING WITH YOUR NOTHING

In 2006, the Nintendo DS Lite was released as a mobile gaming platform that specifically targeted women audiences. Along with this new product, a marketing campaign ran in several special interest magazines such as *O: The Oprah Magazine, People,* and *Martha Stewart Living.*[1] The campaign used the slogan "Do Something with Your Nothing" and featured situations where people are often bored (such as doctor's office waiting rooms and bus stops). Rhetorically, the advertisements suggested that video game play should be done not as an act of leisure for the sake of leisure, but rather to fill snippets of time. For example, one advertisement suggests, "The average wait in a doctor's office is 23.4 minutes. Do something with your nothing" (Figure 6).[2] These ads often accompanied the slogan with images of happy people—primarily women—playing, while bored people enviously watched them.

The "nothing" being referred to in the "Do Something with Your Nothing" campaign was, of course, time.[3] In order to play video games, in order to enjoy them and become a good player, a person needs time more than anything else. The idea of games and apps to keep oneself constantly occupied has become increasingly relevant with the ubiquity of mobile devices. Mobile gaming can be seen as an intensification of this trend—at the core of the iPhone game sits the inherent contradictions between productivity and play. But time is a complicated factor within the lived experiences of many women, and these complications have become part of the designed identity of the theorized woman player. The importance of time as a factor in the designed identity of Player Two is apparent given that "time positive" is its own category in the chart from the previous chapter.

The average wait in a
doctor's office is 23.4 minutes.

Do something with your nothing.

You have time. That nothing time. The time in between everything else you have to do. Touch Generations is a series of games that easily get you in, out, and on with the rest of your day. In just a few short minutes, you could make a dent in a Sudoku puzzle or play three holes of golf. It's your nothing time. Do something with it. For more games and information, go to **TouchGenerations.com**

Figure 6. The Nintendo DS "Do Something with Your Nothing" magazine advertisement. This spot ran in *O: The Oprah Magazine, People*, and *Martha Stewart Living* in 2006. The ad illustrates a desire to sell women on the idea that playtime should be done in small, interstitial snippets of time.

Being "time positive," and being flexible in how a game can be played, therefore, is a core concept at the root of both the lived realities as well as the perceived lives of women players.

In this chapter I demonstrate the delicate balance between time, play, and gender as it relates to the designed identity of Player Two. As noted in the introduction, many women have a specific and complicated relationship with leisure activities, often leaving leisure partitioned into small blocks of time. Since second-wave feminism, with its influx of women returning to the workforce in the 1970s and 1980s, women's leisure has become pocketed into small moments uninhabited by perceived productivity, due to what Arlie Russell Hochschild refers to as "the second shift."[4] The second shift pronounces the notion that women often work full-time jobs both in offices and in household management. Yet, again, time is what video games require—without it games do not get played. In this way, the designed identity of the woman player in many video games deals with managing time both in the game world and in the real world. The resulting play never fully engages the player and never allows for the comfort of uninhibited leisure within digital play. At the same time, it is impossible to ignore that it does allow and make time for play, even if that play is segmented. Playing with time is about allotting specific moments for productive play and giving new players entry into the medium.

Time management, of course, is a tricky topic in video games. Alison Harvey, for example, demonstrates ways that families often limit screen time in general, but that video game screen time also plays an important role for many families in terms of togetherness within the domestic sphere.[5] Thus we don't often associate playing video games with managing time. Time management tends to be relegated to the world of business or the management of the household. Time management is in the spirit of using one's time in the most efficient way possible, whether that is getting projects done on time, attending meetings, or taking the kids to soccer practice. We associate time management with the efficiency of everyday tasks, not with the free-form nature of leisure, which is theoretically *not* meant to be managed. Leisure, as we tend to understand it, is about freedom from the structures of the everyday. The purpose of leisure involves the specific pleasure of *not* thinking or worrying about time. Video games, one would think, fall under this purview—while one might schedule free time for playing video games, the game itself is rarely full of the everyday obligations implied by the monotony of time management. Thus there is a push-and-pull when video games are specifically designed with women in mind. They are often designed with an understanding of the complex relationships between women and time, but also with an understanding that time is what is necessary to draw in more players and create a depth of play. This complicated situation often plays out in the designs, narratives, and mechanics of a genre often referred to as "time management games."

It is impossible to put too much emphasis on the significance of time management games and their descendants in terms of their implications for Player Two. This chapter interrogates the contradictory nature of time and leisure, primarily through this lens of time management games. At their core, such games often employ the thematic subtext of time management in both virtual and real worlds. More specifically, the genre seems to be primarily intended for women players, with most of the games in this category scoring well above a 6 on the continuum from the previous chapter, and many have the thematic relevance that positions them for feminine audiences. Because time management products are primarily marketed to women,[6] it is no coincidence that such games are designed with this perceived audience in mind.

Thus the designed identity of Player Two cannot be disentangled from the mechanics, narratives, and play style of time management games. Starting with what I identify as the urtext of time management gaming, *Diner Dash*, I explain how this game, and its successors in the series, advocate for specific uses of time during play. I then explore three different modes of "time management" as they have pertained to games since the popularity of the *Dash* series (specifically analyzing the games *Island Tribe 4*, *Magic Life*, *Cake Mania*, and *Sally's Salon*). Additionally, I demonstrate how this category turned into a new gaming trend within the last five years—what is referred to as "invest/express" games by industry professionals. Zynga's *Ville* games (e.g., *FarmVille*), *Restaurant Story 2*, and *Kim Kardashian: Hollywood* are all examples of the invest/express category.

TIME IN VIDEO GAMES

In considering the importance of time in narrative, it is useful to factor in the medium in question: specific forms of media affect the structure and expectations of temporality. For example, Paul Booth has cleverly illustrated ways that the shifting aesthetics of television have shaped new paradigms for temporality in that medium. Booth argues that specific conventions have been built into our current televisual landscape through modes of "temporal displacement" that occur "when television programs play with time, using flashforwards, flashbacks, time travel, and/or changes in the protagonist's memory to heighten the spectacle of the television narrative."[7] These temporal displacements have the capability of engaging the audience in ways that allow them to turn the plot into a kind of game.[8] Thus this mode of temporality is specific to the serialized, televisual format that audiences have adapted to over time. Different media are able to engage with temporality in different ways, depending on the affordances of the structures, formats, and audiences of that specific medium.

Given the parameters and complexity of the medium, it is useful to consider how video games engage with temporality. In their research on time, Jose Zagal and Michael Mateas suggest the use of "temporal frames" to consider how time functions within formal analysis of video games. They explain, "Relationships between events constitute time; it follows that all of these events contribute to the temporality of the game. Rather than developing a single 'temporal domain' consisting of the set of relationships between all these events, we found it useful to identify specific event subsets, define a temporality relative to that subset, and then identify interactions between the times established by these different event subsets."[9] In other words, in order to analyze temporality in a game, it is necessary to consider all the ways that time might function simultaneously within that space. Zagal and Mateas then break down temporal frames in video games into four primary categories: real-world time (how time occurs in the real world during game play), game-world time (time that is established by the events occurring within the game world), coordination time (events that are in coordination with multiple player actions), and fictive time (large chunks of time passing that might occur between single rounds of a game).[10]

Using this framework, this chapter primarily focuses on the interplay between real-world time and game-world time, as they relate to time management games and their successors. Time, I argue, is structured in such a way in this gaming genre that it necessarily implies specific modes of time and time management in the real world. The anxieties implied by real-world time management seep into the very structure of time management games. Player Two and her designed identity are affected by the expectation that the player will use her game-world time—time that is often suggested as frantic, manic, and out of control—in order to better manage and structure her real-world time. This complex interplay between temporality in the game world and the real world becomes inextricably linked to expectations of women's relationship to leisure, making campaigns such as "do something with your nothing" an essential pitch to Player Two, who is presumed to not have large chunks of free time but, rather, tiny slices of time.

As described in the introduction, women's leisure tends to be typified by small bursts of free time. Given this, the interconnections between these temporal frames take on increased significance for understanding how play is designed for Player Two. At the same time, increasingly, the modes of time management gaming (particularly those in the invest/ express category as typified by *FarmVille* and *Kim Kardashian: Hollywood*) seem to involve an exponential amount of game-world time in order to play the game properly. This game-world time expands outward, turning into real-world time and blending them together. In this way, one might argue, the designed identity of Player Two might actually be supporting more time for leisure.

THE TIME MANAGEMENT GAME

Time management products are those that help organize how we spend our time in our everyday lives. Products such as day planners, software, books, and phone applications are all meant to illustrate to consumers how to properly use their time in the most efficient ways possible. In Arlie Russell Hochschild's *The Time Bind: When Work Becomes Home and Home Becomes Work*, she asserts that many products for time management are specifically marketed to women. She explains, "Like men, women absorb the work–family speedup far more than they resist it; but unlike men, women are the ones who shoulder most of the workload at home. Naturally, then, they are more starved for time than men are. It is women who feel more acutely the need to save time and women who are more tempted by the goods and services of the growing 'time industry.' They are the ones who shop for time."[11] This time industry, according to Hochschild, preys on the complicated schedules that many women navigate upon reentering the workforce after having children. In other works, as mentioned above, Hochschild describes this problem as "the second shift" wherein women are expected to work the equivalent of two full-time jobs, managing households and careers.[12] The organization of their time then becomes essential to the lived, everyday realities of many women, which can then easily be marketed as products. In these ways, it seems likely that time management games are targeting busy, working, female players, perhaps even mothers. While the games themselves are not time-savers, the "time management" label might have particular appeal to this demographic.

Certainly, parallels between casual games and the aforementioned research on women's leisure are undeniable. Both seem to be characterized by the snippets of time described in the introduction of this book. Casual games not only accentuate these small bursts of time but are also often "cheap or free," much as Rosemary Deem characterized typical leisure for women.[13] The ease with which casual gaming is able to fit into many women's leisure patterns makes the assumptive links between women and casual games unsurprising. In short, casual games are often structured in series of short levels, wherein the player is able to complete a small portion of the game in fifteen minutes or less.

Time management games, though, push issues of time and leisure further than many other kinds of casual games. The time management game is unique in that its very structure uses constraints and expectations of women's leisure (or lack thereof) in order to insist that women *should* play with their free time, but also serves as a constant reminder that women don't *have* the leisure time to comfortably play. Essentially, in time management games, players are generally charged with work-type tasks—waiting on tables, making products, serving customers, guiding employees, or cleaning and reordering spaces—within timed sessions. Time management games are often in the service of the non-player-character customers. In order to be successful in the game world, the player must move quickly and keep customers happy to curry their favor and earn large tips. But in order to do these things, speed is always of the essence.

Even the descriptions of games under the label "time management" often suggest few playful attributes. For example, Big Fish Games advertises a large selection of time management games on its website and encourages the player by suggesting that he or she "manage time, customers, and money in games for the serious goal setter." The lack of playfulness in this definition is notable, but also notable is the (re)use of time management as a marketing tool. It would seem that time management, as an often-gendered consumer product, has been neatly shuffled into a gaming category. Thus, within its game-play style, time management games can be seen as exacerbating these preexisting issues with women and leisure. Computer games in this category include *Diner Dash, Cake Mania, Sally's Salon, Ranch Rush, Island Tribe 4, Magic Life, Burger Shop, Turbo Subs*, and hundreds of others. Similarly, myriad time management games can be found on mobile devices, increasingly referred to by the video game industry as invest/express games, such as Zynga's *Farm-Ville* and *CityVille*; Storm 8's *Restaurant Story 2* and *Castle Story*; and Glu Mobile's *Kim Kardashian: Hollywood* and *Katy Perry: Pop*.

Each of these games, when even marginally popular, subsequently spawns dozens of sequel games and clones (often from other mobile game companies) that offer similar (often identical) game play. Thus the success of *Sally's Salon* might lead to the development of half a dozen distinct (yet slightly different) games. Like other casual games, they are cheap or free to play and involve bursts of activity. But, at the same time, time management games constantly invoke themes of time in the game world in a way that plays off perceptions regarding women's anxieties about time in the real world. To borrow terminology from Zagal and Mateas's work on temporal frames, they suggest a slippage of game-world time and real-world time.

By analyzing the structure of game play in several video games within the time management sphere, I illustrate how the designed identity of the woman player plays with, and into, expectations of women's real-world time. The label "time management game" is an apt one—not only do the games thematically involve work-related issues, but the mechanics of time management games have underlying themes of work embedded in the objects of play. Given this, it is useful to consider these games as a kind of "third shift." Hochschild explains that the third shift might be used for "noticing, understanding, and coping with the emotional consequences of the compressed second shift."[14] Alternatively, Michele Bolton characterizes a third shift as a kind of inner dialogue that functions as a psychological workspace for many women balancing home life with work life.[15] If Bolton's assessment is true, then the third shift of gaming is complementary: it functions as both an iteration of and release from the psychological burden of this mental weight.

DINER DASH: ESTABLISHING A GENRE

As mentioned above, the game *Diner Dash* is the urtext of the time management genre. Created in 2003 by the game designers Nick Fortugno and Eric Zimmerman, the series follows the adventures of Flo, a hardworking waitress/restaurateur who functions as the player's avatar. The game has been credited with inspiring a "trove of restaurant-themed casual games."[16] Additionally, though, it inspired an entire genre of game play— the time management game—which pushes its influence far beyond its waitressing roots. Though the game specifically targeted forty-something females,[17] its conventions helped shape the future of all time management games. The game's popularity initiated the development of dozens of spinoffs, many considered successful from an industry perspective. The company that oversaw the production of these games, PlayFirst, has since been acquired by the mobile game company Glu (responsible for publishing *Kim Kardashian: Hollywood*).[18] In this way, recent iterations of *Diner Dash* are slowly turning to the invest/express model, detailed below. To this end, the traditional time management game has become somewhat obsolete, slipping into a position where invest/express is now the more all-encompassing version of the format. Yet examining the roots of the time management game emphasizes the ways time has grown more elastic in this genre. In other words, by looking at the trajectory from *Diner Dash* through to *Kim Kardashian: Hollywood*, I am able to illustrate the subtle but impressive shifts that have occurred in women's gaming over the last decade and a half.

While *Diner Dash* does not represent the entirety of time management games, it helped establish the roots of the genre as well as several modes of iteration. In the subsequent section, I branch out and describe later iterations of the genre (including invest/express games), as well as how this style of gaming has developed into other franchises with respect to themes of time management. I go into more detail on the *Diner Dash* series than I do about many of the other games discussed in this chapter. Having spurred the initial format for this style of gaming, and being the game that several others clearly modeled themselves after, it is important to illustrate how work and play are structured in the *Diner Dash* series. Additionally, because several other games replicated the format (with often minimal game-play modifications), there is a certain degree of redundancy within this genre—particularly the early games that were deliberately modeled on *Diner Dash*, such as *Cake Mania*. Because of this, I use *Diner Dash* as a model, and then describe other variations that have helped to structure subgenres within this area.

Diner Dash, initially a computer title, has now become a complex network of games, including portable versions for smartphones and multiple gaming platforms. Several of the computer versions have been networked for limited online gaming. The series includes *Diner Dash, Diner Dash 2: Restaurant Rescue, Diner Dash: Flo on the Go, Diner Dash: Hometown Hero*, and *Diner Dash:* BOOM! The most recent release, in 2014, reverted to the name *Diner Dash* as Glu's newest mobile version of the franchise (Figure 7). Some versions have modular premium restaurants that can be added to the base game, which places the main character in a variety of surreal situations. For instance, *Diner Dash: Flo through Time* is an

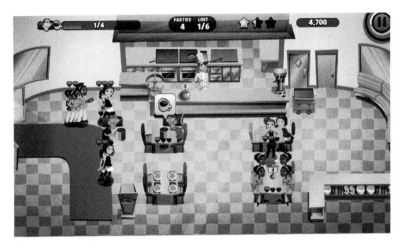

Figure 7. A screenshot of the game *Diner Dash*, originally developed by GameLab and published by PlayFirst in 2003. *Diner Dash* was the earliest example of a time management game—a category particularly marketed to women. The image shows the more recent version of the game, after Glu Mobile acquired the series.

addition to *Diner Dash: Hometown Hero* that uses time-travel predicaments to create more variation in the game play. Other restaurant adventures place Flo as a protagonist in fairy tales and use various seasonal themes. The series of *Cooking Dash* games feature Flo trying to take over a kitchen when her cook is away. Additionally, there are several other *Dash* games, where Flo makes cameos either as a participant (in the *Wedding Dash* games she serves as an occasional waitress), customer, or confidante. The other *Dash* games include *Wedding Dash, Dairy Dash, Fitness Dash, Parking Dash, Fashion Dash, DinerTown Detective Agency, DinerTown Tycoon,* and *Avenue Flo*. Additionally, while many of these listed games are older, each of the games has more recent iterations that have subsequently been released within the series. Most of the games in the *Dash*-verse have women protagonist avatars, and all feature Flo in some form.

The mechanics of *Diner Dash*, and all of the iterations to follow, are fairly simple. The customers request specific things (seats, menus, food, drinks, service, cleaning) and the player (playing the role of Flo) must click on the customer and serve their needs before they get ruffled, angry, or decide to leave the restaurant altogether. If the player serves customers speedily enough, she makes more money and—with enough money—is able to move on to the next level, which generally increases in difficulty.

The happiness of the customer gauges the player's progress within the game—a series of hearts over the customer's head indicates to the player how well they are doing at serving customers. Each game in the original *Dash* series is structured with fifty levels. After every ten levels Flo moves to a different location (usually a new restaurant), thus pushing the narrative forward. In each level the game play changes subtly, but the overall purpose of serving the customers to keep them happy—through the management of time—remains the same.

What can be considered the "time management" elements in these games involves a complex relationship between work and play that underlies the premise of the original game, as well as the premises of subsequent games in the series. Work and play become conflated and combined through elements of narrative and game play. Time management functions both as the narrative drive fundamental to the game worlds as well as the immediate mechanics that the players need to excel at, in order to properly function within that world.

Flo's "origin story" helps to set up this complex interplay between work and play. We are introduced to Flo in the first *Diner Dash* game while she is working at an office. She is shown as a business executive constantly harangued by bosses and coworkers. The initial comic frame opens with the text "Somewhere in a dreary office . . ." and shows Flo sitting at a desk. Several coworkers ask Flo for various reports and repeatedly chant her name. In frustration, Flo runs out of the office exclaiming, "Man, there's got to be something better than this!" As she attempts to escape her coworkers, she happens upon a restaurant for sale and exclaims, "Of course! My own restaurant!" This setup is very telling of the construction of Flo's situation. Flo literally travels from one job where she is being harassed and harangued for things to another job where the same thing happens—but this time serving customers. Time management, as it occurs in *Diner Dash* and subsequent games, is not about managing your own time, but managing another person's time. In this way, the narrative helps set up the reality that we will be inextricably linked to Flo's relationship to time and location.

At their core, all the *Dash* games, and *Diner Dash* in particular, create a nuanced relationship between work and play, resonating through both narrative and game play. While the games are intended for play or leisure time, thematically they involve workspaces that bear a great deal of similarity to work outside the game world. The drudgery and repetitiveness involved in waiting on customers often feels more like work than play. This evokes issues discussed previously regarding women and leisure time: like many women's real-world leisure experiences, the game never disentangles work from play. Time management is the key way to separate these things, and so by conflating work with play our job becomes managing time for Flo or other protagonists.

Through Flo, the player is constantly being forced to mix work with play and to engage in time management activities. During each level, the player takes the role of Flo, maintaining the actions necessary for the character to move on to the next task. At the same time, the player is judged by Flo at the end of each level, determined by whether the player has passed the parameters of that level. As such, the player has three different relationships with Flo: (1) she watches Flo in the cut scenes that occur at the beginning and end of the game, much like how one would watch a film character; (2) the player acts out the role of Flo, identifying with the work the character must do to complete each level; and (3) the player is judged by Flo, in terms of success or failure of that level. As such, the relationship between the player and Flo is nuanced. The player is Flo, is watching Flo, and is judged by Flo. This relationship between the player and Flo (where Flo is avatar, character, and judge to the player) continues to exacerbate problems where video games become work, rather than a play space. Because the player's actions and Flo's actions are constantly being conflated and interchanged, what is Flo's work becomes the player's playtime, and vice versa. While the player's actions are distinct from Flo's actions (they are pressing buttons and using game controllers), it is potentially the work aspects (the on-screen parallels) that resonate with the player. For some players there may be difficulties in disentangling this relationship, and playtime could simply become work time. While *Diner Dash* is only one example of a time management game, the format has been replicated to many others. Essentially, in-game work stresses reenact stresses many women experience in the real world. Time management becomes the primary mechanism to mediate these anxieties.

This tension between work and play is obvious at the beginning of *Avenue Flo*, an iteration of the *Dash* franchise. While *Avenue Flo* is not a typical time management game—it is more of a puzzle game where Flo wanders around DinerTown attempting to help her friends find things and do things—work versus play becomes an important theme as soon as the game begins. The opening cut scene of the game provides a song-and-dance musical number with all the members of DinerTown, but specifically featuring Flo (Figure 8). The lyrics of this song are as follows:

SKIP

I JUST DON'T HAVE THE TIME TO RELAX.

Figure 8. A screenshot of the game *Avenue Flo*, developed and published by PlayFirst as part of its *Diner Dash* franchise in 2009. The image shows the opening number, a song-and-dance cut scene with the line "I just don't have the time to relax"—easily a theme song for the perceived female audience's lack of free time.

I just don't have the time to relax
Gotta keep those diners in the black
The coffee is brewing
The customers are chewing
Your life seems like an interlude
When you're serving up cartoon food, so . . .
I just don't have the time to sit down
On the busiest street in all of DinerTown
Some call this Florida Street
But they're not in the know (no, no, no)
We, call this Avenue Flo

The lyrics of this song are notable for a video game. It is difficult to imagine a game geared toward Player One (such as *Halo* or *Grand Theft Auto IV*) beginning with a primary avatar uttering the words "I just don't have the time to relax" and following this up with "Your whole life seems like an interlude" and "I just don't have the time to sit down." Not only does this song seem to be suggesting that the players of the game might be too busy to play, it seems to be celebrating that fact (evidenced by the song-and-dance style). *Avenue Flo* seems to be, on the one hand, suggesting that it is a game that specifically understands women's lack of time. On the other hand (and with a wink), the song also infers, "But we all know that women don't have free time"—certainly not for play. The *Dash* series and its spinoffs set up not only conventions for styles of game play, but also expectations regarding women, time, and time management.

Monotony is both the curse and the blessing of this initial iteration of the time management game, as typified by *Diner Dash*. Monotony characterizes the banality of the space, the necessitation that the game world is not so different from our everyday lives. Monotony is, then, a factor that potentially made *Diner Dash* a hit and an inspiration for so many clone games, which all similarly deal with the mundane elements of the every day. Yet that very monotony is what roadblocked the genre—there was only so much variation that could occur within this specific model. In turn, subsequent variations took several different paths, particularly in computer gaming.

BEYOND THE *DASH*: EMERGING SUBGENRES

Diner Dash, with all its vast iterations and slight modifications to gameplay style, established not only the time management game genre but also a series of subgenres. In this section I outline three distinct modes of time management games. While I treat the three subgenres as though they are separate, in more recent invest/express games (characterized in detail later in this chapter) the three modes ultimately begin to collapse into themselves for more robust styles of gaming. Importantly, all the games in this established space are about time management, but time also becomes managed alongside other elements. In other words, time is never the only thing managed in a time management game.

As time management games developed as a genre, three different modes began to take form: time–people management, time–product management, and time–resource management. Each of these subgenres has a similar feel in terms of game play—they all produce hectic styles of play. Similarly, they all seem to focus on the mundane rather than the fantastic—even when given supernatural themes. For example, the game series *Magic Life* is a time–resource management game that allows players to develop their "skills" in a magic-based world. Yet the primary game play focuses on the mundane—players must regularly eat and sleep in order to level up their resources and become increasingly magical.

In many ways, the seeds of several of the subgenres were established within the *Dash*-verse. While *Diner Dash* uses very specific game-play mechanisms (waiting on tables, delivering orders, entertaining customers, cleaning up after customers), over time different iterations defined new variations on the game play. For example, while *Diner Dash* itself functions well as a time–people management game, subsequent games in the series such as *Cooking Dash* helped to establish what I identify as the time–product management subgenre, and *DinerTown Tycoon* became an early version of time–resource management. Within all of these, the *Dash*-verse has remained a centralizing force on the casual games industry.

In what follows, I briefly unpack each of the subgenres in time management games. The purpose of this unpacking is manifold. First, we can better understand the different possible meanings of "time management" within the context of the game worlds. Second, it is important to remember that "time management game" often becomes a catchall term for any game that implies extreme busyness in game play. By breaking these out we can understand the ways the genre has become interpreted and reinterpreted into many different things. Finally, and importantly, with dozens of games in this subgenre, many titles are overlooked. By putting a spotlight on small, often-unnoticed games we can start to see specific patterns that arise.

Diner Dash can be considered a time–people management game. This distinction means that the primary concern is around specific customer "types" who have different wants, needs, and desires. Time–people management in many ways taps into the management of emotions (a topic discussed in more detail in chapter 2). Games that use time–people management game play work under the presumption that the role of the player is to keep those around them happy. The "time" element in this kind of game then becomes the speed with which a player is able to serve other people.

The proto-game in this subgenre is, of course, *Diner Dash* itself. Yet PlayFirst also expanded the time–people management game, specifically with other styles of service beyond table waiting. Other PlayFirst games that maintain the expectations within this subgenre are *Wedding Dash*, *Hotel Dash: Suite Success*, *Diaper Dash*, and *Fitness Dash*. Other casual game companies similarly tapped into this market, making games where one needs to manage a range of different kinds of people in a short span of time. For example, *Sally's Salon* is a popular game series that involves managing and moving around different people receiving spa treatments and haircuts. *Jane's Hotel* uses similar mechanics to *Hotel Dash*, where the player arranges people and manages in a hotel situation. While generally time–people management is about moving people around, sometimes it is about moving products around a screen in a way that people move themselves. For example, in *Supermarket Management 2*, stocking shelves with specific products keeps customers happy by making them move to their proper locations in a game store.

The appeal of the time–people management game is typically about controlling a diverse pool of customers. Most often, the player plays the role of an owner or manager in these games and thus has personal buy-in to the success of a small business. As in the original format for the time management game, the frantic energy revolves around the bustling activities of keeping non-player characters happy. The tension in this style of time management gaming centers on other people's sense of time, not the player's own sense of time. The player is tasked with making sure other people's schedules and lives stay on track for her own success. At the same time, this management of humans seems, in many ways, to replicate social dramas: the player is being tasked with keeping customers happy not only with the business owner, but also with other non-player characters. For example, a core aspect of game play in *Wedding Dash* is keeping specific wedding guests apart from each other, per their requests. Failure to do this properly turns the bride and groom into Bridezilla and Groom-Kong, respectively (Figure 9). The emotional pressure of negotiating human feelings replicates a different kind of work than simply a conflation of the work/domestic sphere. In chapter 3 I will discuss emotional/affective labor in more detail. Yet, at this point, it is important to consider the role of people management on the familiarity and monotony embedded into time management gaming. Here, the everyday labor of women becomes gamified in distinct ways.

Similar in some ways to the time–people management game, the time–product management game also features customers as the purpose of game play. While certainly this subgenre has proliferated with the success of the time management game, in many ways its roots go back much further to the 1982 arcade game *BurgerTime* (Figure 10). *BurgerTime* was a platform-style arcade game that tasked players with quickly assembling hamburgers. The time–product management style of gaming that has become increasingly popular pushes this original game style further: while the player still needs to quickly construct products (often food), there are now often visible customers to negotiate and an increasingly complex menu of different product types.

Figure 9. A screenshot of the time management game *Wedding Dash*, originally developed by ImaginEngine and published by PlayFirst in 2007. The image shows the player losing, with the bride and groom turning into Bridezilla and Groom-Kong, respectively.

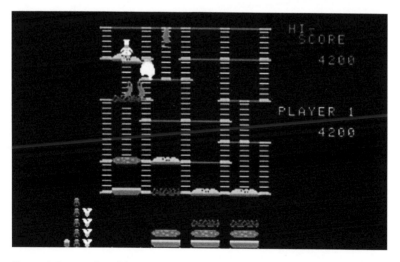

Figure 10. A screenshot of the original *BurgerTime* coin-op arcade game, developed by Data East and Mattel Electronics in 1982. The game signifies an early iteration of time–product management in a game world.

Cake Mania illustrates an excellent example of the combined mechanics and game-play style between the time–people management game and the established product-making style of *BurgerTime*. In *Cake Mania* the player assembles a variety of baked goods at a mom-and-pop bakery shop while customers make specific and personal requests and variations (Figure 11). *BurgerTime* was unemotional assembly work. While assembly-line-style work is certainly involved in a game like *Cake Mania*—or other time–product management games—so is the personal people-style management of the *Dash* franchise. Unlike in *BurgerTime*, the player is not making products for unknown masses but personally fulfilling customer requests. Yet the primary mechanics of these games still focus on building a specific product, rather than the movement of and service to non-player characters.

Food is certainly a popular theme in this style of gaming—bakeries (the *Cake Mania* and *Cake Shop* series), sandwich shops (*Turbo Subs*), and other restaurants (*Cooking Dash*) are fairly common in the subgenre. Amusingly, and presumably paying homage to the success of *BurgerTime*,

Figure 11. A screenshot of the time management game *Cake Mania*, developed and published by Sandlot Games in 2006. The game is a more recent example of time–product management gaming.

some time–product management games use hamburgers as the primary product line (such as the *Burger Bustle* and *Burger Shop* series). Food is not necessary for this style of gaming, however. *Shopmania* involves putting together *Tetris*-like shopping carts. Another variation is jewelry-making games, such as *Youda Jewel Shop 2*. Similarly, several fashion games (*JoJo's Fashion Show*, *Fashion Rush*, etc.) rely on the product management of putting together themed outfits during specific spans of time.

Ultimately, the time–product management game is, to some extent, still about managing people, but more specifically it is about managing people's personal tastes in material goods. The materialism inherent in this subgenre helps to support the notion that the designed identity of Player Two is necessarily as a consumer of material goods. This relationship between material consumption and designed identity will be discussed in more detail in chapter 4.

Finally, the time–resource management game is another subgenre of time management gaming. Time–resource management in many ways pulls from another popular gaming genre, often referred to as resource management games. Well-known game series such as *SimCity*, *Black & White*, and *Sid Meier's Civilization* are examples of this genre. The time–resource management game uses several game-play elements from these titles but tends to function on a smaller level. In the *Dash*-verse, an example of a time–resource management game would be *DinerTown Tycoon*, a game that has Flo managing the resources for several restaurants and looking at restaurants as a larger system. Yet, unlike games such as *Civilization*, the time–resource management game has always functioned at smaller systemic levels—the systems being designed are not meant to encompass entire worlds but rather smaller management systems. The player in a time–resource management game is rarely a god—he or she is another person trying to make sense of the game world around them.

Some examples of the time–resource management game include *Island Tribe 4* and *Magic Life*. These games tend to focus on quests or tasks that have players collecting small amounts of resources to complete subsequent tasks—for example, gathering wood to fix a broken road. Another variation of the time–resource management game style plays off the mundane quality of every day—titles such as *Life Quest 2: Metropoville* and *Magic Life* gamify the process of starting at the bottom of life and working one's way to the top. These games use the premise of capitalist markets as subtext, suggesting that with enough hard work anyone can be successful. And while a game such as *Magic Life* suggests fantasy and supernatural themes (thematically appropriate to women audiences, according to chapter 1 of this book), the actual content focuses on everyday life (Figure 12). Despite being magically inclined, the player still must endure the monotony of daily existence: sleeping, eating, and working. The games in the time–resource management category involve the most variation, and also seem to diverge the furthest from the original *Diner Dash* format. Rather than keeping individuals happy, games in these categories tend to focus more on keeping systems functional. Yet they do not have the complexity of large-system games such as *Civilization*, instead tending to simplify the conceptual frameworks of resource management games into small tasks that are recognizable in everyday life.

Obviously, time management games can mean several different things, and management itself is fluid. While I have made a point of breaking the space into several subgenres, it should be noted that they are not always this distinct. Several of these subgenres often combine with one another to allow for different modes of simultaneous time management in more recent games. Since the emergence of Zynga as a force in the video game industry this includes invest/express games, which frequently combine time–people management, time–product management, and time–resource management seamlessly into a more robust, and more

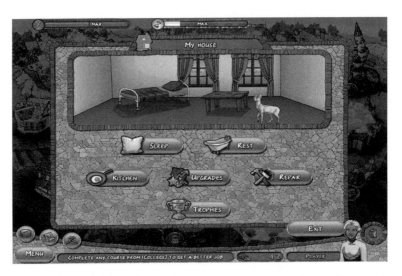

Figure 12. A screenshot of the computer game *Magic Life*, developed by Meridian 93 and published by Big Fish Games in 2010. The game illustrates time–resource management in a game world.

consuming, style of time management game. Within the newer style of invest/express video games, the player's relationship to game-world time becomes even more fluid, increasingly creating a slippage between game-world time and real-world time.

THE EMERGENCE OF THE INVEST/EXPRESS GAME

More than any other video game company, Zynga can be credited for the emergence of what is commonly referred to as the invest/express model by video game developers. Zynga was founded in 2007 and early on acquired *YoVille*, a virtual networking game world.[19] Soon after, Zynga expanded the *Ville* model, first developing *FarmVille* and then other related titles such as *CastleVille*, *CityVille*, and *FrontierVille*. The *Ville* model started as Facebook games, but rapidly migrated to other platforms, notably iOS and Android mobile devices. In turn, other game companies such as Storm8 and Glu have made their own games in the invest/express model.

Typically in an invest/express game, the player is given a sparse, small space and the ability to decorate it. The player is presented with a series of tasks and/or customers that provide small errands or assignments that gradually push her or him to increase the size of the space and the work done within that space. For example, in *FarmVille* the player begins with a small plot of land and a few animals and must farm the land, combine ingredients, and tend to the animals. *CastleVille* does a similar set of things but with a slightly less bucolic theme and more fantasy-based elements. In Storm8's *Restaurant Story 2* the player is given a small restaurant and access to certain ingredients in a store, which the player must use to cook items for customers. In these games there is an ongoing interplay between time–people management, time–product management, and time–resource management. This integration creates an opportunity for the player to constantly engage with the game-world space to complete a variety of tasks, and also forces the player to return to the game world at regular intervals (very literally, managing her time). Just as soon as one assignment ends, the next set of instructions are given to the player, making play appear to be endless in many respects.

The payment structure in invest/express games is similar to many others on the casual market: while players are given a small amount of in-game money to begin, they "earn" more money the more they play. Players are also given the option to use real money according to exchange rates that vary from game to game. Generally speaking, the player can usually progress reasonably well (albeit slowly) without spending his or her own money, although spending money always means spending less time leveling up in the game world. In other words, time always equals money in the invest/express model. These games are commonly referred to as either "free to play" (F2P) or "freemium" games, meaning that the game is free to download but better content comes with a monetary investment. Chapter 4 will go into more detail on the F2P format.

The name "invest/express" is not a consumer name for the games but rather how the video game industry refers to the model. In an interview, one game designer explains the breakdown of the words "invest" and "express" and how they function in this industry category:

> The "invest" portion typically refers to the investment of time/effort on the part of the player. While one of the normal channels of monetization for F2P casual games involves bypassing the time investment, players who wish to progress without paying can almost always do so.
>
> The "express" portion refers to the player being able to create a board that reflects their preferred aesthetic. For instance, some players want to create very realistic layouts, while other players use their board as a canvas to create something wholly separate from the presumed point of the game (e.g., designing a farm).

So, put briefly, "invest" refers to the investment of either time or money while "express" refers to free expression. But it is notable that these terms have quite a bit of fluidity built into them. The time/money aspect of the "investment" portion suggests that time and money are equivalent and interchangeable (which, of course, they are in the game world). Express, while specifically referring to "self-expression," can also refer to the speed of play—play is done on "express" (or sped-up) time, and the more you invest, the faster that play moves. Time seems to be interlinked and necessitated within the invest/express game, wherein temporality and the use of time has become the primary mode of play.

At the same time, invest/express games structure the player's real-world time in such a way that one cannot play endlessly. Generally speaking, the model in these game worlds (as well as other casual puzzle games such as *Candy Crush Saga* and *Polar Pop Mania*) is that over time a player "earns" more energy (game "energy" equals the ability to play). For example, in *Kim Kardashian: Hollywood* the player is given a specific number of energy points that cap out, depending on what level she is at. Once those energy points are used up she must wait for the game to re-allot her more energy points (a new point is given every five minutes). At the same time, another in-game clock is running and the player is expected to complete tasks in a specific period. For example, a player may be asked in *KK:H* to complete a photo shoot in three hours, but the number of energy points given means that she must come back in a specific amount of time to complete the shoot, or she does not get full points for the task. Other games are slightly less demanding. *Candy Crush Saga* and *Candy Crush Soda Saga*, for example, dole out one energy credit every twenty minutes, and the number of possible credits cannot exceed five. One energy credit, however, only equals one turn of play. These different mechanisms, again, reinforce a ludic interplay between time and money. The player can always buy more energy credits, or she can wait and come back to the game later. In *Candy Crush Saga* there are no repercussions for this, but in *KK:H* the player can lose her status on the A-list if she ignores the relevance of time.[20] Yet, *Candy Crush Saga*, while a popular casual game, does not fit into the invest/express model—it is simply a casual puzzle game. Thus invest/express seems to place more importance on the notion of time.

To this end, invest/express has expanded on the most compelling aspects from the time management game. The games in this space are about staying busy, persistent movement, and constant work (even within play). For example, the official game description for the mobile game *FarmVille 2: Country Escape* (Figure 13) reads as follows: "Running a farm is loads of fun in this fresh sequel to a classic world-builder. Zynga's latest offering presents a wealth of activities to keep you busy, including milking cows, harvesting fruits and vegetables, fishing, unlocking new areas, decorating your property, and even selling items to friends." This description is compelling for both its conflation between work and play, and its use of the words "fun" right along side of the phrase "keep you busy." The presumption of this game world is that by doing chores (in this case, bucolic chores) the player will in some way quell their desire to stay busy and feel "productive" as well as fill a need for "fun." The description is written deftly to conflate the two activities and naturalize work as a mode of play. It is also notable that the final phrase of the product description ends with the claim that "it's a delight for any gamer." Perhaps this marketing copy is overreaching about who plays *FarmVille* (and what kinds of players self-identify as "gamers"), or (alternatively) perhaps it is an attempt at expanding the term "gamer" itself.

In many ways, it would seem that the invest/express model provides

Figure 13. A screenshot of *FarmVille 2: Country Escape*, developed and published by Zynga in 2014. The title is an example of the invest/express style of video games. The image shows the game description given by Zynga, which conflates productivity and play.

the perfect setup for the perceived Player Two. If the common cultural understanding of femininity and adult women is that they are busy—too busy for play—then a game that functions in snippets of time while also focuses on having the player return for subsequent game-play sessions would be an ideal format. In this way, invest/express seems to be a perfect articulation of the perception of the female player's leisure habits. The realities of this leisure, of course, lie somewhere between the cultural perceptions and the lived experiences. The maturation of time management games into invest/express games seem to illustrate a desire to capture women audiences on their own terms.

Not all invest/express games are intended for women. For example, chapter 1 alluded to *Clash of Clans*. In some ways, *Clash of Clans* (and its clones) can be seen as the masculinized version of the *FarmVille* style of video game, replacing bucolic themes with battles. This would seem to imply that invest/express as a game style and category has begun to exceed gendered expectations. And in many ways this is true. But perhaps the larger takeaway from the popularity of *Clash of Clans* is a suggestion that as masculine roles continue to shift in our culture, there is a desire to see this feminized style using more acceptably masculine themes. Because designed identity itself is not gender-specific, the concept helps to illustrate the changing perception of multiple markets—men included.

TIME MANAGEMENT WITHOUT TIME

Above I noted that time management products—not just the games discussed, but actual time management aids—are most commonly marketed to women. What is remarkable, however, is that many of the time management games discussed in this chapter have no real-world relationship to time. While this is not particularly peculiar for a video game, it is certainly odd for a time management product. Real-world time rarely seems to be present as an element in the game world. Time management games, of course, erase the rest of the background of computers and smartphones— all elements, including the clocks. In other words, in a time management game the one thing that players are not able to manage is their own time in the real world. A notable exception to this rule is the invest/express game *Kim Kardashian: Hollywood*, which specifically times tasks, forcing the player to return to game play. Yet even in *KK:H* time functions in abstractions from real-world time: the game never tells you to come back at a specific hour (related to your clock and time in the real world), only that in a specific amount of time the gig expires, taking away points from the player if she hasn't completing her tasks.[21]

Those who study clocks and other artifacts of time might remark, however, that the absence of a clock is only a consequence of how humans understand their relationship to time. A clock, of course, is not an actual representation of real time, but a tool to help direct the way we think about time. Kevin Birth refers to objects of timekeeping as "necromantic objects" or "tools by which the dead think for the living."[22] The time recorded by a clock is only a representation of our ontological expectation that time exists as it has been presented to us in cultural and social contexts. Perhaps, then, the lack of real timekeeping mechanisms within most time management games *is* logical—after all, it is the game time being managed, not the real-world time.

Yet there seems to be some trickery embedded in the gendered designed identity within many time management games. The presumption of the label surely indicates to players that by playing in smaller units of time, by doing something with their nothing, they are—in some measure—managing real-world time. In this way, the conceit of time management games is that the games, perhaps, do help to manage a person's time. If stealing seemingly "productive" time is the goal of a video game—or any leisure activity—then the time management game is tasked with implying that players gets to have their cake (mania) and eat it, too.

However, the lack of clocks becomes almost sinister in this way. A parallel of this experience can be framed best by research on gambling at casinos. Natasha Dow Schüll refers to the time experienced at a casino, particularly while machine gambling, as being "elastic." She explains, "The machine zone's elasticization of time, like its elasticization of money, distills key elements of contemporary social and economic life. Clichés like 'time is money,' 'time is running out,' and 'life moves fast' captures a phenomenon of which machine gambling is only one example—namely, that capitalism operates at increasingly high speeds."[23] To this effect, an elasticization of time can be seen in time management games as well, where time seems to be both never ending yet always running out. Indeed, truisms like "time is running out" could easily characterize the monotonous yet addictive play inherent to time management games.

It is through this lens that we need to begin to consider gendered designed identity in time management games. The elasticization of time helps to structure play that is never fully developed and always somewhat tenuous. Inside the game worlds, players' "time" is not their own—it is more often than not dependent on the time of non-player characters. Outside the game world, time does not belong to the player either. She is expected to play for only short bursts of time—a mechanic that is sometimes simply implied, and other times structured into the very core of the game, as with the pay mechanics of F2P games. She is playing within a kind of third shift, where her play always and necessarily resembles work activities. As with Bolton's depiction of the third shift, it somehow becomes an interiorized critique of how players spend their real-world time outside the game. Additionally, there is no reason why the third shift cannot be fun.

Above I suggested that it is impossible to put too much emphasis on the significance of time management games. As evident from the examples given here, time becomes structured in terms of game-play time and real-world time, but the two are often conflated. The nonstop negotiation of other people's time in game worlds such as *Diner Dash* means that time management is always about negotiating the expectations of others. Yet the structure of the games, forcing players to play in snippets or bursts of time, aligns with the real-world expectations of women and anxieties about time and time management.

But the elasticization of time has positive implications for Player Two as well. If leisure time is fleeting for many women, and they are therefore compelled by the time management game genre, the elastic nature of game-world time implies that the game is creating more time for play where there previously was little. The designed identity of Player Two has little or no leisure time to spare, but somehow the game worlds—particularly those in the invest/express category—seem to constantly be squeezing in more time for play. Part of the trickery of all time management games is that while they suggest a nod of "we know you don't really have leisure time" (as implied by the opening song in *Avenue Flo*), they somehow make an elastic time for leisure that, hopefully, spirals outward into the lived experiences of busy players, women or otherwise.

SPEED, HYSTERIA, AND MANIC BODIES

There is a manic quality to many casual games, and time management games are no exception. The time management game's frenetic undercurrent always implies temporality, but in relation to speed. Apart from the realities of game play—which does, indeed, have players moving their avatars around quickly—naming conventions help to support the idea that speed is necessitated through game play. In this way, the aforementioned temporal frames that draw a neat line between real-world and game-world time are very specific in the kind of time they imply: fast time. Bodies in the game world are expected to move quickly and efficiently. Game titles use words such as "dash" (*Diner Dash, Wedding Dash, Diaper Dash, Doggie Dash*), "hustle" (*Busy Bea's Halftime Hustle, Hospital Hustle*), "rush" (*Fashion Rush, Roller Rush*), "haste" (*Hospital Haste*), "bustle" (*Fitness Bustle, Burger Bustle*), "scramble" (*Kitchen Scramble*), even pushing things up to a "turbo" speed (*Turbo Subs*), or simply declaring pure "chaos" (*Costume Chaos*). The speediness helps to maintain the distinction that players should continue to make use of all available time and space—through the constant movement referenced in these titles—in order to do "something with [their] nothing" (as the Nintendo campaign slogan suggests). This also gets reinforced (within the industry at least) with the "express" nomenclature associated with invest/express games. Leisure time, according to these titling conventions, is not about relaxing but about using time as quickly and efficiently as possible—short of falling into pure chaos.

Yet, at the same time, there is another trend in the naming conventions implied by speed: that of hysteria. Several games in this genre use names in their titles like "mania" (*Cake Mania, Nanny Mania, Bubble Mania, Shopmania, Babysitting Mania, Gourmania*), "craze" (*Ice Cream Craze, Fashion Craze*), "frenzy" (*Farm Frenzy, Rescue Frenzy, Fitness Frenzy*), and "fever" (*Deco Fever*), or combine them to convey nothing short of hysterical madness (*Fever Frenzy*). While on the one hand these titles might imply similar themes as the "dash"-titled games (mania in terms of quick movement and speed), they simultaneously imply fanaticism and hysteria. This pushes the speed and movement implied by the dash-titled games even further—the in-game movement is, potentially, not within the player's control. The play, it would seem, has gone too far.

By tapping into this notion of "crazy" within the designed identities of Player Two, there is an implication that the play is guided by and toward hysteria. For hundreds of years hysteria was primarily defined via femininity, and only since 1952 has the term lost credibility in the psychological community.[24] Despite this, "hysteria" is still used as a descriptor to suggest extreme and irrational femininity. The condition of hysteria was marked by a potpourri of potential symptoms, including (but not limited to) fainting, shortness of breath, loss of appetite, muscle spasms, and nervousness. In *Technology of the Orgasm*, Rachel Maines points out that "the panting and shortness of breath associated with the hysterical paroxysm, and eventually the disease itself, came to be called the 'suffocation of the uterus' or the 'suffocation of the mother.'"[25] In fact, the term itself is derived from the Greek word for uterus. Of the gendered nature of hysteria, Maines astutely remarks that "there is no analogous word 'testecical' to describe, for example, male sports fans' behavior during the Super Bowl."[26] In other words, masculinity is permitted to lose control in ways that for women might be considered "hysterical." This point is particularly poignant when applied to games and play, suggesting that within play designed for women there is a loss of control, whereas within play designed for men it is normal and expected.

It is in this space—where movement necessarily implies fast movement (dashing) and subsequently links to hysteria (mania)—that we can inevitably see how the management of time inherent in feminine designed identities links back to the management of emotions. Additionally, we can see how all of this quick play designed for Player Two, if taken too far, could ultimately lead to a kind of hysteria. If play gets out of control—if it goes too far, if leisure time is not properly managed—women's lives can become purely hysterical. The control necessitated in time management games, then, is about controlling that hysteria—specifically, holding it back. Emotions, like time, occupy a specific gendered role in play designed for women—a role that, in this way, overlaps with time management. The underlying implication seems to be that if we let our bodies play too much, if we are unable to control our time properly, we might move into a space of emotional unreliability, where hysteria is inevitable. In the following chapter, "Playing with Emotions," I continue this thread by illustrating how the designed identity of Player Two involves emotional management.

3 *Playing with Emotions*

"MY WII STORY"

In 2007, soon after the release of the Wii gaming system, Nintendo launched an advertising campaign called "My Wii Story." Through the Nintendo website,[1] people were invited to write in stories about the transformative powers of the Nintendo Wii and how it helped their lives and families. While both sexes wrote in to "My Wii Story," the majority of the submissions came from women. Several stories were turned into magazine advertisements, often appearing in special interest magazines such as *O: The Oprah Magazine* and *Martha Stewart Living*, and all of these magazine versions were written by women. The advertisements did not necessarily promote that women play more, but rather that they use play as a means of connecting their families (and connecting *with* their families).

All of the "My Wii Stories" that appeared in physical magazines start off with a testimonial quote about what people like about the Wii gaming system. Below each of these testimonies is a woman's signature—a personal advocacy for the product. For example, one story author, Nancy Ponthier, attests that the Wii promoted family togetherness, which is reinforced by a picture showing a mother playfully hugging her son while negotiating the Wii remote (Figure 14). Her headline quote says, "It's the first video game I've really enjoyed playing." The testimonial continues, "We really like playing together as a family, so we quickly moved it from my son's room to the living room. We even like making Mii characters together. They're funny and we get a kick out of describing each other. I took a crack at making my own Mii. Then my kids told me it wasn't 'pretty enough' and made it better. I thought that was sweet. They were just so happy I was interested in a video game." This testimonial nicely implies that for her the system is not meant for play, but rather to facilitate the emotional happiness of her family. Further, it suggests that her children love her more—even think that she is *prettier*—because she played the Wii with them. In this, the subtext of play becomes a form of what I will identify below as "emotional labor." Other "My Wii Stories"—both in magazines and on the original website—carried similar themes of emotionality and nurturing modes of play.

Certainly we are all permitted to enjoy emotional experiences in, and because of, video game play. "My Wii Story," however, illustrates a different kind of emotionality—one that hinges on the well-being of others. While in the case of "My Wii Story" the emotional well-being is that of real family members, games intentionally designed for women often employ a similar emotional register for fictional, non-player characters. One consistent theme—which I will be highlighting throughout this chapter—is how emotional labor and the work of caring come to the forefront in the designed identity of Player Two. The interplay of emotional labor with themes of productivity and work, I argue, helps to create games where women's in-game labor is always linked to emotional countenance. Yet the emotionality felt within video games is powerful and can resonate in everyday lives. While emotional labor can take its toll, in-game emotional labor often brings positive effects with it. While in the real world emotional labor is often thankless and unsatisfying, in the game world it can result in satisfying, positive in-game outcomes. As with the management of time, emotional labor in games is a mixed bag.

In the previous chapter, I ended with a discussion of how the notion of "mania"—and all of its gendered stereotypes—helps to create a kind of expectation that women's play necessarily broaches instability and insanity—that women's emotional state is always on the verge of hysteria, and that one small drop in the bucket might push her over. I illustrated the underlying implication that by playing too much, and not being able to control their play, women might become emotionally unstable. In this chapter I offer the flip side of this argument. On the one hand, too much play might cause manic behavior, but on the other, it offers a means of emotional caregiving. Caregiving becomes a more "acceptable" emotional outlet for women, a controlled state that infers a form of domestic labor. The designed identity of Player Two is always inextricably linked to some kind of an emotional state. This emotional state can create an extra layer of labor for the intended female audience, but it also has the potential to

Figure 14. A screenshot of an example from the Nintendo Wii "My Wii Story" advertising campaign. Advertisements in this series—including this one in particular—appeared in *O: The Oprah Magazine* and *Martha Stewart Living* in 2007 in an attempt to get more mothers to engage their families in playing the Wii console gaming system.

create emotionally satisfying experiences that replicate real-world emotional labor in more rewarding ways.

As I illustrate throughout this chapter, because women are often charged with performing social functions and caregiving in the domestic sphere, this kind of play often projects a false idea of how women are expected to perform leisure. It would seem the designed identity of Player Two is inextricably linked to an anticipation of women's emotional state, which often seems to bounce between the unstable (the manic) and the nurturing (the necessitated emotional). By exploring how emotional states become designed into video games, I illustrate how these technologies help to manage and play with identities. I break down the emotional countenance experienced in gendered gaming into several categories. First, I discuss *Diner Dash* (and its successors) once again, exploring how emotionality is an important element within time management games. Next, I discuss hidden object games, using the game *Surface: The Noise She Couldn't Make* as an example of how emotional labor functions in this genre. Subsequently, I discuss caregiving games including *Cooking Mama*, virtual pet games, and *The Sims*. Finally, I end the chapter by discussing social network games (such as *FarmVille* and *Words with Friends*) to explore how virtual emotional labor often spills into real-world interactions.

EMOTIONS IN VIDEO GAMES

Of course, many games—or at least good ones—can produce an emotional response from players. The presence of emotional content does not necessarily imply an intended female audience. For example, game designer David Freeman describes the process of engineering emotions into games as "emotioneering." He explains, "People go to films, watch TV shows, and listen to music that moves them. Emotion will be one of the keys to the mass market in games as well. Thus, from the point of view of economics, emotioneering in games is good business."[2] The designed identity of emotional play for Player Two more specifically involves emotional labor, defined in detail below. Yet it is worthwhile considering the role of emotions in gaming spaces in general and how they affect our experiences of play.

In *Better Game Characters by Design: A Psychological Approach* Katherine Isbister uses the game character (both player and non-player) as a major factor in good game design, arguing that by designing better facial expressions and emotional tone to voices, players will relate better to game characters overall. She explains, "Good character designers direct player emotions by using player-characters to underscore desirable feelings (such as triumph or suspense) and to minimize undesirable ones (such as frustration)."[3] Using games such as *Super Monkey Ball 2* and *The Legend of Zelda: The Windwalker* as examples, Isbister illustrates that by creating better emotional links between game characters and players, players will feel more connected with the game. In this book, she suggests that a future direction for game design might be "emotional detection," wherein game characters know, in real time, how to respond to a player with an appropriate emotion through voice cues.[4] In Isbister's more recent work, *How Games Move Us: Emotion by Design*, she furthers these points by claiming that games, in general, have more potential emotional impact than any other medium because of the ability of players to make choices and the importance of in-game flow.

Similarly, Shahrel Nizar Baharom, Wee Hoe Tan, and Mohammad Zaffwan Idris repurpose Don Norman's Human Computer Interaction work on the emotional design of objects (an important concept in the HCI field) to suggest that those premises might also be applicable to game design.[5] Norman's book *Emotional Design* suggests that good design provides emotional connection on one of three levels: visceral (aesthetic), behavioral (functional), and reflective (political). Building off this idea, Baharom, Tan, and Idris suggest that game designers should seek out the emotional response of players by using these categories simultaneously within their designs in order to engage audiences more effectively.[6]

While a focus on emotional game design might help to foster better links between player and character, as Isbister has suggested, Eugénie Shinkle makes an argument that all video games, at their core, are related to emotional and affective response. Shinkle suggests that the medium itself is prone to this kind of potentially emotional connection—in a way that other media might not be. In particular, Shinkle argues, while we often prioritize other senses (vision, for example) when we discuss gaming, we should pay equal attention to proprioception, or "the sensory feedback mechanisms which determine the body's location and movement in space."[7] By considering games in terms of the physical, Shinkle's work expands Isbister's argument on the value of emotion in game design. While Isbister emphasizes characters and narrative, Shinkle suggests that emotional design might be part of the physical space and responses within the process of gaming.

Yet, within this, Shinkle also suggests that while traditional game controllers limit emotional and affective expression in gaming, the recent move toward alternative game controllers has pushed forward the affective potential of video games: "For the gamer, emotional and physical discipline quite literally go hand in hand: get too caught up in a game and you risk swapping precision technique for frantic button-mashing. The limitations of this control language haven't stopped the joystick and its descendants from becoming industry standard, though: the game industry has traditionally paid little attention to the ways that the expressive effects of player emotion might be incorporated into gameplay mechanics."[8] Ultimately, Shinkle's argument is that we are moving closer to a moment where affect and emotion have become a more effective way of understanding the relationship between gamer and game. As gaming audiences and styles expand, so does our emotional relationship to digital play.

At the same time, specific kinds of games might trigger emotions somewhat differently. Tom Apperley and Nicole Heber demonstrate that digital pets and games that emulate this kind of play style specifically engender a kind of "emotional relationship" that is "characterized by both mutuality and hierarchy, and involves the simultaneous exchange of both affection and of capital."[9] The authors' explanation continues: "Emotional expression is one way in which relationship is guided, produced, and streamlined toward a particular end."[10] Therefore, this kind of expression of an emotional relationship expands beyond the relational affect of simply a non-player character that we like. Other games play with emotions within their very construction; Hanna Wirman has noted that as a feminine-designed game, *Super Princess Peach* specifically uses the promise of emotion (such as "joy," "gloom," "rage," and "calm") as an extension of a game mechanic.[11]

Certain kinds of game characters, and certain kinds of games, engender specific forms of emotionality within play. In terms of game design, of course, more emotional response can be a positive aspect. An emotional bond can help foster a stronger relationship between the player and the game. Yet, as I continue to explore throughout this chapter, emotion can also create complicated expectations within the designed identity of Player Two.

WOMEN, EMOTIONAL LABOR, AND AFFECTIVE LABOR

We assume that emotional affect in gaming is always a good thing. Emotions, as Isbister and Shinkle both nicely illustrate, connect us more coherently to both the characters we are playing and the ones with which we interact. Good gaming necessitates an emotional response—as we would expect of any popular media object. The complexity in this response, however, lies in how emotion parses back to the individual players and the specific kind of results they incur. This chapter rests on the premise that the designed identity of Player Two relies heavily on the use of "emotional labor" (also sometimes referred to as "affective labor")—and in this way creates a potentially problematic space for female players who already perform tasks of emotional labor in the real world.

In *The Managed Heart: Commercialization of Human Feeling*, Arlie Russell Hochschild coins the term "emotional labor" as that which "requires one to induce or suppress feeling in order to sustain the outward countenance that produces the proper state of mind in others."[12] In other words, emotional labor is labor where the worker is forced to sublimate his or her emotions and take on the burdens of another person's emotional state. Hochschild's primary example, the focus of her study, is on flight attendants whose stressful position, and need to keep patrons subdued, perfectly illustrates the complexities of emotional labor. What is notable is that emotional labor is not just a function that is blindly internalized—it is institutionalized. Using the flight attendant example, Hochschild quotes from training material advice, such as strategies for avoiding anger—for instance, "to focus on what the *other* person might be thinking and feeling" or to fall back on the thought "I can escape."[13] This institutionalization helps to illustrate how emotional labor is dictated through systems of power. Regardless of an ability to "escape," the providers of emotional labor are essentially powerless.

Women, Hochschild argues, are the primary purveyors of emotional labor. She suggests, "As traditionally more accomplished managers of feeling in private life, women more than men have put emotional labor on the market, and they know more about its personal costs."[14] In her definition of emotional labor, Hochschild is ultimately referring to the professionalization of domestic and private labor into the public sphere. Given the large number of women who partake in these careers (including waitressing, nursing, or working within the child-care system), emotional labor involves turning stereotypes about women and caregiving into jobs.

Researchers often use the term "affective labor," which functions similarly to emotional labor, although it is generally applied more to the domestic sphere. This form of labor is also referred to as a kind of "immaterial labor." Kylie Jarrett refers to immaterial labor as "labor done in the home—women's work—[which] is a necessary input to capitalist circuits of exchange, producing healthy, socially adept, well-nourished laboring bodies."[15] In other words, as many Marxist feminist theorists have noted,[16] labor that is culturally assigned to women is often overlooked or derided as not being legitimate. Jarrett has demonstrated how this form of physical, social labor can easily parse into digital spaces, such as Facebook, arguing that "intensifying affective states and building affective connections is the essence of the work we do when using social media, which in turn places affect at the core of the digital economy."[17] Affective labor, then, complements emotional labor and the categories blur into each other. Emotional labor is one form of affective labor, but it also exceeds the implied domesticity embedded in the term.

Emotional and affective labor becomes a cornerstone of the designed identity of Player Two. Just as careers of emotional labor are often labeled as women's jobs, leisure activities involving emotional labor are often labeled as women's play. In the same way that emotional labor complicates women's work, so does emotional play. Similar to emotional labor, these play and leisure activities often include suppressing personal needs in order to elevate the desires of the family. In video games that involve emotional play, there is a risk that women players might not be able to disentangle play activities from the emotional engagement of others. Players who are particularly attuned to caregiving or emotional labor careers are at risk of conflating work and play activities. Beyond this, the gendered assumptions of domestic labor mean that affect is necessarily part of the feminized experience in terms of sociality and caregiving.[18] It follows that because emotional labor is often considered women's work, when women's play overlaps with caring, caregiving, and expectations of family play a tension arises between play and productivity. In essence, game designs often construct women as being social- or care-centric players—a stereotype that ultimately moderates aspects of play—while focusing on features that construct the feminine player as the facilitator of family leisure time. This often turns video game play into something else entirely.

It is not surprising that emotional labor is a mode of women's labor. In effect, it is the result of cultural and social expectations about how care is constructed in gendered ways. In her essay "Women and Caring: What Can Feminists Learn about Morality from Caring," Joan Tronto writes about the sexual politics of who is permitted to care about what in our society: "The script runs something like this: Men care about money, career, ideas, and advancements; men show they care by the work they do, the values they hold, and the provisions they make for their families. Women care for their families, neighbors, and friends; women care for their families by doing the direct work of caring. Furthermore, the script continues, men care about more important things, whereas women care about less important."[19] Tronto further makes a distinction between caring "for" and caring "about": "Caring is engendered in both market and private life. Women's occupations are the caring occupations, and women do the disproportionate amount of caregiving in the private household. To put the point simply, traditional gender roles in our society imply that men care *about* but women care *for.*"[20] In her essay "Caring: A Labour of Love," Hillary Graham suggests that this is linked to socially constructed gender expectations in Western culture: "Men negotiate their social position through something recognized as 'doing,' doing things based on 'knowledge' which enables them to 'think' and to engage in 'skilled work.' Women's social position is negotiated through a different kind of activity called 'caring,' a caring informed not by knowledge but by 'intuition' through which women find their way into 'unskilled' jobs. Thus, caring is not something on the periphery of our social order; it marks the point at which the relations of capital and gender intersect."[21] Notions of "caring" are always already designated as inherently feminine, helping to structure what women's work—and, in turn, women's play—ought to be. Caring, and representations of women caring, helps to reinforce gendered hierarchies.

However, looking at emotional labor, and the work of caring, as a *primarily* cultural stereotype is still complicated. These stereotypes arose, in part, because of expectations wherein women perform the cultural function of motherhood—distinct from the biological function of childbearing. Motherhood can be seen as a subset of caregiving, and one that most often maps to femininity. The corollary often is true, here, where femininity translates to nurturing behavior because of an expectation of maternalism. Thus, regardless of whether women fill the identity role of "mother," they are often treated as necessarily maternal. The designed identity of Player Two very often aligns with caring and motherhood.

Motherhood stands in a strange place within the constructs of gaming and play. In *Of Woman Born: Motherhood as Experience and Institution*, Adrienne Rich explains that rather than being a natural "human condition," motherhood "has an ideology" that is "more fundamental than tribalism or nationalism" and imbued with patriarchal overtones.[22] She explains:

> Throughout patriarchal mythology, dream-symbolism, theology, language, two ideas flow side by side: one, that the female body is impure, corrupt, the site of discharges, bleedings, dangerous to masculinity, a source of moral and physical contamination, "the devil's gateway." On the other hand, as mother the woman is beneficent, sacred, pure, asexual, nourishing; and the physical potential for motherhood—that same body with its bleedings and mysteries—is her single destiny and justification in life. These two ideas have become deeply internalized in women, even in the most independent of us, those who seem to lead the freest lives.[23]

Thus, according to Rich, motherhood sits at one end of a stereotype of how women are perceived—as the sacred mother, caregiving would be one of her primary attributes. The idea that motherhood is the "single destiny and justification in life" reinforces its importance in play. Playing with one's children becomes a justifiable mode of leisure aligned with the asexual image of motherhood. This image of woman as nourishing mother problematizes much of the play designed for and marketed to women. At the same time, it helps to construct a familiar pallet from which to work.

As such, in the opening of this chapter I described the "My Wii Story" campaign, one that is entirely based on the maternal expectations of the feminine player. Rather than being sold as purely fun, the gaming system suggested that women's play is neatly integrated into family play, a mode that is necessarily part of a mother's work. Other examples abound, though—while one mode of caring, caregiving, and emotional labor is constructed within the scope of playing in order to garner the love of one's family, other video games manage women's play through in-game emotional labor and in-game caregiving activities. By structuring play as necessarily linked back to modes of emotional labor and caregiving, that play becomes designed in such a way that those who serve these primary functions in the real world have, in turn, potentially troubling relationships with those things in the game world. In this chapter I illustrate how representations of women as caregiver and emotional laborer facilitate the designed identity of Player Two. These aspects of gaming emotionality often turn the game world into a form of domestic labor. Because caring is often understood as women's work, games that use caring activities as central mechanics and overall themes help to maintain a distinction between masculine and feminine video game play styles. These play styles designed into the video games are both positive and negative. They reinforce gendered modes of labor but also potentially offer satisfying emotional experiences within a safe space.

TIME MANAGEMENT AND EMOTIONS

In the previous chapter I described time management games and their relationship to the management of time in the real world, paying special attention to the *Diner Dash* game series. Certainly, the *Dash* games help to manage women's time, often conflating work and play in complicated ways. Yet the labor of time management games isn't simply a conflation of work and play; emotional labor is also always an underlying feature. Other time management games, such as the *Delicious Emily* series, further combine these elements in complicated and compelling ways.

The work of emotions was designed directly into the *Dash* games. According to game designer Nicole Lazzaro, *Diner Dash* is successful because of its focus on character emotions, and their relationship to player emotions.[24] Unlike many other casual games, *Diner Dash* and similar clones use human emotion to capture more of a range of emotionality than do typical casual games.[25] A white paper by Lazzaro's company, XEO Design, presents a more in-depth analysis of *Diner Dash*: she argues that the game mechanics of the *Dash* titles (and the games that followed) are unique in terms of our typical expectation of games to inspire emotional response. Serving others and causing joy is a different set of emotions than solving a crossword puzzle, winning a car race, or inflicting pain in a first-person shooter. According to Lazarro's white paper, the focus of the *Dash* game mechanic is emotion on top of the pattern matching you would find in *Tetris*, *Bejeweled*, or a jigsaw puzzle. The mechanic is one of helping instead of hurting people and creating joy in life rather than the loss of it, making the game appealing to more diverse audiences. Compared to other games in its category *Diner Dash* offers players a unique emotional profile.[26] While the intentionality of the designers does not always correlate to the actuality of experience, this focus on emotional impact allows players to relate to characters differently than they might relate to those in a first-person shooter. The emotional experiences that occur during game play may be nuanced depending on the real-world experiences of players. The narrative, design, and mechanics of the *Dash* games create a complex landscape where different players might interpret the game in different ways.

Diner Dash, and the similar games that followed it, fall into the category of what Aubrey Anable refers to as "affective systems" that "mediate relations between players and devices, workers and machines, and images and code (and our feelings about those relations)."[27] As such, Anable describes how affect functions as a mode of "women's work" within these gaming spaces and is "always culturally situated in relation to the gendering of the bodies and objects of mass media culture."[28] Within this, it becomes important to consider ways that time management games help not only to manage women's time, but also to manage their emotional affect—and how that affect might impact the real lives of players in both positive and negative ways.

Flo's relationships to customers (and the mechanics that follow these relationships) provide hints that she is far more interested in others than she is in her own needs. In the game, customers are cantankerous, quick to anger, and often impatient—not unlike the customers Hochschild describes in her description of the jobs of flight attendants. Each customer behavior relates back to different aspects of game play and strategy. For example, to keep a "businesswoman" happy the player must serve her as quickly as possible; to keep "seniors" (senior citizens) happy, the player must be patient and know that they will order and eat slowly, despite impatient customers around them; to keep groups of "teens" happy the player must seat groups of girl teens and boy teens near each other so that the player gets a "flirt bonus"—failure to do so results in upsetting other customers, because the teens will talk loudly on their cell phones. Management of all these people creates a situation that replicates socially dictated domestic work—keeping some people together, others separated, and managing the emotions of all parties.[29] Just as real-world emotional labor involves a multitude of dissatisfied customers, so does the game world. Other non-*Dash* time management games, such as *Cake Mania*, *Sally's Salon*, *Fitness Frenzy*, and *Delicious Emily*, all share the same parameters in which different kinds of customer behaviors help to suggest different difficulty levels.

To illustrate customers' degrees of happiness, each table of customers in *Diner Dash* bears a series of hearts hovering over them (Figure 7). As the player works harder to please the customers, the hearts fill up. Alternately, as the customers get increasingly angry, their heart level goes down. In many respects, the player is serving and cleaning for others in order to win their love. Hearts are a fairly common measure of health in games, and on the one hand, their use to show player status in *Diner Dash* might seem unsurprising; on the other hand, though, while hearts ordinarily depict the health of the avatar, in time management games they illustrate the happiness of the customers. While this distinction might seem slight, it is telling. In most video games players are concerned with their own health level, but the hearts in the *Dash* games signify the well-being of others. In some ways, this gendered treatment of hearts in video games evokes Lynda Birke's discussion of hearts in *Feminism and the Biological Body*. Here, Birke notes that while discussions of heart disease and the mechanics of the heart have masculine connotations, emotional associations with the heart are almost entirely feminine: "The heart is gendered, not least through its symbolic association with emotionality. Even in the discourses of biomedicine, its apparently neutral status as 'merely a pump' carries connotations of gender . . . Not only is heart disease so often portrayed as though it were a disease uniquely affecting men (and captured in advertising campaigns urging housewives to 'look after your husband's heart' by avoiding butter), but even representations of that hearty pump in scientific texts can be read as gendered."[30] It seems compelling that these gendered interpretations of the heart are so neatly folded back into video games, which returns us to the emotional labor of the player. As with the dynamic Birke suggests occurs in medical metaphors, the diseased heart losing life belongs to more masculine avatars, while the more feminine Flo is concerned with others' emotionality. Her life is directly connected to the well-being of others and her own performance of emotional labor.

Yet the emotional labor that occurs in the *Dash* games and other time management titles can be very *satisfying*. While one cannot necessarily win the love of family members, customers, or coworkers by providing emotional labor in the real world, in the game world the player can actually win. The surplus of hearts is pleasurable as a mode of emotional labor—the affective work being done is rewarded on-screen and the player is constantly reminded of the love of non-player characters. Hearts brightly light up the screen to tell the player that she has done well and performed her labor successfully.

Emotional and affective labor plays an equally interesting role in the *Delicious Emily* series. The game play in this series is strikingly similar to that of *Diner Dash*, with only slight modifications. Emily owns a restaurant and we are charged with helping her keep the proper flow of patrons and products. Like *Diner Dash*, the *Delicious Emily* games use hearts to signify customer happiness. But the games also structures emotionality into strategic cut scenes. In the game *Delicious Emily's True Love*, the title character meets Patrick, a florist, and begins to date him. After each completed level, we earn one more story via short cut scenes. Subsequent games have Emily and Patrick getting married (*Delicious Emily's Wonder Wedding*), moving into a home (*Delicious Emily's Home Sweet Home*), and dealing with the difficulties of motherhood and marriage (*Delicious Emily's New Beginnings* and *Delicious Emily's Hopes and Fears*). By the time we arrive at *Delicious Emily's Hopes and Fears*, the cut-scene narratives have shifted from the romance and honeymoon of earlier games, and often feature passive-aggressive spousal bickering or confessional moments between the partners (Figure 15). In other words, while the *Dash* games have a certain emotional distance regarding Flo's inner life, the *Delicious Emily* series revels in Emily's emotionality, anticipating that the audience has a desire for this level of melodrama.

And within all this we can begin to see the conflicted nature of emotional labor in the game worlds and how this labor maps to the designed identity of Player Two. On the one hand, time management games create

Figure 15. A screenshot of the mobile game *Delicious Emily's Hopes and Fears*, developed by Blue Giraffe and published by GameHouse in 2015. The screen shot is a cut scene (between playable levels) where there is a particular amount of melodrama between the protagonist and her husband. It concludes with the particularly passive-aggressive line, "LEAVE THEN. I do everything here myself anyway . . ." as Emily's husband threatens to leave town in an effort to find a cure for his daughter's mystery illness.

a link between work and play, making them impossible to disentangle. Yet, on the other hand, that work is always the type that is necessarily associated with feminized and emotional labor. Emotional labor functions in a way, here, that the player is forced into a role that might emulate the labor he or she might practice at home or work. The continuity of this has the potential to be both rewarding and limiting.

HIDDEN OBJECTS OF EMOTION

Time management games are not the only gaming style where players are asked to perform emotional labor. Hidden object games, another casual genre, are also replete with examples of this kind of feminized work. For example, in one hidden object game, *Surface: The Noise She Couldn't Make*, the player is asked to play the role of a psychic who must venture into the mental space of a critically injured and mentally ill woman in order to save her life. Early in the game, a nurse pleads with the player in a short cut scene: "We don't normally work with psychics but we're desperate. We found her at the edge of the forest. No name, so we can't contact her relatives. No visible signs of injury but she won't wake up. She's getting weaker, as if something's hindering her treatment . . . psychologically. Please. . . . Can you reach her . . . psychically?" As the game proceeds, the player is forced to puzzle through the character's mental state, taking on the burden of her inner emotional turmoil while images of the young girl occasionally plead with the player for help. While the player avatar, herself, is anonymous—invisible in the game world—the girl is full of personality and life. It is almost as though the psychic player becomes lost, ensconced in the mental state of an unstable person. The player is being asked to take on the emotional burdens of a non-player character, and this example is by no means unusual for the genre. This section will explore how several different hidden object games replicate this process of emotional labor within the experience of play.

Hidden object games are most commonly point-and-click-style adventure titles, which have the primary mechanic of players locating objects in a room after being given a list of items to find. In addition to the "found objects" portion of the game, there are generally larger spatial puzzles, and the player must listen to the clues and narratives of non-player characters (such as those described in the *Surface* game). Generally speaking, the player navigates through this world, finding puzzles and objects in order to solve a larger mystery. While most hidden object games closely follow the mystery-telling style, others push into romance or supernatural genres. Most hidden object games would rank at either a 7 or 8 on the scale I used in chapter 1 of this book.

Though I focus on the narrative for the *Surface* game in particular, there are hundreds and hundreds of games that follow similar kinds of trajectories and play styles. A small sampling of game titles include:

- *Mystery Case Files: Return to Ravenhearst*
- *Redemption Cemetery: The Island of the Lost*
- *Mystery Tales: The Last Hope*
- *Mysteries of the Ancients: Deadly Cold*
- *Riddles of Fate: Into Oblivion*
- *Grim Legends: The Forsaken Bride*
- *PuppetShow: Destiny Undone*
- *Grim Tales: The Stone Queen*

The list of this genre on the computer game portal Big Fish Games contains hundreds of games, and hundreds more can be found on other websites.[31] Additionally, many of the titles function as part of a larger branded series, hence the use of colons within the titling styles, creating a sense of each brand carrying dozens of similar-yet-different video games that repeatedly offer the same experiences. (For example, there are several games in the *Mystery Case Files* series and the *Grim Tales* series.) The genre is clearly popular and resonates with audiences, but the play styles—as well as the emotional labor implied by the games—are worth studying. For the sake of simplicity, my focus in the discussion below is on *Surface: The Noise She Couldn't Make* as a representative game—games in this genre are so often narratively similar that it is easy to use any game out of the stack to illustrate the larger whole.

In some ways, the work/play tension of hidden object games might appear to share some similarities with time management games. Many scenes in these games take place in large, cluttered rooms full of "missing" objects that the player, often placed in the roll of a detective, must navigate. Once a hidden object has been found, it disappears from the larger image (Figure 16). At its core the hidden object mechanic is not a puzzle so much as a *cleaning* mechanic—the player is cleaning a messy room in an effort to bring order to a chaotic situation.[32] Cleaning, as a leisure activity, helps establish a complicated relationship between work and leisure in the game world. Hidden object games, then, have several

Figure 16. A screenshot from the computer game *Surface: The Noise She Couldn't Make*, developed by Elephant Games and published by Big Fish Games in 2012. The screenshot shows a typical hidden object messy space, which must be cleared (or cleaned) by removing objects.

possible meanings, particularly in terms of maintaining a kind of domestic order. At the same time, the space can never be fully "cleaned"—only certain objects can be selected and removed from the environment. This simple mechanic thus implies an endless cleaning experience with little resolution or satisfaction.[33]

In a similar way, to progress narrative flow, players pick up objects throughout the game world and must use them in larger puzzles. For example, in the game *Surface: The Noise She Couldn't Make*, the player must cross water at one point. In order to cross the water, she must have previously picked up an ironing board, found elsewhere in the game. While the player might pass thousands of other representations of boards in a variety of locations in the game, it is not until she puts the ironing board in the correct location that she can move on to the next set of puzzles. This kind of brainteaser combines a *MacGyver*-esque logic (i.e., using things in ways other than their originally intended purposes) while limiting the player to specific solutions. The inevitability of these mechanisms does not imply the best possible solutions, but rather the most inconvenient solutions to complex physical problems.

Yet, when examining the narrative conventions of the hidden object genre, it is worth considering how emotional labor plays a major role. While the overall scope of the games vary wildly (some take place in our current world, some in fantasy worlds, and others in the past or future), the setup of the hidden object games are all strikingly similar. The player functions as an outsider to a place where a mystery must be solved by combing through frozen-in-time geographic locations in order to find a series of physical and textual clues. The games inevitably involve some kind of victim—often women or children, but also sometimes an entire town of victims or, occasionally, adult male victims. In the *Surface* game mentioned above, the player's emotional labor functions by being asked literally to get inside the head of a young, abused, comatose woman and take on her emotional burden. Yet, other games function with similar kinds of emotionally wrought tales. For example:

- The *Ravenhearst* series has the player uncover the Gothic tale of an abusive husband, whose ghostly wife (and, later, children) must be freed.
- *PuppetShow: The Mystery of Joyville* involves tracking down missing children in a small town formerly famous for its puppet show.
- *Grim Tales: The Bride* asks the player to explore her (fictional) sister's past and memories to try and figure out whether she died.
- *Fearful Tales: Hansel and Gretel* involves having one's own children kidnapped and embedded in the famous fairy tale—the player's job is to save her own children.
- *Mystery Chronicles: Betrayals of Love* involves uncovering the story of a gruesome murder of a countess.
- *Grim Tales: The Stone Queen* has the player saving not one individual but a town of frozen people.

This list only touches the surface on the similar-yet-different narratives offered by the hidden object game genre. In all of them, by solving unsolvable mysteries of victims and hearing their pitiable narratives, the player is constantly doing the work of emotional labor: fixing the problems of those who cannot help themselves. While this may not contrast deeply with other media intended for female audiences (romance novels and melodramatic films, for example), it is strikingly different from the narrative style constructed in games designed for masculine audiences. It seems unlikely to find *Metal Gear Solid*'s protagonist, Solid Snake, reaching out to the player to help him release the ghosts of wronged people or to tell the story of an abused wife.

At the same time, the player is invisible within the story, both literally and figuratively. The hidden object game is almost always without an avatar; the player's embodiment on-screen is invisible. Even when using tools to solve puzzles, the tool floats in midair as if held by a ghost. Yet, in a figurative sense, the player is still invisible: she arrives after the crime or tragedy has taken place, solving mysteries for people who cannot see or appreciate her. The player's invisibility makes her emotional labor fruitless. There is no personal gratification in solving mysteries, as her invisibility makes her incapable of recognition. In the hidden object game, the most hidden thing is the player herself. The use of domestic labor within play taps into emotional labor, helping to form the player's designed identity. The player is lost within the game and invisible within her ongoing tasks of emotional labor.

A few hidden object games eschew the mystery stories for romance plotlines, although romance serves as a less compelling means than mystery for moving a player forward through a narrative world. Games such as *Harlequin Presents: Hidden Objects of Desire* place the player in the role of the (female) protagonist in a romance story, while games such as *Love and Death: Bitten* push the player back and forth between the masculine and feminine roles in a supernatural (vampire) romance story. These kinds of games maintain the visage of emotional labor by asking players to explore the inner selves of the romance protagonists. The *Dream Day* series (*Dream Day Wedding, Dream Day Honeymoon*, etc.), in particular, rebukes the mystery part of hidden object games and replaces it with a more direct form of emotional labor: wedding planning.

CAREGIVING GAMES

Caregiving games sit in a strange place in terms of how designed identity functions for Player Two. Games that center on the care of others are not necessarily designed for an audience of *women*; there often seems to be a tacit assumption that younger people are the primary and presumed audience for these games. Yet, part of a designed identity is that the process of identity production does not start at the point of adulthood—obviously, from a young age girls are encouraged to replicate and perform tasks relating to motherhood and domestic care. Therefore, while caregiving games are not necessarily meant for adult women, their replication of mother-hood helps to construct them as games for both girls and women, regardless of who is playing them.

Games such as those in the *Cooking Mama* series nicely suggest this ambiguous space of how caregiving games act as a training ground for girls yet a familiar space for women. In this series, the player takes on the role of Mama (an ambiguous character we do not ever see in an actual motherhood role) as she cooks, gardens, crafts, or does other domestic-themed chores.[34] In terms of the game's play with emotional affect, Mama's rejoinders regarding the player's success or failure at cooking become one of the most notable aspects. Success at the completion of the recipe results in the response "Perfect! Just as good as Mama!" Conversely, failure to complete the recipe properly invites the fury of Mama, whose eyes turn to angry flames: "Don't worry. Mama will fix it" (Figure 17). (Mama always refers to herself in the third person.) There is an unsubtle reminder of women's roles in the domestic sphere here, suggesting that motherhood

Figure 17. A screenshot of the video game *Cooking Mama*, developed by Office Create and published by Taito, originally in 2006. The image shows the "fail" screen when a player does not succeed at a recipe. Note Mama's burning eyes aligned with the semi-threat, "Don't worry. Mama will fix it."

is constantly in the mode of fixing problems. With her flaming eyes and curt tone, there is a slight note of threat in her negative response, almost as if she is saying, "Don't make Mama come fix that."[35] Mama serves as a reminder of the woman's role in the domestic sphere, wherein she is constantly in an iconic position of fixing other people's problems. The more recent iOS version of the game features Papa, a difficult-to-please character to whom the player is expected to serve meals. The game itself is ambiguous in terms of its intended audience: it could be meant for children taking on the role of mothering, or mothers performing the role in a game world. In either case, the *Cooking Mama* games are an example of how the behaviors behind caring become a meaningful mechanic in a game world. In many ways, *Cooking Mama* teaches players (regardless of age) the mechanics and nuance of emotionality within motherhood.

This is even more the case when a player is asked to care for a virtual pet or creature—a consistent mode of caregiving in a game world. Several games designed for an intended female audience simulate love and caregiving within the game mechanics of virtual pets and characters. Recently popular games in this space include *iLive*, *FooPets*, *Egg Baby*, *My Boo*, and *My Baby (Virtual Pet)*, with many others using a similar style. It seems inconsequential in these games whether the player is raising an animal, a monster, or a child—only that the player must constantly be in the process of grooming and caring for that creature, keeping it healthy and happy in a maternal way. Largely, these games were based off earlier games such as *Nintendogs*, *Hamsterz*, *Baby Pals*, *Horsez*, *Purr Pals*, and *GoPets: Vacation Island*, and their mechanics have not changed substantially over the past decade.

As discussed above, caregiving is considered women's work: Tronto nicely summed up how women are expected to care "for things" whereas men are expected to care "about things." Just as emotional labor is integral to many women's careers, emotional play is an example of how many games are designed for and marketed to women. Caregiving play was not invented in video games; the 1990s saw trends such as the Tamagotchi (a key chain–sized creature that must be fed, cleaned, and loved on a near-constant basis to keep it alive) and the Furby (a stuffed animal version of the Tamagotchi). The popularity of these earlier games helped to foster video game versions. Sherry Turkle's research on children and Furbies found "that children describe these new toys as 'sort of alive' because of the quality of their emotional attachments to the objects and because of the idea that the Furby might be emotionally attached to them."[36] A similar kind of response can be found in more recent games that involve virtual pets and creatures. Virtual pets are all about emotionality and the work of emotional labor. At the same time, Lauren Cruikshank suggests that these games are not just "mommy simulators" and are "not necessarily simple or faithful to the scripts established by official game objectives or by cultural gender play expectations."[37] Caring games are more complex than we often give them credit for; they help to produce affective and emotional labor, but at the same time they produce a familiar space in which female audiences feel authorized to play.

As already noted, while many of the caregiving games are geared toward child audiences, *Nintendogs* in particular became well-known as an early game that attracted an adult female audience. This shift was best witnessed by the newspaper comic strip *FoxTrot*, which in 2005 featured a story line where a mother kept stealing her son's Nintendo DS to play *Nintendogs*. This six-comic run shows a son begging his mother to give his Nintendo DS back, while she neglects her domestic caregiving duties (such as making dinner). In the final cartoon, the son asks his mother about dinner and she responds that she just fed "Cutie Paws" (her Nintendog) two hundred biscuits. Her son angrily yells back, "I meant OUR dinner!" Interestingly, the cartoon presents an example of a woman not only playing the game, but playing the game to the detriment of domestic chores. The popularity of *Nintendogs* with feminine audiences is also reinforced by a Nintendo advertising campaign titled "I Play for Me" in which pop star Carrie Underwood plays the game. Thus *Nintendogs* and other caregiving games, while perhaps designed for younger audiences, seem to have slippage and get parsed as a part of adult female culture as well.

Most striking is how the game's primary goal is the simulation of love and affection. There are several different versions of *Nintendogs*, each associated with various breeds of dogs, allowing players to have a more personal and specific relationship with the exact dog of their choosing. The player names the dog, uses voice commands to train the dog, feeds the dog, takes it for walks, plays with it, and grooms it. Ultimately, if a dog is poorly cared for it will grow up untrained and unruly. Alternatively, if the player cares for the dog properly he or she is rewarded with love and affection—the game's goal.

More recent research on virtual pets has illustrated the important role that emotional design plays in these games. Apperley and Heber examine how the game *Kinectimals* creates a space for potential intimacy between the player and the virtual pets, describing how emotion is "not used as a tool for training but is itself entrained"[38] within the process of training the player. Yet that emotionality would be impossible to disentangle from other forms of emotional labor. The caregiving elements of tasks are necessitated by the upkeep of virtual pets. Because emotional labor is so often understood to be women's work, the corollary is that emotional play also becomes a kind of women's work.

A compelling alternative to the typical virtual pet game is *Neko Atsume*, a "cat collector" game in which the player is given a small environment to design (similar to the setup of invest/express games), along with cat toys and food for in-game purchase (Figure 18). The player sets up their space with cat toys and puts food in the food bowl, which automatically invites cats to drop in, eat, and play. The player has no sense of "ownership" of the cats—different cats wander into the game space randomly. The cats reward the player with in-game currency, which can then be used to purchase more food and cat toys.[39] The distinction between this game and virtual pets is that the player is in no way responsible for the

Figure 18. A screenshot of the mobile game *Neko Atsume*, developed and published by HitPoint in 2014. The image shows the player caring for several cats, including my personal favorite, "Sassy Fran."

overall life and well-being of the cats she serves. Once the player stops feeding the cats, they simply disappear, presumably to go to someone else's house. Yet there are no repercussions or guilt if the player begins the game again, many months later. Rather than being confronted with hungry and angry cats that have wasted away, the cats simply return to the yard when the player puts out new food. *Neko Atsume*, then, has all of the benefits of gaming affect with none of the Tamagotchi guilt. It balances the desire for affective engagement without the consequences of negative emotional baggage.

The Sims (in its many versions and expansions) can also be considered a caregiving game, situated in the work of emotional labor. Many scholars have noted that *The Sims* has a history of being popular with female audiences in particular.[40] In many ways the game seems like a grown-up version of virtual pet games, but rather than nurturing a single creature the player is tasked with nurturing families and larger social networks. According to Katherine Isbister, it is the open-ended, nongame style (as well as domestic themes) that may be what makes it particularly attractive to feminine audiences: "It is not a highly goal-directed game—players can determine their own subgoals and can move from one to another freely. A player can devote time to building her Sims characters' careers, their social lives, or their houses, in any order, at any time. Destruction and violence are not primary game activities. *The Sims* metaphor—families with careers and children—is quite close to everyday suburban life (with some entertaining twists, of course)."[41] Thus *The Sims* integrates an ongoing theme of domesticity, specifically in terms of how it relates to the social. A player's primary goal is the caring for in-game characters, treating them as though they were extensions of one's own families. While some have noted incidence of Sims abuse,[42] the primary mode of play—the correct mode—is one of nurturing and caregiving. Emotional labor is inevitable as characters from *The Sims* are entirely dependent on their godlike creator, who is the only one that can improve their overall well-being. These themes of caregiving then relate back to domesticity in expectation of minding the lives of one's family and of the production of daily tasks.

PUZZLE GAMES AND TINY ACTS OF LOVE

The complexity of emotional labor in gendered gaming can occur in both large and small ways. Certainly, emotional labor is central to much of the work performed in time management and caregiving games and functions as a narrative undercurrent within hidden object games. Yet the power of emotional labor allows for tiny acts of affect in unexpected places. These acts are not necessarily fully developed or clearly articulated—they happen in small moments and in minor ways as a constant reminder to players.

Many casual puzzle games contain these subtler elements. Bubble shooter games (a variation of the match-3 genre) provide a rich example of how emotional labor can function in a game world, even without it being a primary premise for play. The player is given a series of multicolored bubbles that appear at the bottom of the screen. The player is tasked with matching colors and shooting bubbles of similar colors.[43] If the bubble lands on a set of two or more other bubbles of the same color, the entire set of bubbles disappears. Overall, this gaming setup would appear to be without politics or an excess of extra-game meaning. As with many games in the casual puzzle category, the setup is innocuous and generally free of narrative.

Yet many of the popular bubble shooters use graphic skins that *do* imply some degree of meaning and narrative. *Polar Pop Mania*, for example, uses the character of a mother seal as the mechanism to shoot the bubbles (the seal throws bubbles at other bubbles in order to pop them). The rationale for the bubble throwing is that some of the bubbles (generally speaking the ones at the top) encase the seal's babies we are tasked with saving. As the game description explains, "Cecilia the Seal needs YOUR help finding all her playful little pups that have ventured out all over the world! Toss and match colorful bubbles to save the seal babies and reunite them with their siblings." When the player fails (which, in my experience, is quite often), Cecilia the Seal and her babies cry miserably (Figure 19). Affect, here, is the punishment for not playing well. In turn, the seals cheer happily when the player succeeds at the rescue.

Of course, *Polar Pop Mania* is only one game. But as often is the case with casual games, there are at least a half dozen other bubble shooters that function identically, including *Bubble Mania* (where the player rescues baby cats) and *Panda Pop* (where the player rescues baby pandas). Other games, like *Hungry Babies Mania*, use a more typical match-3 format but include a light narrative about feeding hungry baby animals. The objects being matched in *Hungry Babies Mania* are food items (fruits, vegetables, waffles, etc.). As the player matches three or more of each food type, he or she feeds cute, big-eyed animals such as puppies, foxes, ducks, and pigs.[44] Each animal has a threshold of how much "food" they

Figure 19. A screenshot of the mobile game *Polar Pop Mania*, developed and published by Storm8 Studios in 2015. The image shows the player "fail" screen, with Cecilia the Seal crying because the player could not save all her babies.

need to stop being hungry, and the player wins by hitting that threshold in the allotted number of turns (Figure 20). Upon failure the player is told curtly, "You didn't feed all the babies." While the game's narrative content is low, it still manages to have embedded within it themes of affective and emotional labor.

There is another strange mode of subtext in how emotional labor functions, particularly in Storm8 games. Several games produced by Storm8 use the word "mania," which I suggested in the previous chapter contains baggage for feminine audiences. But beyond the histrionic implications of "mania" there is a strange visual effect to how the word is printed. When the title screen for *Hungry Babies Mania* is viewed quickly, the font kerning of "Mania" appears to almost look like the word "Mama" (Figure 20). This is not likely an intentional decision by Storm8, but that does not

Figure 20. A pair of screenshots from the mobile game *Hungry Babies Mania*, developed and published by Storm8 Studios in 2015. The left screen shows how the kerning of the word "Mania" makes it look slightly like "Mama." The right screen shows the feeding of cute baby animals in acts of caregiving.

make the effect any less jarring. Given these factors, it becomes increasingly evident how small, seemingly meaningless puzzle games can have larger implications regarding emotional affect.

THE SOCIAL AND THE EMOTIONAL

My focus in closing this chapter is on social games: a meditation on how the increased sociality in video games helps to maintain modes of emotional labor. This distinction of referring to specific kinds of gaming as "social" is complicated—after all, despite an unfounded reputation of video games being played alone, in the dark confines of a basement, many games are somewhat social. In considering the designed identity of social gaming, as opposed to the social behaviors already inherent in gaming, it is useful to consider Bart Simon, Kelly Boudreau, and Mark Silverman's consideration of "designed sociality" versus "played sociality" within their examination of social play in the game *EverQuest*. Of the social behavior of *EverQuest* players, they explain:

> We want to refer to this as the played sociality as opposed to the designed sociality of the game. That is, while we acknowledge that forms of sociality or social structures have literally been hardwired and soft coded by the programming choices of the designers and the mediating conditions of the hardware interface, at base the meaning of social interactions in the game rests on the active interpretation by the players who engage with the design. Not only does meaningful social engagement in *EQ* depend on the player's active interpretation, but as a consequence, the specific forms of played sociality experienced by players may differ from the designed sociality intended by designers. While the latter must certainly influence the former we are primarily interested here in drawing attention to played sociality as a distinct object of analysis.[45]

In many ways, the most effective social play is going to combine designed and played sociality. The two help to structure what is expected as well as the lived realities of the player.

The core question concerns how designed and played sociality becomes parsed as a form of emotional labor and affective labor within the designed identity of Player Two, and what the repercussions of that might be. Social play is complicated by expectations that social engineering is understood as women's work. In short, social gaming brings with it the potential to appeal to new players but also helps to demarcate them, pushing them toward specific modes of play that foster affective and emotional labor. This can be seen most clearly in both the popularity of and pushback against Facebook games and other social network games (SNGs).

Social network games[46] are games that are embedded as a part of social networking websites, particularly Facebook,[47] but also have become increasingly freestanding as part of mobile gaming. The interplay between games and social media suggests that in order to play properly you must make requests of existing "friends" on social networks. The friend-play creates more opportunities to share items, get bonuses, and complete certain kinds of quests or goals. This social element, according to Mia Consalvo, is a large part of the draw with SNGs, allowing for "the opportunity to play alongside one's friends and family—either by helping one another to advance or through engaging in friendly competition."[48] Consalvo demonstrates that through the process of friending, gifting, neighborhood interactions, regular communication, and challenges, players are given specific game mechanics that are meant to enhance social relations, although the affordances of these mechanics are quite limited.

SNGs have ushered in a new mode of gaming and have also invited in new kinds of gamers—including women. While the number of actual women playing social media games is just a bit above average—somewhere around 54–55 percent[49]—the specifics of which games they are drawn to help illustrate why certain games in this category very specifically appeal to women. So, for example, while more men are more likely to play the SNG *Texas Holdem Poker* (75 percent), more women play *FarmVille 2* (69 percent) and *Words with Friends* (63 percent).[50] Of the games on this list, *FarmVille 2* certainly involves the most caregiving and emotional labor–related tasks—keeping up with the grounds of friends' farms, keeping crops from withering, sending gifts to help other friends excel. These are the types of games that seem to be more heavily played by women.

The often-required sociality of SNGs—such as the never-ending barrage of messages that integrate with personal and social spaces, the nature of gift giving and receiving, and the ongoing interactions with friends and family members—positions social media games in such a way that they become a mode of affective and immaterial labor.[51] At the same time, it *transforms* in-game emotional labor back into the real world—in most cases the people with whom we play SNGs are those we already know. The affective work of SNGs is in their use of emotional labor. After all, one's interest in whether the digital crops of a friend or loved one wither away is based on the premise that you care about that person, that you want to keep their space from entering modes of entropy. At the same time, friend players offer this service back, by pushing gifts and providing reciprocal affect in response to emotional labor. Much like in the emotional labor of *Diner Dash*, that of *FarmVille 2* (and similar games) is satisfying—you get material proof of the love of those around.

Yet, while the designed identity embedded in social gaming helps to reinforce the value of emotional labor, the format has been often insulted by individuals in the video game industry. The original *FarmVille* game won "Game of the Year" in 2010 at the Game Developers Association Conference, yet the video game industry has been primarily indifferent or outright insulting regarding this feat.[52] Academic and game designer Ian Bogost made fun of the primary mechanics of *FarmVille* by creating his own (critical) game, *Cow Clicker*.[53] It would seem that just as affective labor is devalued in the real world, so is it devalued in the gaming world and as a form of play.

There is some slippage between what is labeled an SNG and an invest/express game (a category discussed in detail in chapter 2). Many SNGs, over time, have transformed into the invest/express format and lost some of their social elements. The category of SNG, in many ways, overlaps with invest/express games. By looking at the similar games under the umbrella of "SNG" here, the idea is to consider how the social and time management aspects can affect the same games in different ways.

Some invest/express games have different layers of emotion that trickle into game play. For example, in *Kim Kardashian: Hollywood* (discussed in more detail in chapter 4), the player's emotional labor primarily centers on dating. The player can "date" a real-world friend but also is given opportunities to date a variety of non-player characters that shuffle in and out of the game. As the player becomes more prominent in the game world (moving closer to the coveted A-list), her avatar is increasingly approached by strangers interested in dating her. Often, the non-player characters will use passive-aggressive tactics such as "I will stop eating if you won't go out with me!" When a player rejects a non-player character, the response is sometimes emotionally heated. When a player begins to seriously date a character, if she does not take a significant other out often enough, the paramour will call angrily and threaten to break up with the player if she does not spend in-game currency (K-Coins) on them. Other games that deal with dating themes, such as *Campus Life* and *EnchantU*, similarly involve the negotiating of emotional situations. The emotional labor in these scenarios can be characterized differently from many of the ones mentioned above. Rather than being domestic in nature, these games deal with romance and the potentially abusive responses of spurned lovers. These moments also disentangle the affective labor from other SNGs, as the player is (hopefully) likely to receive less potential abuse from actual friends and loved ones than from NPCs in the game world.

In later versions of *Kim Kardashian: Hollywood* the player is able to have a baby through adoption. While this ability suggests a resonance between *KK:H* and some of the caregiving games discussed above, in reality the player has little interaction with the baby and is not tasked with any emotional labor in order to care for her.[54] In fact, while there are repercussions for not maintaining a love relationship in the game (the player will be dumped by her partner), there are no consequences for ignoring one's baby. Like the cats in *Neko Atsume*, the baby is there when you want her but does not disappear if you forget to feed her.

SNGs are not the only form of affective labor in social gaming, and also not the only kind specifically marketed to women. The idea of the family gaming system became part of the video game landscape with the Nintendo Wii. What has been called "family-centered video gaming" began with the first generation of the Wii in 2006, although Xbox and PlayStation have both since jumped in on this trend as well.[55] This affective mode of play as it relates to the social (specifically the family) was apparent with the "My Wii Story" advertisements that began this chapter. The Wii system was unique, not only in its game controllers but also in the manufacturer's desire to appeal to families in a household (as opposed to one or two individual gamers). The "My Wii Story" advertisements illustrate that the center of this household, the person meant to facilitate family gaming activities, is a maternal figure. The emotional labor of the Nintendo Wii occurs not in the actual labor of gaming but in being the organizer of play. Desire to play does not center around the organizer's own activities, but rather around the enjoyment of other people's play.

In many ways, the Wii (and other modes of family-centered video games) provide a noteworthy space for the emotional labor of the designed identity of Player Two. The family gamer has no interest in gaming for herself—or so we are to believe if we understand the "My Wii Story" advertisements correctly. The family gamer and organizer of these games is more interested in the affective labor of making sure her family functions well

4 Playing with Consumption

"ROLL HOME PHAT"

A 2013 commercial for the video game store GameStop features a mother as a household consumer of video games. In this ad, we see a middle-aged white woman, in a beige sweater, wearing light makeup, with her hair pulled back, driving a white minivan. The mother character—we do not know for sure that she is a mother, but she appears to be embodying that role—has thumping bass music playing loudly, blasting out of her suburban vehicle. She owns the role, nodding lightly to the seemingly mismatched music. Along with the tunes, the minivan is trailing down the street—its back end is weighed down so that it hits the pavement, referred to as a "rolling" car in low-rider culture. The minivan rides low enough that it creates sparks on the street. As she drives down the street, she passes a concerned black police officer, giving him a menacing two-finger gang-style salute. The police officer has pulled over a white male, who is positioned solemnly with his hands on the car. The soon-to-be-arrested man looks wistfully at the low-riding mom. Then, in slow motion, she passes a younger man, who appears to be Latino, in his own low-riding vehicle. The young man nods approvingly at the white mother in her absurd, bass-thumping minivan. She returns the nod and smirks, pleased.

The commercial ends with the mother pulling up to a white suburban home, lit with bright, non-garish Christmas lights. As she pulls up and opens the back of the minivan, we see the reason why she was low-riding in the first place: the back of her vehicle is completely packed with GameStop bags, video games, controllers, an Xbox, and a PlayStation. The weight of everything she purchased had pushed down the car to such an extreme that it emulated a low-rider. The announcer reinforces the theme of the commercial with the voice-over, "This holiday, roll home phat[1] with the hottest tablets from Samsung and Google."

The television commercial is fascinating in a variety of ways. It attempts to broach a conversation about authenticity—the video games in the back of the car seem to be granting the white woman a kind of trespass into a cultural aesthetic that is traditionally neither white nor feminine. Yet there is clearly a tone of appropriation here—the mother is not fully invested in the othered culture in which she trespasses, and she concludes her voyage in potential deviance within the safety of her white, suburban, nonthreatening home. The contrast between whiteness and non-whiteness in this commercial is jarring. Not only is the woman white, but her whiteness is reinforced by the white minivan and white home (drizzled with white lights). Those she encounters, however, are primarily not white: the black police officer and Latino driver are both reminders of her appropriation of other cultures. Her physical appearance is not what allows her to represent in othered cultures. It is the consumption of the video games that weigh down her vehicle that permits her appropriation.

Yet what is truly fascinating about this commercial is that she does not appear to be purchasing these games and gaming systems for herself. Her ticket into othered cultures, her questionable behavior, and the perception of her "gangster" style is presumably related not to her personal tastes but to those of her family. Nothing in the commercial is meant to indicate that she actually plans to *play* the minivan full of video games she has purchased. Her consumption is not her own—it is de facto consumption for her family. As she pulls into her safe suburban space we know that we have all been played, just a bit. She has been able to "roll home phat," but only because she has purchased gifts for her family. In many ways, this woman is other within the cultures she is fronting—she is both othered from the low-rider culture she has emulated, and she is simultaneously othered from the video games and systems she has bought in great surplus.

The commercial is not particularly surprising. While video games might not be frequently advertised to women as players—with an obvious exception being the Nintendo campaigns discussed in the previous chapters—women are still the primary shoppers in most households. The commercial functions as a signpost toward a long history of constructing women as household consumers—an image that, in turn, has become socially expected behavior. In a 2013 study by the Private Label

Manufacturer's Association, two-thirds of all women report that they do most of the household shopping.[2] While these numbers do not specifically reference the purchase of video games, they do logically imply that while there is not always a perception of women as video game players, there is an understanding that middle-aged women might often purchase (or enable the purchase of) video games. Given that, it seems logical that a commercial would suggest that by purchasing a minivan load of video games—so much so that the minivan itself becomes subsumed in nonwhite cultural aesthetics—a mother might appear cooler and more "phat" to her family.

But this raises a larger issue—one that underlies how all video games are marketed to Player Two, both inside and outside of game spaces. Women's play/work is often associated with consumptive practices. These practices are then central to the role of what are allowable acts of play for women consumers. Because of long-standing associations between women and shopping, these playful acts of consumption help to justify the presence of women within gaming. They imply that women are there not to play but to *consume*—by purchasing either for themselves or for others. This consumptive play is then baked in to the design, the style, and the culture of video games designed for Player Two. Yet the play also manages how those consumptive practices should occur, and how women are expected to be consumers—in very deliberate and predictable ways that reaffirm historical and social constructions. Still, it is important to acknowledge that consumption is a path toward a certain degree of mobility in many spaces, including gaming. Women's consumption within the casual market over recent years has caused many in the video game industry to take note and rethink gaming audiences. Just as with previous chapters on time and emotions, playing with consumption is a mixed bag.

In this chapter I analyze these modes of consumption in video games, as it particularly applies to the designed identity of Player Two. Within this, I look at how consumption is part of many game mechanics in a multitude of ways: disappearing objects (such as the hidden object games discussed in chapter 3), fashion aesthetics, alternative forms of gaming currency, and F2P (free-to-play) purchasing mechanics all help to suggest that women can consume their way into specific portions of video game culture, reinforcing traditional cultural ideologies. At the same time, the rest of the gaming community often marginalizes games that highlight these mechanics. In particular, this chapter will look at several games that use different kinds of consumptive mechanics, paying particular attention to *Kim Kardashian: Hollywood* as a game that taps in to several modes of consumptive practice simultaneously in its attempts to appeal to Player Two.

GAMES AND CONSUMPTION

Video games, like all forms of popular culture, cannot be disentangled from the realities of industry and consumptive practice. That is to say, most video games are made with the goal of the creators to make money, and all video games (regardless of their market value at any given moment) cost something to the player: actual currency, time, or the cost of relinquishing personal information to corporations. Furthermore, as major corporations continue to collapse into one another, it is often difficult to discern the specific costs of media consumption. In "The Culture Industry," their prophetic work from 1944, Max Horkheimer and Theodor Adorno explain, "The dependence of the most powerful broadcasting company on the electrical industry, or of film on the banks, characterizes the whole sphere, the individual sectors of which are themselves economically intertwined."[3] Though Horkheimer and Adorno predated the video game industry, their point still stands—corporate conglomeration makes playing mainstream (non-independent) games an act of consumptive practice. Video games, like all popular culture, sit at the intersection of art and commerce, involving "numerous disciplines rooted in a particular culture producing creative, artistic, and culturally important works."[4] The struggle between art and commerce—as in other forms of popular media—often becomes a driving force for what games are made and what images are represented in those games.

Yet there is also something unique to how video games perform consumptive practice. While watching film or television or listening to music involves varying degrees of agency, the process of interacting with specific mechanics and avatars in a virtual world increases the agentic appeal of a game. In other words, we might *choose* to watch a television program, but when we purchase a video game to play ourselves, our relationship to that game is as active as the game world predicates. It is not only the process of purchasing and viewing, but a will to consume and continue to consume that helps leverage the interactions between players and their games. That process is ongoing—to consent to play one must maintain an ongoing consumptive relationship. This is even more to the point with the growth of "freemium" or "free-to-play" games, where a player does not lay out money at the outset of a game, but consumes in ongoing ways throughout the process of play. The relationship between the free-to-play model and the consumptive practices of play are broken down in detail below. Part of the complicated nature of considering the role of consumption in video games is that the term "consumption" can mean several things, often simultaneously, in this environment. Tapping into older research on consumers, Morris B. Holbrook and Robert W. Chestnut make distinctions between buying versus consuming, choosing versus using, purchase versus product involvement, and informational versus transformational advertising as it applies to video games and enjoyment of those games, suggesting that future research focus on experiential models. They argue that the combination of these elements contribute to the "hedonic (i.e., pleasurable) components of the playful consumption experience."[5] While games have changed over the years, there is still some complexity in the relationship between how we can understand the experience of consumption in gaming. For the purposes of this chapter, consumption in gaming can refer to the following:

- *Material consumption*: This refers to the initial purchase and or download of a video game. Regardless of the cost of the game (or whether the game is free), the player's consent to play and placement of the game on a technology (computer, mobile device, console system, etc.) is an act of consumptive practice. All games involve this form of consumption at the point that the player/consumer chooses to add that game into her library of potential games.

- *Content consumption*: In this term, I am referring to the consumption of time, space, and data in the game world. Content consumption is the process of consuming a video game within the parameters of that game's world. While a player might engage in material consumption (downloading the game), she might participate in varying levels of content consumption, depending whether she choses to actually play through any of the content of that game. In other words, for a game that is purchased in a store, the player might engage entirely in material consumption habits, but then consume only 25 percent of the content of that game.

- *Mechanical consumption*: This term characterizes the process of small objects in a game "disappearing" when a player completes an action or mechanic, such as in *Bejeweled* styles of gaming, or when a player consumes energy points during the process of play.

- *In-game purchasing*: This refers to cases where the player spends only fictional, game-world money in order to succeed in the game world.
- *Extra-game purchasing*: This refers to cases where the player spends real-world money in order to succeed in the game world. Many games conflate in-game purchasing and extra-game purchasing, creating a seamless space where the player might not always easily equate his or her in-game spending habits with real-world money. While extra-game purchasing implies material consumption, I am breaking the two apart—material consumption occurs at the point when the player is first downloading or consenting to play the game, whereas extra-game purchasing happens during game play.

In addition to the above modes of consumption in gaming that easily can apply to many popular video games, I would like to propose two final categories for consumptive practices in video games that specifically are marketed to female audiences:

- *Fashion-based consumption*: This refers to video games that specifically emulate the process of "trying on" and cycling through different articles of clothing and accessories, usually to place on the player's avatar but also often on non-player characters. Sometimes fashion-based consumption can be linked to in-game purchasing or extra-game purchasing, although it should remain a distinct category because of how it plays into gendered expectations of use in fashion.
- *Culinary-based consumption*: Culinary games often also involve a kind of consumption, which I will touch on toward the end of this chapter— they suggest a form of literal consumptive practices (eating), but also a denial of the actual pleasure associated with culinary arts. In other words, a player is able to create virtual foods but never actually eat them.

These different modes of gaming consumption often occur simultaneously, allowing the pleasures of consumptive practice to function on a multilevel, reward-based system. As this chapter continues, I will talk about several themes within consumptive behavior, explaining how they relate to one another in gaming environments as well as how they construct subjectivities of consumption.

Yet consumption also implies purchase. Given that, it is important to consider what it is that the consumer is *purchasing* in all these exchanges, as they relate to video games. Obviously, when considering what is purchased, the game itself is often the primary purchase. However, as many cultural studies scholars have noted through the years, the purchase portion of consumptive practice is often more than buying *products*, but also about acquiring *status*. Another way of thinking about this is through the lens of what Thorstein Veblen calls conspicuous consumption. According to Veblen, "The utility of consumption as an evidence of wealth is to be classed as a derivative of growth. It is an adaption to a new end, by a selective process, of a distinction previously existing and well established in men's habits of thoughts."[6] Certainly, many have written about how the consumption of goods helps people attempt to exceed their current social class. More recently, Lynn Spigel has coined the term "conspicuous production," wherein smart technologies (e.g., "smart homes") turn sites of leisure into a spaces where "the resident is meant to be seen working all the time."[7]

It is in a similar capacity that we can understand the layering of conspicuous consumption/production within video game spaces. Alternative identities within game worlds are more calculated than our real-world identities (i.e., we often are able to define our identity in more strategic ways in a game world). Because of this we are able to see ways that conspicuous consumption *and* production might create a space of excess desire and labor within game worlds, wherein women players are always trying to buy their place at the arcade machine. Given the already-noted dominance of white masculinity in gaming spaces, perhaps it is useful to consider the possibility that the desire to "consume" functions as an attempt to gain a foothold and prosper in alternative ways. In the television commercial described at the start of this chapter, we saw a perfect example of this kind of conspicuous consumption—the character was attempting to pass in cultures other than her own through the consumption of goods. Here consumption functions as a kind of "permission slip" for play: the player has purchased things and is thereby permitted to exist (in part at least) within that culture. Those permission slips are powerful yet ephemeral. They become even trickier when the play is designed with gender-normative modes of consumption. Games that are too centered on consumptive mechanics are often dismissed (such as free-to-play or fashion games) and are not accepted as part of the broader (masculine-based) gaming culture. In this way, because of designed identity, women players are theoretically able to buy their way in to video game culture, but they are never able to fully embody the nuances of that culture. Just as Veblen's "conspicuous consumption" suggests that shifting social class through consumption is only partially effective, the same applies for the gendered modes of conspicuous consumption in video games. Games that highlight consumerism and consumption create a mode of designed identity wherein women are expected to pay to play—that is, in order to be part of gaming culture they must consume. At the same time, as often is the case in other examples of conspicuous consumption, this creates an experience that is only partially satisfying; buying into a culture is not the same as being an authentic part of that culture. Furthermore, purchasing one's way into that culture can mean having to continue to consume, ad infinitum. Those very consumptive practices, though, as conflicted as they might be, are also helping to form a path for emerging audiences in gaming.

WOMEN, SHOPPING, AND PRODUCTIVE CONSUMPTION

Many years ago, when I was in the earliest phases of this research project, I approached my mother and began to badger her on a regular basis. She had no interest in playing games—or insisted as such—and I was dubious of her claims. I would call, e-mail, and pester her in person, repeatedly asking what might make her want to play video games. One day, we sat on the phone and I brought it up again: "But there must be *something* that might make you play," I pleaded. In an exasperated tone she replied, "I don't know, Shira. How about a nice shopping game?"[8] This moment gave me pause. *A nice shopping game.* At what point, I wondered, did shopping—an entirely productive task—become a mode of leisure. As I followed this thread, it became apparent that this was only a form of leisure for women—when I mentioned this as a gaming possibility to men, they seemed to be impervious to the charms of shopping play. Further, the notion of a shopping game implies a middle-class or higher ideal— one can only think of shopping as a form of leisure if he or she has the wealth, time, and means to partake in this pastime.

Philosophers and scholars have often considered the relationship between production and consumption, showing connections between the two as part of a circuit of capital. The majority of theoretical work on consumption and consumer practices focuses on "things": much of it takes Marxist or postmodern standpoints to understand how desire for material goods is constructed and facilitated. Most notably, in *Critique of Political Economy*, Karl Marx deftly explains the symbiotic relationship of production/consumption:

Production is simultaneously consumption as well. It is consumption in a dual form—subjective and objective consumption. Firstly, the individual, who develops his abilities while producing, expends them as well, using them up in the act of production, just as in natural procreation vital energy is consumed. Secondly, it is consumption of the means of production, which are used and used up and in part (as for instance fuel) are broken down into simpler components. It similarly involves consumption of raw material which is absorbed and does not retain its original shape and quality. The act of production itself is thus in all its phases also an act of consumption. The economists concede this. They call *productive consumption* both production that is simultaneously identical with consumption, and consumption which is directly concurrent with production.[9]

This notion of "productive consumption" allows me to illustrate the nuanced relationship between the two. Productive consumption, as I will demonstrate, is not always economically based, but can also be part of complex gendered activities. Furthermore, I would argue that productive consumption is something particularly applicable to women—women are expected to be the primary consumers in a household, expected to enjoy it, and are simultaneously culturally critiqued for wanting to "shop 'til [they] drop." In Marx's worldview, we are always already playing a "nice shopping game."

The relationship between women and a perceived desire to shop is complicated. It involves what Joseph Turow and Nora Draper would refer to as an "industrial construction of the audience," where media and corporate practitioners play a role in this system.[10] While this construction might appear to be natural, it is not. The roots of the consumer being designed as feminine can be traced back to the Victorian era.[11] Celia Lury illustrates that a parallel between women and consuming cultures creates negative perceptions of women.[12] Stereotypes of women as shoppers help to situate women as the ultimate consumer, rather than producer, of goods. According to A. Fuat Firat, this corresponds to the perception of women as consumer and, more important, as "shopper": "The female— specifically, in visual culture, the female body—became the representation of the feminine, which was the *ideal* consumer in Western culture. She 'went shopping' while he worked. She spent his money or earnings. Her frivolity in buying and consuming became a major topic of jokes in the culture. She was such a consumer that he had always to restrain her appetite for consumables."[13] Thus women play a particularly complex role in consumer culture; essentializations of women automatically map them as the primary consumer in the consumption/production relationship. This essentialization is reinforced by the aforementioned statistics demonstrating that women are the primary purchasers of products in a household. By combining these aspects, shopping is automatically stereotyped as a mode of feminine practice. At the same time, women's shifting roles in society (moving them out of the household and into work domains) also creates more responsibilities: in the last thirty years women have increasingly become both producers and consumers. Therefore, it would seem that women like to shop—they like fashion and they enjoy conspicuous consumption—or so we are told. This middle-class ideal that women find pleasure in the process of shopping is a standard assumption in popular culture. Commercials, songs, television shows, and films all play off this notion, often turning it into a punch line. Women are "material girls" (per the classic Madonna lyrics) and need to tone down their tendencies toward being shopaholics (per the popular *Confessions of a Shopaholic* book series and film). Constructions of females as shoppers cross boundaries of ethnicity, social class, and age.

By tapping into Marx's definition of "productive consumption" and Veblen's "conspicuous consumption," in this chapter I illustrate a complex relationship between gender, consumption, and production. These complementary ideas, bolstered by the gendered implications within the designed identity of Player Two, illustrate ways that gaming uses several of the consumptive modes, discussed above, in order to configure and essentialize specific kinds of games as (a) necessarily feminine, (b) necessarily productive, and (c) unable to achieve the lofty desires implied by the label of "conspicuous consumption." In this way, the designed identity of Player Two configures a perceived feminine desire, which cannot be disentangled from shopping, purchasing, and consumptive practices. At the same time, those very consumptive practices are *allowing* her into the space.

CONSUMING MECHANICS

As discussed earlier in this chapter, consuming mechanics can take on a variety of meanings. Different modes of consumptive mechanics (material consumption, content consumption, mechanical consumption, etc.) all come with a distinct set of implications, but often they become even messier when different versions of these mechanics happen simultaneously.

Given the complicated nature of consumption in video games, I will begin with the simplest version—what I refer to as the consuming mechanic. This mechanic is not bound to games that involve shopping, products, or currency. The consuming mechanic is one where the player's goal is to perform a series of maneuvers that make an object or series of objects disappear, visually creating a sense that the object has been consumed.

In his book *A Casual Revolution: Reinventing Video Games and Their Players*, Jesper Juul discusses the history of match-3 games, suggesting that they belong to a genre that has begun to wane in popularity. Juul suggests that the channel of downloadable casual gaming distribution creates "an inherent conflict between innovation and cloning," in part accounting for some of the difficulties in this genre of the casual.[14] In other words, match-3 games necessarily need to look and feel identical to one another (the cloning aspects) in order to achieve popularity, but simultaneously they need to feel innovative in ways that help them to attract new audiences. However, Juul's writing predates the moment when *Candy Crush Saga* (and its many clones) grabbed hold of the market. His work suggests that players and game designers want different things within this model. While a game designer might push toward product innovation, the player is more likely interested in a game that is instantly and easily playable. This discrepancy accounts for the waxing and waning popularity of match-3 games. Most certainly, Juul has a point about the ease of learning as being integral to this style of game. Additionally I would also like to suggest that there is also something *inherently satisfying* within the game mechanic itself. This mechanic is enjoyable because of the disappearing elements, which has the effect of neatly clearing the screen.

We already saw the satisfaction of the "disappearing object" mechanic at play in the genre of hidden object games in the previous chapter. I previously identified the process of selecting in a hidden object puzzle as an act of cleaning—because the player is able to understand the landscape of a room better after finding and clicking on an object (and making it disappear), I argued that this process replicates gendered domestic tasks such as cleaning. However, at the same time, this process of clicking on an object so that it disappears is also *consumptive*. By this I mean that once the object is used, it disappears from the landscape in a way that makes that virtual object consumed—it is no longer at play in the game world. Here, consumption and cleaning work simultaneously to create a liminal space and, while solving the puzzle, puts the player constantly in a mode of consumptive practice. Certainly, the satisfying nature of this work of consumption exceeds gender divisions—perhaps accounting for the widespread popularity of the match-3 game—but the thematic relevance of hidden object games tied with the consumptive mechanic helps to map the idea of "cleaning as consumption" intended as a kind of gendered domestic chore.

Consumptive mechanics as a primary mode of play are common in the casual market. Games such as those in the *Bejeweled* and *Candy Crush Saga* series have had hundreds of iterations, all replicating the game-play style. In these games, the player's goal is to match several items that are similarly shaped and colored, so that they disappear from the screen, making way for an endless string of new items to match. The result is that the player enables a game space where the goal is the consumption of small, meaningless objects. This consumption is the satisfying moment of play—the win condition that the player is meant to find thrilling. Watching objects disappear from the game space gives a jolt of satisfaction, indicating that we have properly consumed elements of the game board.

While this setup is not the primary focus of the chapter, I like to think of the consuming mechanic as a priming one, preparing players for a continued form for consumption throughout the process of gaming. Players might not be engaging in literal shopping or branded-product consumption in these games, but the mechanic helps to shape a style of game play that elicits further consumptive practices. For example, the F2P model, discussed in detail below, hinges entirely on the consumptive mechanics of disappearing objects—whether those objects are physical or more ephemeral. Therefore, if players are already in a mode where they are in the constant act of consuming objects, they are likely more easily primed to spend actual money on that game. Similarly, games such as *Kim Kardashian: Hollywood* are stacked with one consumptive mechanic upon the next. The consumption of imagined game currency helps to disconnect the player from the realities of real money, priming a player to potentially spend more of his or her cash. Yet the jolt of disappearing objects on the screen, physically consumed into nothingness, helps to create an environment where the player has no choice but to continue to consume.

FASHION GAMES AND SHOPPING GAMES

As already discussed, narratives of women as consumers dominate popular culture. Jennifer A. Sandlin and Julie G. Maudlin suggest that women consumers are framed in popular culture as out of control and impulsive, unable to control their consumptive desires.[15] These stereotypes also construct their representations in terms of race and class, suggesting more and less desirable forms of consumptive behavior along racial lines. Historically, consumptive practices for women are articulated through fashion and makeup, creating subjects that believe they can push past race- and class-based boundaries through the purchase of specific products.[16] In our current times, this was articulated most clearly through what Laurie Ouellette refers to as the "invention" of the "cosmo girl," helping to establishing the consumptive practices of fashion as a method to reconstruct identity.[17] In these ways, fashion and beauty products are primarily marketed to women as a form of "self-expression." This taps into what Elizabeth Wissinger refers to as "glamour labor,"[18] pushing it to a consumer level.

Given fashion's gendered nature, it would seem counterintuitive that fashion would play a role in many video games. But as game designers attempted to get more girls and women to be gamers, an increasing number of fashion games began finding their way to market. Ever since the oft-commented-on girl game of the 1990s, *Barbie Fashion Designer*, fashion games have held an ongoing, although somewhat secondary role, in games intentionally designed for female audiences. *Barbie Fashion Designer* was a unique game for girls when it was released—not only because players could select from themes and styles, mixing and matching clothing, but because the goal was the ability to print out clothing that a Barbie doll could actually wear. In Kaveri Subrahmanyam and Patricia Greenfield's study of girls playing *Barbie Fashion Designer*, they concluded that girls liked playing with the software because they "like nonaggressive play activities that allow them to create fantasies set in familiar locations with familiar characters. The *Barbie Fashion Designer* allows girls to do just this and becomes one more accessory in their role play."[19] While these aspects may be true in the case studies done for that essay, it is impossible to consider the *Barbie Fashion Designer* game and its predecessors outside the lens of consumptive practice. Fashion games—past, present, and future—create a space of entitled yet productive consumption, where a player's game work is automatically associated with the purchasing and appearance of clothing and accessories. These games help to tease out underpinning gendered narratives such as self-transformation, self-expression, and identity play.

Of course, *Barbie Fashion Designer* was never meant for women, but rather girls. While it is impossible to disentangle the age associated with intention, several other "fashion" games have found market prominence over the years—games that highlight the material edge of consumptive practice by giving players an opportunity to try on clothing and to mix and match ensembles. For instance, *Covet Fashion* is a mobile game where players are asked to put together outfits for events, in a way that seems to echo the content-sharing website Pinterest (Figure 21). Players are able to purchase the designs they have "discovered" through *Covet Fashion* in the real world, making a seamless transition between the implied consumption of a fashion game and the actual consumption practices of shopping. The artwork is realistic, not cartoonish, and seems to suggest a kind of grown-up paper doll using high fashion. *Covet* works with existing brands by showcasing their actual clothing and gives players the ability to purchase that clothing in the real world. The demographic for the game is explicitly stated to be women twenty-two and older.[20] One of the game's cocreators explains in a *VentureBeat* interview, "It is a lot like dressing up in real life. You feel good about yourself and you get feedback."[21] The consumptive elements of *Covet* are entirely productive: they suggest that the player's consuming behavior should directly link back to real-life decisions. Further, the name itself articulates desire in its purest form: coveting suggests the emotionality of aspirational ownership.

While *Covet* pushes toward fashion realism, other fashion-centric games are more cartoonish. Games like *JoJo's Fashion Show* and *Style Quest* are computer downloadable games that do not use real branding and offer instead more cartoonlike models (using the "lush" aesthetics described in chapter 1). Often, more cartoon-styled games do not allow the player to see all angles of the outfit—the in-game purchase of a cool outfit might only give access to the clothing from certain perspectives, and it might even be two-dimensional. The player cannot examine the clothing up close, generally, and cannot purchase that clothing in the real world. *Covet* seems to be one of the only games where this is an exception: after all, the purpose is in the game's title, to "covet." The player's role is not to be satisfied with what she can buy within the fictional game world but to create desire outside the game world.

Many games directly associate the stereotype that women and girls love to shop with modes of play by simply turning a video game into a form of paper dolls. From this perspective, paper doll mechanics are a "bonus" within a game world—for instance, it may be something that can be done as a small reward when a player finishes a level. In several of the games in the *Diner Dash* series, players can select alternative wardrobe

Figure 21. A screenshot of the mobile game *Covet Fashion*, developed and published by CrowdStar in 2014. The game combines typical fashion gaming with a Pinterest visual style and real-world clothing that the player can purchase.

options for Flo as she continues through the game. Sometimes these items give the player some kind of game bonus (e.g., sneakers that allow Flo to move faster), but others are just decorative, allowing the player to slide different clothing options on her avatar, implying that aesthetic form is sometimes more valuable than function. While different armor options in massively multiplayer online games and role-playing games like *World of Warcraft* offer better play, most fashion game upgrades are not meant to imply that the player can actually navigate the world more effectively, but rather, that the player gets to beautify her avatar. It neatly enfolds the labor aspects of Wissinger's "glamour labor" into game play.

This focus on having players *create* fashion (from preordained templates) echoes Brooke Erin Duffy's work on fashion bloggers and the use of consumers to generate content in digital spaces. Duffy argues that fashion blogs become a form of "immaterial labor" in commodity culture.[22] However, while fashion bloggers are sometimes given opportunities to touch, hold, and access the fashion they create, the two-dimensional, paper doll fashion creations in the game world seem to be copies of copies—they lack real cultural markers that allow for material consumption in satisfying ways. *Covet Fashion* tries to bypass this stopgap, but even in that the consumption offered to players is shallow and abstracted from reality—it does not account for body types and assumes a level of material wealth. This game, which appears to offer unlimited forms of play, is actually quite limited.

So, how about the "nice shopping game" suggested by my mother? Indeed, there is a history of games that seem to function around shopping as an activity. Certainly *The Sims* can be understood as a "shopping game" of sorts, where (ultimately) consumption rules. But other games have similarly toyed with consumption. *Shopmania*, for example, has the player working for the fictional superstore called Spendmore (Figure 22). As the player moves up the ranks (and through several departments) she is given a series of customers and shopping carts to be filled properly—in many ways a cross between *Tetris* and a time management game like *Diner Dash*. The game is not about shopping for oneself but about negotiating consumption for others. Superficial shopping choices (such as color matching) are rewarded, and the goal is to satisfy customers by making them consume as much as their carts will allow.

More recent shopping-centric games are also available on mobile devices. These games are often surprisingly similar: in the iOS game *Shopping Mall*, the player is tasked with saving the world after an evil

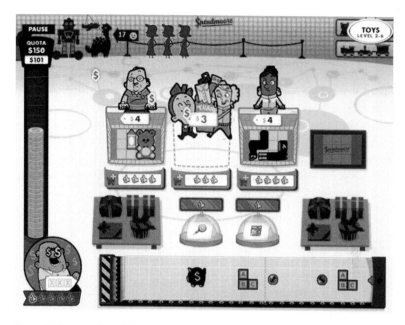

Figure 22. A screenshot of the computer game *Shopmania*, developed by Brighter Minds and published by iWin in 2008. The game focuses on consumptive themes, using a *Tetris* style of puzzles within levels.

businessman, Mr. Zog, has destroyed it. The primary means of doing so is by rebuilding a shopping mall.[23] Another iOS game, *Shopaholic World*, is a fashion-centric title with a shopping theme. Often, shopping games and fashion games bleed into each other. For example, while the primary mechanics of a video game might involve shopping, the reward system could involve receiving increased fashion choices for the avatar. The absurd scenarios presented (such as in *Shopmania* and *Shopping Mall*), wherein shopping and malls are always necessary, suggest that consumptive practices are not only "what women want" but also necessary and normalized in a basic human way. They help create a productive element to consumptive behavior while simultaneously reinforcing playful possibilities.

Without question, shopping-themed games imply and reinforce issues of conspicuous consumption, turning the act itself into gaming. This link between shopping, fashion, and gaming is naturalized, with suggestions that these activities had gaming elements all along. For example, *Glamour* magazine's blog post write-up of *Covet Fashion* suggests that many readers already consider shopping to be gamelike.[24] This naturalization between shopping and games helps to justify these games as a presence on the market. In most cases—other than *Covet Fashion*—the shopping behavior is only a simulation, a cartooned-up version of consumptive behaviors that we may or may not replicate in the real world. Even if playing *Covet* doesn't lead to purchases outside the game, the player continues to circulate normative feminine behaviors within the designed identity of the constructed audience. But how might simulated fashion and shopping games lead to real-world consumption? The answer can be found in one industry term: free-to-play.

THE FREE-TO-PLAY MODEL

Of course, many games cost money—for a long time the model of paid gaming was either an upfront purchase from a retailer, or a subscription-based model (as with massively multiplayer online games like *World of Warcraft*).[25] An alternative model—free-to-play (F2P, sometimes referred to as "freemium")—helps unpack the complicated relationship between play and consumption in gaming. The term "freemium"[26] was coined by the venture capitalist Fred Wilson in 2006.[27] F2P games (usually based off either social media or mobile devices) are initially free for download, but for premium play users must engage in micropurchasing. Micropurchases in these games might range from buying increased in-game energy (i.e., being able to play for longer periods of time), in-game money that can be used to purchase things in the game world that would otherwise not be attainable from regular play, or other intangible benefits, depending on the game. For example, in the most recent mobile versions of *Diner Dash* (now owned by Glu, the company that also publishes *Kim Kardashian: Hollywood*), the player would have a difficult time achieving a reasonable score by play alone. The game recommends that players increase their play power by adding things like faster sneakers to help Flo move more efficiently between tables. Those sneakers then cost a specific amount of in-game money, which translates to real-world money.

To give a sense of scope of how influential the F2P model is in the video game market, 76 percent of all iPhone purchases in 2013 came from in-game acquisitions in the United States, and in the Asian market those numbers were even higher.[28] This number becomes slightly more startling when combined with recent reports that less than 1 percent of mobile gamers are responsible for those in-app game purchases.[29] That means that a very small number of people are spending a very large amount of money on games that are, theoretically, free. These high-spending players are often referred to as "whales,"[30] a term appropriated from the gambling industry.

Consequently, the F2P model has often been called into question. An episode of the television show *South Park* (titled "Freemium Isn't Free") highlights the complexities of the F2P market when young Stan spends both a great deal of money and time to beat a never-ending game. Game developers and critics have questioned the "morals" of this model, and some have even suggested that F2P games are potentially hurting the overall game market and, in particular, independent game developers.[31] Mia Consalvo and Christopher A. Paul document how developers and game journalists refer to the model as "evil." In response to claims that the F2P model is not a "real" game, Consalvo and Paul argue that "to spend money on this system at all is to legitimize it, and to call into question all sense of what makes a game real—its developer, its mechanics and its revenue model."[32] In other words, because players chose to spend money on the game, their purchasing power makes the F2P model a valid gaming style, regardless of any criticism.

How might we connect consumptive practices in games with F2P mechanics? Certainly not all F2P games are marketed to women, and not all of those games have elements of fashion and shopping embedded in them. In fact, recent numbers suggest that whales are more likely to be men. However, as I have explored several times throughout this book, actual demographics are irrelevant—part of game design is about perceived demographics, wherein games are structured with a sense that women will play and might possibly spend money. After all, when a *Kotaku* article declares in its headline "Who Are the 'Whales' Driving Free-to-Play Gaming? You'd Be Surprised,"[33] it is clear that there is a perception that women should be driving the consumptive practices that are allegedly "ruining" the video game industry. F2P games happened at the same cultural moment in which the video game industry began to attempt expanding its audience (as illustrated by the Wii advertisements in the previous chapter and many of the games described throughout this book). If perception matters more than actual demographics, then there will always be an assumption that women are central to consumptive practices. Furthermore, there is an additional expectation that those women gamers are only equipped to game as a mode of excess and through consumption. The woman is not a primary gamer; she is the person with a white minivan full of games, prepared to disperse them to her family. Within this perception, gaming is only another form of currency.

Yet many women *do* play F2P games and indeed pay for them. While we can argue about whether *Candy Crush Saga* or other puzzle games with consumptive mechanics might be gender-neutral at their core, it is difficult to look at shopping and fashion games with a sense that they had been built as though intended for both men and women. It is worth considering ways that the process of shopping in a game world and the process of simulated and productive consumption in that game helps to prompt the player toward real-world consumptive practices. This might happen in very direct ways—the transitional shopping mechanics of *Covet Fashion* suggest that players purchase in-game clothing in the real world—or in subtler ways wherein shopping is so fluid in the game world that the player is more in tune with fashion and shopping because of the use of in-game currency. Shopping becomes a normalized practice in F2P games, and the preestablished stereotypes about women, shopping, and consumption help to suggest that women will always already be consumers. If they want to play, women must pay.

THE KARDASHIAN FACTOR AND OTHER CELEBRITY GAMES

The video game *Kim Kardashian: Hollywood* was released into the wild on June 25, 2014. The game was almost immediately both addictively popular[34] and widely criticized.[35] The game itself was only marginally novel—many of the mechanics and play styles were derived from the semipopular game *Campus Life* and Glu's own game *Stardom: The A-List*—but the combination of a clean interface, a celebrity spin, and a dizzying amount of alternative forms of currency and rewards made the game an instant hit. Following *KK:H*'s initial rise to fame, several clone games replicated the game-play style and mechanics, such as *Celebrity Girl* and *Love and Hip Hop*. Additionally, the actress Lindsay Lohan released an appallingly bad game called *Lindsay Lohan's The Price of Fame*.[36] While Lohan's game did not feature the same game-play style as the other celebrity games, it shared such conceits as a basic game-play element where players needed to spend money in order to get fans. Pop star Demi Lovato recently partnered with Pocket Gems (the creator of *Campus Life*) for the interactive narrative game *Episode: Choose Your Story* with a specific series of Lovato episodes, beginning with "Demi Lovato: Path to Fame." Recently Glu Mobile released the game *Katy Perry: Pop* as well as games branded for Britney Spears, Kendall and Kylie Jenner, and Jason Statham,[37] with a Nicki Minaj game on the horizon.[38]

The proof of *KK:H*'s success was apparent almost immediately in its financial reports. Mere weeks after its release the game had a projected income of $200 million for its first year, driving up Glu's market share by 42 percent.[39] As with most games, there is little official demographic data on who actually plays, though the presumed influx audience—in terms of how it is written about—is almost necessarily women and girls.[40] One author for the feminist pop culture website *Jezebel* reported spending almost $500 in a single week of play.[41] All of this is to say, the game is popular, it is different enough from the rest of the market, and it has made a lot of money. And the target audience for *KK:H* is a perceived audience of women and girls.

In what follows, I discuss several aspects of *KK:H*, theorizing how the style, branding, mechanics, and currency all help to imply very specific modes of consumption that design a kind of expected woman gamer. Because the game itself is far too complex to deal with in terms of all of the minutiae of consumptive practice, I will focus on three core elements of game play: the monetary systems, the use of fashion, and the promise of celebrity status as a consumptive model. In chapter 5 I will return to *KK:H* in order to discuss the construction of normative bodies in gaming.

For a "casual" game, *KK:H* is deeply complex and requires an unbelievable amount of player time.[42] Given that, the link between *KK:H* and the casual market is tenuous; it can only really be considered a "casual" because it is played on mobile platforms and because of its presumed women audience. The player begins at the bottom: she lives in a low-rent Los Angeles apartment and works in a local clothing shop. When celebrity Kim Kardashian comes into her shop, she is given opportunities to join up with Kardashian and is given modeling gigs, acting opportunities, and other forms of celebrity appearances. Other non-player characters become the "competition" and create "drama," which acts as one of the key elements holding the player back in her path from the "E-list" to the "A-list" (Figure 23). This list status is the primary factor driving the player's progress (although in addition to list status the player is also marked by a "level" that determines what clothing she is permitted to purchase and how many energy points she is able to get).

The primary method of moving from the E-list to the A-list is through accepting gigs. At a gig, a player must select a series of progress bars to complete tasks. For example, when at a celebrity party, the player might

Figure 23. The main screenshot from the popular and lucrative game *Kim Kardashian: Hollywood*, developed by Blammo Games and published by Glu Mobile in 2014. The game, known for its connection to the celebrity, drove up Glu's market share by 42 percent.

use her energy points to "Do a Shot," "Make New Friends," or drink "The Good Stuff"—these tasks each take varying amounts of energy points. In some ways, the repetitive nature of these social tasks, unique to this kind of casual game, suggests that the presumed woman player is necessarily social and taking on relational tasks (the kind of emotional/affective labor discussed in chapter 3 of this book). Because energy points are limited resources, only reappearing over time (a player gets back an energy point in five-minute increments), it often takes several hours of revisiting the game to complete one gig or event successfully. If a player gets a five-star rating at an event, the "press" will tweet about it, moving the player's ranking up slowly, toward D-list, C-list, B-list, and finally A-list, where the player attempts to move into the number-one slot of celebrity-hood.

There are two different monetary system representations within the game world. The first is a representation of dollars. Different items can be "bought" on the dollar system, such as clothing, furniture, homes, and travel. But there is also an alternative system: the K-Coin. The K-Coin is relinquished to players much more sparingly than dollars are (a player might earn a few hundred dollars per gig or event but would be lucky to earn even a single K-Coin). Players are able to use K-Coins to purchase nicer items and buy the affections of (or to "charm") non-player characters that are higher on the celebrity A–E-lists than the player is. Additionally, K-Coins can be used to purchase more energy. The pivotal nature of the K-Coins, then, makes them the most valuable currency in the game world. This value makes them marketable, and *KK:H* sells additional K-Coins to players to allow them to play the game more effectively. This, of course, is how most players get sucked into spending real money in *KK:H*—to play quickly, and in the most satisfying way, the player needs to spend her own money.[43] Like many F2P games, *KK:H* ties in real money with play money, using exhausting exchange rates that never quite benefit the player or maps to a stable economic system.[44]

The two competing monetary systems have a certain rhetorical power attached to them. On the one hand, the player needs money to function in the everyday world of the game, but money itself is easy to come by. What is more difficult is the intangible monetizing of celebrity power, what is represented by the K-Coin. The K-Coin is treated as practically genetic. Those who are part of the Kardashian clan already have this monetary system built into their lives—but even after the player has gotten to the much-coveted A-list in the game, she must still struggle for the intangible consumptive power that is linked to celebrity-hood. One can pay the game (and, indirectly, the real Kim Kardashian) for more of her specialized money, but then that player is giving Kardashian real-world money—an unsettling thought when you consider the woman's vast wealth. In *KK:H* the house always wins: either the player cannot achieve the pure celebrity power that is wielded by the Kardashian family, or she has to pay them in order to do so.

Fashion play, and the consumptive implications of that, has a complex set of meanings within *KK:H*. The player is constantly asked to go to fashion shoots, but—at least on the surface—the clothing one wears to a fashion shoot is inconsequential. A player can dress her avatar in anything from jeans to formal gowns at these events, and the visual rhetoric suggests that clothing choices do not make a difference; the player is not given additional points for her fashion selections. This, in some ways, makes it distinct from games like *Covet Fashion*, where the player's choices are rated in terms of how well an outfit selection meets the criteria of the occasion in the form of "challenges." Yet the purchase of clothing itself has value and meaning within the game space. Articles of clothing for purchase have either stars or hearts next to them—stars give the player the ability to get a "bonus" for gigs or events, while hearts give players a bonus when going on dates. In order to get a five-star rating either on an event/gig or on a date, it is recommended that the player purchase clothing (or other things such as furniture). These bonuses help the player use less of her personal time in a direct time-equals-money system. In other words, by purchasing the right clothing you can do more things and get ahead in the game faster. Yet a player can "purchase" a formal gown in order to do better at a gig/event or on a date yet not wear that gown for the occasion and still gets those points. In other words, what is valued is not the fashion itself, necessarily, but the act of purchasing. By purchasing more things, the player is better positioned to excel in the game world.

Fashion, then, and the consumptive practices around it, is both essential and irrelevant within the Kardashian world. It does not matter what the player *wears*, but it does matter what the player *buys*. Consumptive practices make items disposable and irrelevant. At the same time, such practices highlight the agency of the player—she can wear what makes *her* feel like a celebrity, not what she is told is celebrity clothing.[45] This is further reinforced when the player's managers declare that she has been placed on the "best dressed" lists—this is an automatic rejoinder, and even more meaningless because all of the player's fashion choices were preselected as Kardashian-appropriate. Because many of the more desirable articles of clothing are attached only to K-Coins (as opposed to dollars) that means that in order to get the best bonuses and in order to dress a celebrity in ways the player deems attractive and suitable, the player must trade real money for K-Coins. Additionally, several items of in-game clothing are part of the Kardashian Kollection—an actual line of clothing produced by the Kardashian family. Other family products are semi-pitched through the game. For example, in the real world, Khloé Kardashian has a cologne line called Unbreakable; in the game the player is asked to pitch for her cologne line Unstoppable. The similarity of branding helps to create recognition for purchase decisions that may occur in the real world.

Wealth is everything in the *KK:H*. Occasionally, plot points center on the purchase of particularly expensive clothing. If the player wants to get married, she must purchase wedding clothing for her avatar, running an average of $1,000 (of game money) or 120 K-Coins.[46] At certain events or on dates, the player must lay out game dollars to purchase drinks or food. The player is urged to look under things for dollars, and screens have several spots where if you click you can find dollars, experience points, or energy points by looking in bushes, under drinks, under birds, or in other non-obtrusive places. This constant process of scavenging about for money seems to replicate *poverty* more than it replicates *wealth*. Unless she spends her own money, the player is deeply poor—poor enough that she must take time out from dates or events to look around and see if she can find cash lying about. Even as an A-lister, there is no satisfying sense of wealth in the Kardashian world, and this, in part, is due to the constant need to update fashion to excel at events and move the game forward.

All of these elements seem to support the promise of celebrity status, what Brooke Erin Duffy might refer to as "aspirational labor,"[47] wherein a person does a kind of creative labor with the intention of gaining social and economic capital. The player is able to "play through" the pitfalls of celebrity by a series of events and decisions. "Dramas" are created for the player to bypass, when other would-be fictional celebrities threaten the player's credibility and the player is asked to make decisions in how to react. Wrong decisions can result in a plummet of fandom; fans can literally disappear overnight depending on how the player handles interpersonal situations with non-player characters. While most of the paths seem straightforward if the goal is reaching celebrity status, consumption is always at the core. In this, the game creates a constant wave of desire to consume, and garner fans, yet not cause too much "drama." This results in a kind of policing effect: the player should *want* but stay within the boundaries of a certain kind of behavior in order to succeed in the game world. At her core, though, the player is never able to fully achieve a real kind of celebrity status because, of course, this is just a game. The K-Coin serves as a perennial reminder to the player that authentic celebrity is unattainable and illusive. Even achieving the top spot in *KK:H* is fleeting—the player must continue to work to maintain that spot over an infinite period of play.[48] Once you stop playing, the celebrity status earned through money—both real and fictional—can dissolve into nothing.

CONSUMPTION AND FOOD GAMES

As I begin to resolve this chapter, I want to suggest a different kind of consumption from what I have previously discussed. While most of the consumptive behavior considered throughout this chapter was about shopping or purchasing material goods (in both virtual and non-virtual contexts), the final portion of this chapter is about the consumption of food. This move is a bit strategic—in order to move on to the next chapter, "Playing with Bodies," it seems valuable to consider the virtual processes of culinary consumptive practices in video games. Given the domestic implications of cooking, it should be unsurprising that several video games catering to women audiences feature cooking as a primary mechanic or discuss the consumption of food in a variety of ways. Even in *KK:H*, the player is able to pay money to consume food on dates or at events in the game, allowing the player to accumulate the achievement of being considered a "foodie" at several different levels. However, as with most virtual games, there is no satisfying consumption with the virtual food—we never see the food, and we are never given the opportunity to taste it, virtually or otherwise. Food consumption, in video games, is entirely without the pleasures of tasting, chewing, and digesting.

While this might seem obvious—after all, how would one actually *taste* virtual food—the very fact that food games are created and commonly designed for an intended female audience is notable. While some of these games fall under the time management umbrella (*Cooking Dash, Cake Mania*, etc.), others have taken on different or more instructional functions. During the height of popularity of the Nintendo DS, a series of instructional cooking games/apps appeared on the platform, including *Personal Trainer: Cooking, Iron Chef America: Supreme Cuisine, What's Cooking: Jamie Oliver*, and *America's Test Kitchen: Let's Get Cooking*. With the exception of the *Iron Chef* game, these DS apps are more instructional than game. These "games" simply teach players how to cook using a mobile game device and would not even qualify as games had they not been made for the DS. With the overwhelming popularity of other mobile formats in recent years (both phones and tablets), this subgenre has been subsumed and no longer qualifies as "gaming"—though the fact that they were originally created as a means to get women "playing" the Nintendo DS has interesting implications. These applications, in theory at least, generate *real* food; they are instructional suggestions to the player that he or she should cook the food as it is presented.

But more fascinating than either the time management or instructional cooking applications are games that simulate the cooking process without teaching the act of cooking or involving the complex, high-stakes environment of the time management game. In this, I am referring to *Cooking Mama* and the clone successors that are now equally popular. Other games in this strange genre include *Lunch Food Maker, Cooking Academy*, and *Milkshake Maker*, among many other iPhone and Android clones. As discussed in chapter 3, *Cooking Mama* involves player instruction by Mama, a small, cherubic, asexual character who tells the player how to chop, stir, broil, and mix a rapid series of in-game recipes. When the player cooks them correctly, she "becomes" Mama—when successful, Mama's rejoinder is "Perfect! Just as good as Mama!" But when the player fails it results in an angry Mama scolding—"Don't worry! Mama will fix it"—with her usually sparkling eyes turning into a threatening blaze. In chapter 3 I discussed how these rejoinders place the player in a position where she must reproduce and perform affective labor (and, in turn, motherhood), regardless of the player's gender, age, or status as parent. Similarly notable is the question of *lack* in this game and its clones—the process of cooking without consuming and reproducing food items that can never be enjoyed. Susan Bordo might refer to this in terms of the "cultural containment of the female appetite," which she describes as situations where "women are feeding and nourishing *others*, not themselves."[49] Similarly, Kathleen Parkin writes about how advertisers use this assumed feminine desire to nourish others as a mode to endear themselves to members of the household: "Food advertisers also exploited the connection between food preparation and love toward women, enlisting mild allusions, floating hearts, and pecks on the cheek to demonstrate how her food selection accorded her affection. The message was clear: when she chose such a high quality, tasty product she was entitled to receive love and credit for her pains."[50] In terms of food, women are not *consumers* so much as *enablers* of consumption. *Cooking Mama* and similar games help to reinforce these practices of self-denial.

Women, it seems, are strangely situated in light of consumptive practices. While shopping is treated as an enabling mode of consumptive practice, something allowable, the consumption of food is rarely wholly acceptable. Women can binge-shop but not binge-eat. However, at the same time, the process of binge-play is also questionable—after all, the anecdote that began this chapter suggested that while it is acceptable for a woman to binge-shop for games that are meant for others, it did not imply that binge-play was equally acceptable. I would argue that, in part, the debates over the F2P format is less about the ethics of the actual genre or any effects on gaming, but rather about the perception that those F2P games are consuming women (regardless of the realities of whale demographics). Women get to be consumers, so long as they don't get consumed. In this way, video games get to control women's consumptive practices.

And yet, for most of this chapter I have ignored an elephant: social class. The intersectionalism suggesting that I address social class looms around these conversations about consumption, purchasing, and video games. After all, the notion of "shop 'til you drop" is only available to those who have the means—both financial and temporal—to consume with little regard to the necessitation of wealth in the process of consumerism. This, of course, applies to all gaming: without time and without money, the binding practices of product consumption are meaningless; the identities that are designed into all games necessitate that social class is both invisible and implied. In this way, the designed identity of the woman player is necessarily middle class and already presumed to be a participant in consumptive behaviors.

When bodies at play are assumed to be feminine, they are already positioned as consumptive, yet also entrenched in a kind of denial. The consumptive practices within video games can take on several forms (material consumption, content consumption, mechanical consumption, in-game purchasing, extra-game purchasing, fashion-based consumption, and culinary consumption), which may be combined in complex ways to reinforce real-world consumer practices. Feminized gaming bodies are pushed to consume—via traditional modes of feminine consumptive practices—but then denied the satisfying consumption allowed to masculine gamers. Bodies are at the root of the problem: bodies that are allowed to create digital food they cannot taste, bodies that purchase games they cannot play, bodies that can buy clothing they cannot wear. These bodies become a host of unrequited desire and, simultaneously, locked into a gendered designed identity; the bodies are necessarily white, middle class, heterosexual, abled, and cis-gendered. In the next chapter, I focus on the paradoxical nature of bodily identity in video games designed for Player Two.

5 Playing with Bodies

"LIKE *TEMPLE RUN* FOR THE VAGINA"

In the summer of 2014, a Kickstarter campaign was launched for a new kind of video game device. The Skea game controller promised to make Kegels fun for women. Kegels, which are exercises often recommended after giving birth in order to deal with issues of incontinence, are meant to strengthen a woman's pelvic floor. Upon the announcement of the Skea campaign, many declared that it was "like *Temple Run* for the vagina" (referring to the popular endless running game).[1] The campaign for the Skea was kicked off with a video featuring its inventor, a man named Tom Chen (referred to as a physicist and game designer). Chen rhetorically asks his viewers, "Which muscle do women need to exercise most? Buttocks? Abs? Not really. It's actually the pelvic floor muscles. Either you want to be more sexy or more healthy." He continues by demonstrating incontinence and other potential health risks by depositing fruit through a net in front of a poster showing the lower half of a lingerie-clad woman's body—a fairly offensive representation of women's anatomy (Figure 24). The Skea ultimately promised to turn "boring" Kegel exercises into a fun game they referred to as *Alice Incontinence* in the initial Kickstarter advertisement. The campaign was successfully funded, bringing in $52,021 for its initial launch.

Of course, game controllers have had gendered and bodily connotations before. Old Sega advertisements, for example, made a point of highlighting the phallic nature of the joystick with the lines "The more you play with it, the harder it gets" and "Something to do with your hands that won't make you go blind."[2] These parallels between the body and digital gaming reinforce the preexisting narrative of Player One: the joystick game

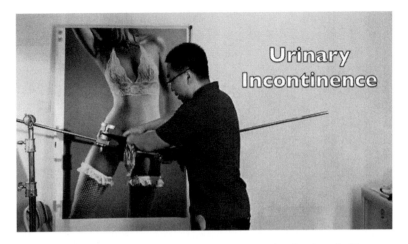

Figure 24. A still image from the Kickstarter campaign video for Skea, launched in the summer of 2014. The Skea promised to be a "*Temple Run* for the vagina"—a way to gamify Kegel exercises. The image shows Skea's creator pushing items down a net, placed over the vaginal area of a lingerie-clad model on a poster. This process was meant to illustrate the idea that the vagina loses elasticity.

controller was permitted to take on phallic connotations because it reinforced the perception of the Sega player, who was presumed to be male.

But the Skea was different—it was designed specifically *for* women's anatomy. As a game controller, the Skea complicates questions of diversity and representation of video game players. On the one hand, a sex-specific game controller holds the potential to invite in new players, but on the other, its very premise hinges on cis-centric assumptions that those who identify as women necessarily have vaginas, and that those very vaginas probably need some kind of fixing (hence the call for exercise). Within weeks another "smart" Kegel device, called the kGoal, offered a similar technology but without a gaming interface, and was also successfully funded on Kickstarter. The kGoal, though, did not promise to gamify the practice of Kegel exercise. Skea, then, stands out as the first attempt at using women's sexual organs in gaming. This move essentializes and prioritizes women's bodies in uncomfortable ways. While we often talk about the relationship between the player and the controller, we generally discuss the controller as a technological apparatus; rarely do we talk about the means of holding that apparatus (presumably, generally speaking, with hands) when we consider those bodily interactions. When the mode of gripping turns from hands to something else—in this case, the vagina—we are left with questions of how the body relates to gaming and game controllers in a physically embodied way.

The Skea, in many ways, was a failure. After being funded, the company that produced the Skea ended up having trouble making a smartphone app that worked efficiently. To this point, *Alice Incontinence*, with its lovely *Alice in Wonderland*-style graphics from the original Kickstarter advertisement, was downgraded to a simple game where long, phallic-shaped tubes fell down on a screen while the player was instructed to "squeeze." This was no *Temple Run*, and the final version of the Skea involved more frustration than actual play.

And so, as a historical artifact and from a biomedical perspective, the Skea builds on a history of masculine authority misrepresenting, commodifying, and essentializing elements of women's health and bodies. Nancy Tuana demonstrates that women's health needs to be reclaimed from the patriarchy of biomedical knowledge making.[3] Similarly, Lynda Birke suggests that much of biomedical literature is written from a masculinist perspective that essentially ignores the lived realities of women's bodies.[4] Emily Martin demonstrates that reproductive mythologies are often written to reinforce cultural narratives of biological determinism.[5] In this way, the Skea fits in—the Kickstarter video wherein Chen describes Kegel exercises as "boring" and flippantly talks about his wife's incontinence following childbirth seems to almost "mansplain" women's bodies to women. For example, Skea inventor Chen remarks in the video of his wife, "When she found herself unable to control her piss . . . she was really pissed off." While medically there are sound reasons for women to do Kegel exercises, there is a discomfort in a man throwing phallically shaped fruit down a basketball net and remarking on the looseness of a woman's vagina following childbirth.

The Skea, in the end, functions as a basic reminder that video games need bodies. Bodies at play are necessary to clutch game controllers, to sit patiently or move aggressively. Bodies at play are both tense and loose—they might hold themselves quietly while completing a difficult task in a *Call of Duty* game, or might wave around freely with a Wii Remote or playing *Dance Dance Revolution*. Without hands or flexible bodies (or, in the case of the Skea, vaginas), we have no method of clutching the controller. Without sight and other senses, we have more complicated interactions with screens. From this bodily perspective, gaming is generally built from ableist presumptions. However, at the same time, the Skea serves as another reminder: gaming bodies are complicated, they are messy, and controlling a gaming body does not always work as intended.

In this chapter, I explore the mess of gaming bodies, paying specific attention to how video games designed for Player Two attempt to manage those bodies, and how those bodies are also integral to larger changes to the video game industry. In her work on eSports, in response to claims that video games are not "real" sports, T. L. Taylor argues that through a variety of constraints, computer games are "deeply interwoven with material, embodied practices."[6] The virtual becomes so over-present in game spaces that sometimes we forget about the importance of bodies in gaming. Of course, as noted above, video games manage all bodies—without the body as an interface, gaming would be practically impossible. Games need bodies, and games control those bodies. At the same time, the concrete masculine history embedded in the video game industry started from a working assumption that most of those gaming bodies were necessarily *male*. This, then, pushes us to the next obvious question: what happens when those bodies are not male? How does gaming manage female bodies differently, and to what extent is this bodily management successful? Further, are there ways we can use our bodies to manage and take control of gaming spaces? I discuss these core questions by dividing the chapter into two main categories of bodily control: the real and the virtual. By "the real" I am referring to the actual physical bodies of female players, particularly as they apply to physical interfaces, such as the Wii and the Kinect. In "the virtual" I am referring to the avatar, how the formation of in-game bodies manages real-world bodies. These categories, as I will discuss, inform on one another in ways that both reinforce the past modes of Player One yet suggest the emergence of Player Two.

DOCILE BODIES AT PLAY

Gaming may need bodies, but not all bodies function equally as gaming bodies. This is not to suggest that, at their core, there should be a positivist notion of "good" or "bad" bodies, but rather, that gaming prioritizes specific procedures, postures, positions, and forms of cooperation, which suggests that some kinds of bodies are preferable. And yet gaming *produces* the bodies it needs. The positions we hold while playing video games are neither natural nor neutral—in order to game well, players must conform their bodies and reform them into what Michel

Foucault might refer to as "docile bodies."[7] By interrogating how gaming bodies become docile bodies, and the implications of this theorization, it becomes easier to elaborate on how bodies are prioritized as acceptable/unacceptable at play.

Foucault's body of work focused on the post-structural implications of large, institutional structures such as medical, disciplinary, and educational institutions. Foucault suggests that within these institutional structures, technologies often take on disciplinary functions, helping to advocate for dominant ideologies within their form and function. Most relevant to what I discuss in this chapter, in *Discipline and Punish* Foucault forms his argument around the idea that progression of technologies of punishment shifted from the discipline of the body to the discipline of the soul. In other words, as society became more "advanced" there was less effort to physically punish individuals with the threat of torture and physical pain, and an increased move toward the punishment that would affect mind and soul, and force individuals to self-punish and self-monitor. Within this shift, he argues, Western culture itself has become increasingly prison-like, with constant institutional surveillance as a means of creating a "carceral texture." This texture helps to make bodies more easily observable but also functions to force citizens to internalize the surveillance that has become integrated into everyday technologies. He explains, "The carceral texture of society assures both the real capture of the body and its perpetual observation. It is, by its very nature, the apparatus of punishment that conforms most completely to the new economy of power and the instrument for the formation of knowledge that this very economy needs."[8] In this way, we can see how institutional structures use actors (both human and nonhuman) to create a sense of order that reinforces dominant ideologies and creates self-discipline. So, for example, the ubiquity of cameras in digitized societies has created a kind of self-discipline—many people automatically assume that they are being watched and monitored, and behave accordingly.

And so it is worth considering how these carceral-influenced technologies use disciplinary processes to mold ideologically coerced bodies, naturalizing specific behaviors—what Foucault refers to as "subjected and practiced bodies," disempowered but increased in their levels of "aptitude."[9] Docile bodies, according to Foucault, are formed within institutional structures as a means of turning individuals into ideologically driven subjects. Within his examples, he uses the institutions of schools and militaries, and how each creates the disciplined subject, although his theoretical work can be similarly applied to other institutions. By limiting the time, space, and movement, Foucault argues, the subject becomes more easily disciplined and manipulated.

This limitation of time, space, and movement is practiced and ideologically driven, according to Foucault. He describes a breakdown of body parts in relation to how their manipulation and precision creates monotony. Said monotony ultimately suggests that the corresponding body can most easily comply with the ideology behind those movements:

> Discipline defines each of the relations that the body must have with the object it manipulates . . . it consists of a breakdown of the total gesture into two parallel series: that of the parts of the body to be used (right hand, left hand, different fingers on the hand, knee, eye, elbow, etc.) and that of the parts of the object manipulated (barrel, notch, hammer, screw, etc.); then the two sets of parts are correlated together according to a number of simple gestures (rest, bend); lastly, it fixes the canonical succession in which each of these correlations occupies a particular place.[10]

These precise movements correspond with an "enclosure," which is a space "heterogeneous to all others and closed upon itself," and in this way becomes a "protected place of disciplinary monotony."[11] In a similar capacity, time becomes structured, limited, and part of a disciplinary process, wherein time functions within a mode of "ever-growing use" and "exhaustion" and becomes the mode of how bodies get situated within the disciplinary process. Institutions and their relational technologies help to form our ideologies by creating docile bodies that have been prepared and primed through all these modes of physical monotony. Just as with the carceral texture of society, bodies become their own prison systems.

Elsewhere, I have applied this particular notion of video game technologies as having disciplinary potential. Using the game *Grand Theft Auto III* as an example, I argued that the precise movements, repetitive motions, and constricted spaces in video games are ripe for Foucauldian analysis.[12] Games, like other technologies, may be constructed as tools (of work or play), but they are also mechanisms for helping to create docile bodies in gaming spaces. With *Grand Theft Auto III*—as I argued in 2005—the disciplinary nature of the game teaches the subject that "crime doesn't pay" by placing them in a relatively unwinnable mode of criminality. Similarly, other games can use disciplinary processes to manage play styles and larger belief systems. In this way, video game mechanics and narratives become essential to understanding the larger perception of players.

In considering the designed identity of Player Two, this notion still holds up. Gaming trains us as subjects, regardless of platform or game, and regardless of the specific intentions of game designers. For example, while someone playing a game on a console system might technically be able to play while standing on his or her head, turned away from the screen, most people are not going to play *well* with their body in that position. The console gaming system suggests certain specific styles of play: face front, sitting relatively close to the screen, generally positioned beneath the screen. The traditional dual-shock style of controllers for consoles require a specific position that trains bodies (and hands) over time, through repetitive motions and precise movements. This precision ultimately has created a reasonably high bar for gaming wherein novice gamers often are unable to properly play on console systems. The intuitive movements necessitated by the Nintendo Wii Remote (and later the Microsoft Kinect) was, in many ways, created in response to this traditional style of console gaming. But even the Wii demands certain kinds of bodies situated properly in certain kinds of spaces. Those playing games on computers are even more bound by bodily situatedness: a player of a computer game (generally speaking) must sit bound to a keyboard and other peripherals, usually in an office chair, straight-backed and attentive. Laptops create more freedom of space, but gaming on laptops is more difficult, in terms of typically smaller screens and less memory capacity.

As we move increasingly toward mobile devices in gaming, there is an inference of improved bodily freedom—after all, now we can play anywhere, anytime that we want without the typical constrictions of time and space implied by console systems and computers. Yet, I would argue that mobile devices such as smartphones, tablets, and the Nintendo DS do not so much remove the bodily boundaries as internalize them. While, perhaps, we can play on our smartphones in any location (a subway, a restaurant, in the comfort of our homes, or any number of places we encounter during our daily routines), we still must position our bodies in specific and rigid ways in order to play. Our bodies become locked into screens—smaller, compact, and unmoving beyond the basic twitching of thumbs and fingers. Rather than expanding space, the mobile device has made our space even smaller. When I play *Kim Kardashian: Hollywood*, my body is fixed in very specific ways to respond best to the small screen and maximize my playtime. While not identical to the "material" and "embodied practices" T. L. Taylor references with eSports, mobile gaming manages the body in similar ways. Taylor explains, "Though it is easy to fall into speaking of computer game spaces as simply virtual and of leaving the body behind, in reality we are continually working through, and with, materiality when we engage in digital play."[13]

To this point, Foucault's discussion of temporal/bodily monotony in his construction of docile bodies in *Discipline and Punish* suggests a return to the discussions of time management games in chapter 2. Designed identity plays with time. This use of time management games creates an exhaustive sense of how one should use gaming to manage time in a disciplinary sense, yet it also creates a kind of elasticity to time. Bodies and the temporal structure become necessarily intertwined here—we cannot disconnect the management of how one controls bodily movements in video game play with how we structure our understanding of appropriate temporal movements both inside and outside the game world. Time management is, of course, inherently part of bodily management: time management tells us what we can do when, how, and where. And if time management products are, as I discussed in chapter 2, more heavily marketed to women audiences, then this, too, feeds into a larger discussion of bodily control within the designed identity of Player Two. Time and bodies, in this way, become interchangeable as subjects of control.

Therefore, bodies can easily be seen as fluidly connecting with their disciplinary technologies. Once again drawing on Latour, as was done in the introduction, while it might initially seem easy to divide humans from technologies and institutional practices, our interconnections grow increasingly harder to disentangle—particularly in terms of the relationship between organic and machine. As Anne Balsamo points out, the Foucauldian tension between the human and the material that defines the human is tenuous. She explains that "at the point at which the body is reconceptualized not as a fixed part of nature, but as a boundary concept, we witness an ideological tug-of-war between competing systems of meaning, which include and in part define the material struggles of physical bodies."[14] Therefore, while it is tempting to see our technologies controlling us, it is also essential to remember that we are indistinguishable from our technologies. The institutions that created technologies are ideologically driven, and it would follow that those technologies are both part of and form our subjects.

All of this to say, video games create their subjects; they create gaming bodies that presumably play games well. Deviant gaming bodies are those that do not easily comply with the expected modes of how the technology *wants* us to play. We become disciplinary subjects of gaming worlds, and this subjection transforms our bodies over time. In this way, gaming is always a body problem—and when the gaming subject is presumed to be a specific gender, ethnicity, sexuality, or abled in specific ways, the gaming technology assists in transforming that subject as best it possibly can. As we continue to interrogate the "body problem" as it relates to video games, it becomes clear that gaming bodies (a) are ideologically driven, (b) necessitate specific bodily actions, and (c) want specific bodily features in order to be a *preferred* gaming body.

However, gaming involves two levels of body: extra-gaming bodies (real people) and in-game bodies (avatars). In many ways, we can see these things as separate—many studies have illustrated that people often chose or design avatars that do not resemble them, and there are many reasons for this distinction. This chapter will interrogate how the othered body, both on-screen and off-screen, necessitates ideological subjects and docile bodies, particularly in terms of the construction of a woman gamer. Yet the chapter also hints at the possibilities that gendered gaming bodies might be in the position to push back against their own subjection.

THE BODY PROBLEM

We have a body problem. While the centralizing topic in this chapter is the larger theme of bodies in video games, particularly as they pertain to a perceived growing woman audience, it is important to recognize that women's bodies are almost always a problem. The goal of this portion of the chapter is to review important literature that suggests that women's bodies are always in flux and always under a critical lens. The popular media, also, often plays into the production of the appropriateness of women's bodies: from popular magazines to diet programs, women are produced in a way that they are necessarily dissatisfied with their bodies. In this, the designed identity of Player Two helps to reinforce other modes of popular media wherein women's bodies are only rarely varied, yet often othered and sexualized. All this is to say that there is a general cultural assumption that women are perpetually dissatisfied with their bodies—in ways that are rarely assumed for men—and representations of these bodies are often problematic. Yet we *live* in our bodies. Our bodies help to facilitate play and cannot be ignored. In this way, the "body problem" is multifaceted and complicated. Essentializing the body to biological function and sex organs is a problem. But so is ignoring the body, those functions, and those organs. In many ways, this paradox is central to all feminist debate on the "body."

Therefore, while many feminist researchers and pundits discuss the body as though it were a problem, the explanation of how it is a problem varies. Susan Bordo's important work *Unbearable Weight: Feminism, Western Culture, and the Body* critiqued the portrayal of body image in popular media, but used more theoretical complexity to tackle the topic. In particular, Bordo characterizes representation of slender women's bodies in terms of Foucault's "docile bodies" as a mode of disciplinary practice: "The exploration of contemporary slenderness as a metaphor for the correct management of desire must take into account the fact that throughout dominant Western religious and philosophical traditions, the capacity for self-management is decisively coded as male. By contrast, all those bodily spontaneities—hunger, sexuality, the emotions—seen as needful of containment and control have been culturally constructed and coded as female."[15] If the containment and disciplinary practices associated with femininity are producing ideologically formed bodies, then gaming bodies create multiple layers of disciplinary practice. In this, Bordo reminds the reader that Foucault's goal was not implicating groups or individuals as singularly oppressive; instead, he argued that institutional structures create bodies that reinforce those institutions.

At the same time, nonacademic books have addressed the body problem, beginning in the 1980s and flourishing through the 1990s. Specifically, many dissected the lived realities of low self-esteem among girls.[16] Popular books such as *Reviving Ophelia: Saving the Selves of Adolescent Girls* illustrated the plummeting self-esteem of young women and girls.[17] In turn, other feminist authors attributed the self-esteem problem to embodied images of women in media. Famously, Naomi Wolf tore apart the cosmetics industry in *The Beauty Myth: How Images of Beauty Are Used against Women.* Similarly, Jean Kilbourne attacked the advertising industry and the physical representations of women and girls with her documentary series beginning with *Killing Us Softly*[18] and the subsequent book *Can't Buy My Love: How Advertising Changes the Way We Think and Feel.* Kilbourne's argument can be summarized with the relatively fair assertion that "the glossy images of flawlessly beautiful and extremely thin women that surround us would not have the impact they do if we did not live in a culture that encourages us to believe we can and should remake our bodies into perfect commodities. These images play into the American belief of transformation and ever-new possibilities, no longer via hard work but via the purchase of the right products."[19] Popular feminist texts focused on the problem with girls, women, and bodies through an attack on popular culture and the images of over-sexualized, thin, and hyper-feminine bodies that pervaded magazines, films, television programming, and other forms of media.

Yet women's bodies are not only sexualized—their life-giving potential (by way of menstruation, ovulation, and pregnancy) is also part of the body problem. Many theorists have remarked on the body problem for women in terms of its reproductive capacity. This places women in what Kathleen Hall Jamieson refers to as the "double bind" wherein they "can exercise their wombs or their brains, not both."[20] This, in turn, leaves women in an impossible position relative to their bodies: either they are nothing more than a womb, or they are "defective" because they do not engage in childbirth. According to Shari Thurer, the processes that define women as mothers bind feminine bodies so that they cannot exceed such barriers: "For thousands of years, because of her awesome ability to spew forth a child, mother has been feared and revered. She has been the subject of taboos and witch hunts, mandatory pregnancy and confinement in a separate sphere. She has endured appalling insults and perpetual marginalization. She has also been the subject of glorious painting, chivalry, and idealization. Through it all, she has rarely been consulted. She is an object, not a subject."[21] Certainly, women are bound by the reproductive assumptions presumed over their bodies. Yet this theorization of the mother-object (as opposed to mother-subject) suggested by Thurer discounts the docile body potential to which a mother-subject can be bound. Part of the "body problem" is that women are disciplined subjects, regardless of whether that subjection is due to the self-denial that creates Bordo's sexualized docile bodies, or the reproductive binding that presumes women must bear children in order for their bodies to be acknowledged as practical on a societal level.

But, then, the other part of the body problem is the question of who counts as a woman. Transgender rights have become a growing issue, with an increasing number of trans persons adding to the debate within feminist literature and academic discourse. To this point, many feminist scholars have begun to acknowledge that a woman might not necessarily need to be born a woman in order to identify as one. This, admittedly, creates some additional complexity when considering the body problem, which has caused territorial rifts among many feminists. Notably, Janice G.

Raymond has suggested that male-to-female transgender women appropriate women's bodies while still embodying patriarchal dominance.[22] In response, many transgender women and men have used their lived experiences to dispute these claims, demonstrating reasons why feminisms should be inclusive of transgender people, and also showing that sex organs do not necessarily "make" a woman.[23] It is important, then, to not be exclusive in a breakdown of the body problem. While women's bodies may be central to the body problem, those bodies do not necessarily need to be *born* as women.

Given all the above, it becomes apparent that part of the *problem* with the body problem is the essentialization of the body—a discourse that suggests that women are necessarily bound by their bodily constraints. The body problem is always just shy of biological determinism, and therefore privileges some bodies over other bodies. According to Lynda Birke in *Feminism and the Biological Body* this often results in a misplaced critique of biology, wherein feminism(s) often speak of a kind of transcendence of the body. To this point, she argues that women seem to be bound by the prescriptive nature of their bodies (unable to disentangle from reproductive organs) while simultaneously pushing to exceed those very boundaries. The results often become paradoxical, resulting in yet more bodily problems. In response to claims of essentialism, Birke asserts that women's bodies are in flux: it becomes easy to forget that the changing nature of women's bodies, the lack of stability, and the lack of stasis are core to an expected identity of women. She continues that perceptions of the body as fixed and unchanging naturalize masculine bodies: "The unchanging body is a masculine one; that is, the masculine body is assumed to be relatively consistent (itself a dubious assumption), against which female bodies, with their ebbs and flows of bleeding, become problematic."[24] So, according to Birke, there are still ways to focus on the body in feminist discourse without resorting to determinism. By focusing on the body as a changing—rather than stable—entity, we are more prepared to consider the discourse of the body in terms of its feminist possibilities. This perspective neatly allows for an acknowledgment of trans bodies without discounting the question of biology. All bodies are constantly transitional, thus making space to broaden the conversation of whose body counts.

And so, in tying all of this back to gaming, much of the body problem is something that has resonated throughout this book without being specifically diagnosed as a "body problem." For example, in discussing makeover and fashion gaming in the previous chapter on consumption, it is extremely difficult to disentangle this from questions of self-esteem and body image. In discussing food games as consumptive practice, along with the self-denial of not eating, it is challenging to consider these things without acknowledging the cultural obsession with the thin female body. Time and time management games are similarly implicated in the double bind, because (after all) time management is a construct that helps women negotiate their dual roles as womb/brain (characterized by Jamieson). The hysteria implied by time management games is inextricably linked to the body, because surely women's hysteria is already linked to their inescapable womb. And emotions are nothing but a bodily response to the implied pressures of the physical world. It would seem, in many ways, that *bodies* have been dancing their way through all of this book's arguments.

WOMEN AND EMBODIED GAMING

Gaming necessitates bodies. But those bodies are often bound and structured according to desires—not the desires of the player but those of the game. Generally speaking, this seemed to be a consistent theme in video game design for many years: game controllers bind bodies to screens. This relationship between bodies and screens goes well beyond discussions of gaming. As Lev Manovich points out regarding our move toward mobile technologies, particularly in light of virtual reality endeavors, "VR continues the screen's tradition of viewer immobility by fastening the body to a machine, while at the same time it creates an unprecedented new condition by requiring the viewer to move."[25] The same can be said for gaming technologies: in recent years a growing number of video games and platforms have allowed for an increased amount of movement in games, but that movement often continues to trap the player, immobilizing him or her into specific physical positions and a limited amount of space.

Yet the movement toward mobile gaming has also afforded the ability for different *kinds* of bodies to be comfortable with gaming. Beginning with the Sony PlayStation EyeToy, through the Wii and Kinect technologies, certain genres and video game platforms have begun to move away from traditional game controllers—controllers that in many ways required years of training to use to a point of perfection—and toward more intuitive, naturalized game controls. This is not to say that traditional, handheld game controllers have entirely disappeared; however, beginning in the early-to-mid 2000s naturalized game controllers began appearing on the market and offered a point of competition. Such combinations of body screen captures, differently shaped controllers, and other peripherals helped to expand the video game market. While the expansion included broader audiences more generally, it very clearly was meant to bring in families and, in particular, women. For example, Alison Harvey has illustrated ways that the Wii has regulated family play.[26] This was certainly apparent from the advertisements highlighted at the beginning of chapter 3, for the "My Wii Story" campaign; Nintendo Wii clearly used the promise of emotional engagement to try and bring in more women.

The first home gaming peripheral to use these more naturalized bodily movements in video games was the Sony PlayStation EyeToy, released in 2003. The EyeToy combined web cam technology with gesture recognition, allowing players to make motions that were understood and reinterpreted on the screen. This led to a variety of naturalized games integrating sports, exercise, music, and other physical activities into one's living room. In many ways the EyeToy was a domesticized version of an increasing number of arcade games such as *Dance Dance Revolution*, which involved complex dance routines on small mats. A few early exergames were developed for the EyeToy, helping to illustrate that there was a market for a different, more physical type of gaming.

In 2006, only a few years following the development of the EyeToy, an entire gaming platform emerged to cater to nontraditional gaming styles. The body was central to Nintendo's Wii gaming system, which involved the use of sensors and a more intuitive controller that could sense movement and did not rely solely on quick button pushes. As already noted, the Wii unquestionably catered to a more diverse audience, with the specific goal of gender inclusivity. According to Steven E. Jones and George K. Thiruvathukal's platform analysis of the Wii, "Nintendo's niche marketing strategy based on certain assumptions about gender and the domestic space in which games are played led to certain design decisions. Those decisions about platform technology have in turn both constrained and enabled specific features of the creative and expressive works—the games created for the platform. And then the games have had an effect on the larger culture."[27] In other words, the emergence of the Wii was almost entirely due to a desire to attract more female gamers, and the games and technology were specifically designed with this in mind.

Wii sales were some of the highest on record for console systems. Subsequently, the creation of the Wii helped to generate the space for Xbox's Kinect—a similarly intuitive system that responds to bodily movements.

The idea of active players was central to the pitch of both the Wii and the Kinect, although the Wii was particularly invested in the notion of using the gaming system to promote family togetherness. The player representations with the Wii were key to the construction of bodies both inside and outside the game world. Each player in the Wii system was represented as a "Mii"—a virtual reconstruction of a player in a cartoonish body. These mini-bodies inhabited many games, mimicking the physical movements performed by the extra-game bodies of the players. The naturalization of those movements has helped to address many of the existing problems in the video game industry regarding the complexity of previous console game controllers. In effect, the Wii was an effective means of appealing to novice players, including women. But just as the Wii was a means of expanding audiences, the Mii limited that very audience: it promised to represent the player yet minimized body types down to the *expected* body of the gamer, albeit in cartoonish ways. Therefore the Wii is simultaneously freeing and limiting. Kinect character creation has similar limitations, although with a far less "cute" output.

The cooperation between the Mii and the player was most clearly seen in the *Wii Fit* games, wherein the player's cute little Mii character performed the exercises done by the player. Jones and Thiruvathukal explain: "That image—the rotating wireframe Mii body being scanned by the system—is a visual metaphor for what's essential about *Wii Fit Plus* and its Balance Board controller as well as what's ultimately essential about the Wii, at least from the point of view of the designers and software developers at Nintendo. It's a figure for the idea at the heart of the Wii as a platform—the idea of focusing attention on the player's active body out in physical space, rather than on the virtual presence of an avatar in an imaginary game space."[28] The Mii frames the body both within the game space and in the real world, creating a hybrid of the two spaces. The game world of Wii Fit portends a certain level of dissatisfaction with the body—immediately upon running the game for the first time, a determination is made about the player/Mii body, and the "age" at which that player performs. Of course, players of all kinds of body types might play *Wii Fit*, but the game gears itself toward framing what a correct body behaves like, parsing that representation back to the Mii. The Wii frames specific bodily behaviors as preferential. While it engages with both gender and age, normalizing both female players and older players, it does not necessarily consider othered bodies: those with disabilities, those who are overweight, and those who have nonbinary bodies are necessarily dictated as not possible within the framework of the software. The edges of the designed identity of Player Two become increasingly visible with the Wii.

Of course, this kind of prioritizing of correct bodies is necessary within exergaming. In order to sell an exergame, a game developer needs to encourage a sense of player unease with his or her own body. All things being equal, both male and female players can be drawn into this dissatisfaction. Yet the body problem, as previously discussed, wherein women and girls are more likely to be critical of their bodies, means that the exergame seems to be vying for a feminine audience that would necessarily be unhappy with their body. It is impossible to ignore that exergames are *built* for specific types of bodies, bodies that occupy disciplinary notions of "healthy" in order to fit into the parameters of the game but are very possibly not in compliance with that vision of "health." Much like the Kickstarter video for the Skea, *Wii Fit* is concerned with the regulation of the properly performing and docile body.

BODIES THAT (DON'T) MATTER: FLATTENING THE DIGITAL BODY

The Wii is an example of how real bodies can interact with game controllers in a way that promises to entice new audiences while also limiting those very audiences. But on-screen bodies are just as relevant as the off-screen bodies. The construction of a digital body helps to send a message about whom a game is intended for and what that player should look and behave like. Digital bodies as gaming bodies give a limitless capacity to expand the body. After all, the abilities of a gaming body are only limited by imaginations and pixels, and such bodies do not necessarily need to conform to bodily cultural expectations. Yet they often do.

Many scholars have studied representations of feminine-gendered bodies in games made for masculine audiences—characters such as Lara Croft are often cited for their unrealistic and hyper-sexualized curves.[29] Often, Croft and similar characters are also portrayed as physically powerful in game worlds, although not necessarily. More recently, there was outrage that *Assassin's Creed: Unity* featured no playable female characters at all. Ubisoft, the game's creator, insisted that this decision was made because it would have "doubled the work" in game creation.[30] Just as in the real world, women's bodies clearly present a problem in digital spaces.

Yet these body problems remark on a different designed identity than the one discussed throughout this book. The body problem of hyper-sexualized characters and missing playable avatars in console gaming resonates with those who play video games that have been designed for intended masculine audiences. Certainly many women play these games, and certainly the representations (and lack of representations) are a problem. But that problem, perhaps, is for a different book.

Instead, this book deals with the designed identity of female players, and the role of bodies in games that are designed with the intention of those players. In short, the avatars designed in the games discussed throughout this book can be characterized in a single word: flat. "Flat" here is not meant to comment on their breast size (in contrast to the over-zealous breast size of many of the playable and non-playable characters in console and hardcore gaming). Certainly, many of these characters are able to enjoy a more reasonable and comfortable chest size than Lara Croft or the catsuited Bayonetta. Flat, instead, refers to the character's lack of visual depth.

In several of the games discussed throughout this book, the characters—both male and female—have a clear flattening effect. Their characterizations are often cartoonish, sweet, childlike, and with no sexuality to speak of. For example:

- Flo of *Diner Dash* is white, ponytailed, petite, with a relatively featureless face (in the original version of *Diner Dash* she did not have a nose at all). Other characters in subsequent *Dash* games have a similar appearance, whether male or female. Flo is most often represented in an apron, although in some versions of the game the player is able to purchase generally bland clothing for her. While some characters have darker skin tones, their features are (generally speaking) white.
- The title character of *Cooking Mama* is short and cherubic, and appears to be simultaneously young and old. She appears to be almost a white mammy, with a kerchief over her head.
- In *Castle Story* the player is able to select between a male and female avatar, though she is not able to personalize that avatar. The avatars are virtually identical (the female has longer hair and a narrower facial structure). Both are white.
- Many of the other cooking- and kitchen-themed games, such as *Restaurant Story 2* or *Kitchen Scramble*, use avatars and non-player characters that look strikingly like Flo, always white and brunette and always with a featureless, sexless body.

- *Candy Crush Saga*, while without playable avatars, is guided by a strange, cartoonlike white girl who embodies the lush aesthetics of the rest of the game.

The sexlessness of the avatars, particularly in time management and invest/express games, makes sense in many ways. Time management is about occupying excess time. In this way, it would seem, bodies are almost besides the point, and having the least possible offensive bodies helps to create a comfortable space for an expected audience of women gamers. Yet this also (uncomfortably) suggests the ideology of slenderness, per Bordo, referenced above. If buxom women are at the heart of games designed for masculine audiences, then slenderness is at the heart of games designed for feminine audiences. The most common visual image in time management games is a slender, ponytailed, white woman.

Fashion game avatars are almost entirely white, desexualized, and featureless as well. The characters in fashion games look so physically similar that to address this point, Figure 25 shows a screenshot of several similar-but-different fashion game icons from my iPhone. The characters are almost identical, mostly white, with nondescript, small features and usually blonde hair (although occasionally brunette). An exception to this can be found in *Kim Kardashian: Hollywood*, which will be discussed in more detail below. Fashion games, unsurprisingly, seem to be promoting conformity of bodies.

Many games designed for feminine audiences bypass the question of sex, ethnicity, and other physical attributes entirely by avoiding human characters and using cute animals as a guide. *Polar Pop, Diamond Quest!, Panda Pop, Hungry Babies Mania,* and several other casual puzzle games use cute, nonoffensive animals as either playable characters or guides for the player. Reinforcing the interviews I performed in chapter 1, the use of cute animals seems to be a specific maneuver to attract women. These animal bodies are certainly the least possible offensive representations, but the desire to not offend audiences seems notable here. After all, when creating a television series intended for a female audience, we would not expect a producer to replace a sexy female lead with a cute panda bear. In many ways, the flattening of bodies in women's gaming seems to be entirely in response to the sexualization of those very bodies in games intended for masculine audiences.

The flattening of digital bodies in these games also suggests other qualities of the designed identity of Player Two. For one, as implied by the

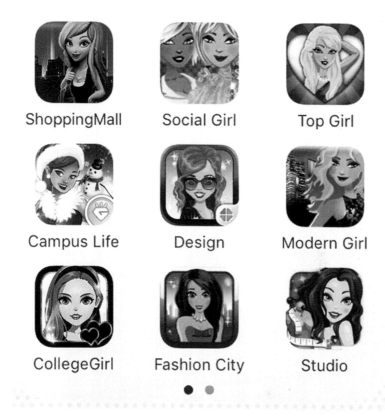

Figure 25. This image shows several icons from my iPhone of various fashion games. Note the similarities between each of the bodies and styles of the women depicted.

games listed above, it suggests that she is necessarily white. Her access to plain, nondescript clothing suggests that she is likely middle class. She is also necessarily able-bodied and physically slim, again resonating with Bordo's ideology of slender women. While Mama from *Cooking Mama* is a possible exception here, in reality, while her face is round and cherubic, her actual body is relatively tiny. She is cis-gendered and probably heterosexual (recent games have introduced us to Papa, who appears to be her spouse). If none of the other patterns previously remarked on in this book gives any indications about the relationship between the expected identities of players and the designed identity within these games, the lack of diversity is surely a tell. From an intersectional perspective this is troubling. While video games are increasingly being made to appeal to a more diverse audience of women, there seems to be a tacit assumption about what women should look and behave like.

THE DEFAULT SETTING AND DESIRABLE BODIES OF GAMING

One alternative to stock character design is to feature designable playable characters in a game. In many ways, this move (while time-consuming for the player) creates more potential for specific kinds of diversity, such as hair color, hairstyle, skin color, and clothing choices. These choices, though, tend to be somewhat shallow. The argument *against* giving a player stock playable characters to chose from (or stock guide characters to take instruction from) is that those characters define what is "othered" in the game world. But when options are highly structured, they rhetorically suggest that the player must become like the character they are creating, rather than the inverse.

While online game worlds such as *Second Life* and *World of Warcraft* have long allowed players to define themselves via personalized avatars, taking another look at character generation in *Kim Kardashian: Hollywood* provides a neater lens to parse how issues of gender, sexuality, ethnicity, and other bodily conceits can both extend and limit the player's in-game persona, reaching potentially to their outer game identities. The focus on *KK:H* in this section relates back to the designed identity of Player Two: while *World of Warcraft* and *Second Life* are intended to be consumed by diverse audiences (scoring a 5 and a 6 on the table from chapter 1, respectively), *KK:H* is clearly intended for women audiences (it scores a 9), as elaborated on in my discussion of "consumption" from the previous chapter.

Bodies in *KK:H* are fluid and mutable—but only to an extent. When the player begins, he or she is given their choice of being male or female, one of the few unchangeable aspects of the player's character. The player is able to chose skin tone, hair color, and hairstyle from a limited pallet that includes both Caucasian and darker skin tones, although is not exceptionally broad. The player is only able to select from five different skin tones in *KK:H*, although in a subsequent Glu title, *Katy Perry: Pop*, the player is given six options (Figure 26). Hair color and style in *KK:H* is similarly diverse but still limited, allowing for some African American hairstyles but leaning toward more Caucasian looks (once again, *Katy Perry: Pop*

Figure 26. A side-by-side comparison of *Kim Kardashian: Hollywood* (developed by Blammo Games and published by Glu Mobile, 2014) and *Katy Perry: Pop* (developed and published by Glu Mobile, 2015). Each screen shows the respective avatar-selection process for the games. A wider number of skin and hair colors were available in *KP:P* than in *KK:H*.

has significantly more options both in hair color and style, likely due to the fact that it is a newer game).

Players are also able to choose facial shape as well as the size of features such as the nose, lips, and eyes. These options, however, seem to be fairly unimportant. On small mobile devices the distinction between different kinds of noses is almost impossible to see, practically indistinguishable.

Furthermore, the facial features, for the most part, appear to be relatively Caucasian and embody an overwhelming sense of whiteness.

The player is permitted to change any of these features—skin color, hair type and color, facial features, and facial shape—at any point in the game, similar to how they might change their clothing. To bring this point further home, when the player receives bonuses and prizes in daily specials, new facial features (a new nose or eyes) is a potential prize. There are no repercussions to changing skin tone, hair, or any other mutable physical attribute in the game world. The avatar can change from one day to the next looking entirely different with absolutely no ramifications to game play.[31] The decision to constantly change these features within the real world becomes completely naturalized, an expected feature of celebrity. While it costs in-game money to change one's name, it costs nothing to change from a white woman to a black woman and then back again throughout the day (so long as your conception of "black" or "white" falls within a specific pallet).

There is a certain kind of liberating appeal to the mutability of characters in *KK:H*. It seems to be post-race and post-sexuality in this way. The game does not respond to a player's whimsical (or serious, for that matter) views about her own bodily associations. The designed identity of the player in *KK:H* does not seem to be bound by plebian notions of physical identity. Want a new nose? Get one. Want darker or lighter skin? It can be changed with a click.

Yet in *KK:H* bodies are still a problem. The only thing that cannot be altered in any way is the avatar's body *shape*.[32] While some more complex game worlds (e.g., *Second Life*) allow the player to transform body types and shapes, most of the games discussed throughout this book—games designed for an intended female audience—tend to offer singular and immutable body frames. In many games (e.g., *FarmVille* or *Castle Story*) this body has a tendency toward an aesthetic of "cute." Usually these non-player characters and avatars are characterized by bearing somewhat larger heads on tiny bodies. At other times bodies are just generally slimmed, giving them no real shape or contour.

In other games there is a more chilling effect of bodies. In both *Kim Kardashian: Hollywood* and *Katy Perry: Pop* (both Glu Mobile games) the player is automatically given a more "Hollywood" body. For male bodies, this parses as slim and muscled (although male bodies in the game world wear less revealing clothing). For female bodies, this automatically becomes an impossible hourglass shape, with clothing that regularly reveals the contours of the pixelated body. Players are only offered a choice between "male" or "female," with no ability to control their contours. While all other aspects of bodies, such as facial shapes and skin tones, can be changed, the player is trapped in her impossible body. Nonplayer characters are permitted bodily variations. The depiction of Kim Kardashian, for example, has larger breasts and hips than the player's character does. Similarly, Kylie Jenner is thin and waifish in her in-game representation. But the player characters must meet the specific bodily expectations of the game world. The game seems to be working under the assumption that there is no other body type the player might desire (or that might be acceptable in Hollywood). These desirable bodies, both the slim body of the *Ville* games and the hourglass of *KK:H*, are the default setting of gendered gaming.

TOWARD A TRANSFORMATIONAL JENNIFER

In chapter 1 of this book I introduced "Jennifer." Jennifer is the idealized player for Storm8's *Restaurant Story 2*. I suggested that Jennifer was, in addition to being a thirty-something woman, also white, middle class, heterosexual, able-bodied, and cis-gendered. We know this from looking at the bland, white, thin, brunette guide that greets us throughout the game's progress. Jennifer is normative and normalized in this game world. Jennifer doesn't just play *Restaurant Story 2*, she is who we assume plays many of the games throughout the book. It is her imaginary (and problematic) body that has guided this book.

If bodies are a problem in games that are designed for Player Two, then it is perhaps an affect of the larger body problem within feminist discourse. Bodies in a game world are both freeing and limiting. They assign an idealized mode of what the gamer should look like, in addition to how that gamer is expected to behave. The desired body of gaming is still most commonly white, middle-class, able-bodied, and cis-gendered. While games such as *KK:H* offer opportunities for remapping the body in terms of skin color, there are still hints of an idealized player body. The body problem becomes a problem when it maps back to real bodies, the lived bodies of actual players that internalize who is expected to play and how that play should occur.

Even hidden object games, such as the *Mystery Case Files* series, suggest a mess of bodies. These games are free of avatar bodies—they function within a spectrum of invisibility wherein the avatar's in-game body is literally unseen. For example, when a player picks up an object in the game, the object floats in the air, as if held by a ghost. As discussed in chapter 3, this makes her invisibility function on both a literal and meta-phorical level—she is invisible from the game, but also from larger industry discourse. Certainly this spectral effect is freeing and implies that the player should imagine herself into the game space. However, by removing bodies entirely, it seems to suggest that the player is weightless, meaningless, nonexistent, and ephemeral. Becoming disembodied is both powerful and terrifying.

The idealism of transformation might be key to reconciling bodies with feminism. According to Lynda Birke we should "think about the biological body as changing and changeable, as *transformable* rather than as a 'tedious universal' machine. Accepting concepts of the biological body as relatively unchanging and universally representative continues to fix it into determinism; by insisting on thinking about 'the biological' in terms of transformation and change, rather than fixity and stasis, we might be able to develop a conceptualization of the biological that is not rooted in determinism."[33] In other words, rather than thinking of bodies as fixed, we should be thinking of them as constantly in flux and looking at the potential beauty of that change. If this is a path to reconciling feminism with biology, then it is equally a potential way to reconcile feminism with the messiness of gaming bodies. In this way, *KK:H* may be the closest to the answer. The fluidity with how it deals with bodily identity is surely on the right track.

When we think of Jennifer, then, we shouldn't be thinking of her white, heterosexual, middle-class, cis-gendered, and able body. We should think of her, and design her, in terms of all the possible things she is able to be. Jennifer can be fluid and changeable. She can be queer. She can be black- or brown-skinned. She can be intersectional in any number of ways and push the identity of the woman gamer even further. She can lead the video game industry into kinds of games and play we have still not even conceived of yet. Jennifer can, and should, be transformational.

CONCLUSION

The Playful Is Political

"THIS WAS THE VALLEY OF MEN."

In the sublime mobile game *Monument Valley*, the player guides Princess Ida, a tiny, voiceless, faceless princess, through decaying monuments, solving a series of Escher-esque, mazelike puzzles. At the fourth level of the game she is stopped by a strange, patriarchal, ghostly figure who proclaims to Ida (and the player, in kind), "This was the valley of men. Now all that remains are our monuments, stripped of their glories. Thieving princess, why have you returned?" (Figure 27). The game, which won the Apple iPad Game of the Year for 2014, seems to be almost speaking metaphorically of the larger predicament of the video game industry that was, indeed, once a "valley of men." To this end, one might continue to consider that, much like Ida's alien world, all that is left in the valley of men are now monuments: the shell of old games that serve as ghostly reminders of the virtual world Player One built. But the most jarring line is the question that follows: "Thieving princess, why have you returned?"

The first time I played *Monument Valley*, this accusation felt directed at me personally. In a post-GamerGate world it seems as though much of the video game community was, indeed, full of indictments regarding the destruction of their well-intentioned monuments. However, while Ida may be a thieving princess, she is also our protagonist. When Ida meets troll-like crows that badger her and push back against her progress in the game, the player is always able to unfold her triumphant path if she plays long enough. If I, the player, am a thieving princess, then I have returned for what is rightfully mine: a strange and tangled path back to play. Upon further reflection, what once sounded like an accusation begins to sound more like an invitation. This is particularly the case because *Monument*

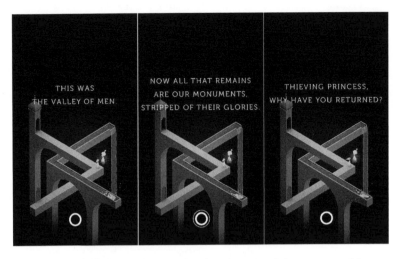

Figure 27. These three images show a series of statements made in a cut scene of the mobile game *Monument Valley*, developed and published by Ustwo Studios in 2014.

Valley, a mobile game with a female protagonist, has met high industry praise and enjoyed great financial success. *Monument Valley* seems to be a forward-looking game, but one that rests on the memorials of the past.

The video game industry is changing rapidly—so rapidly that the discourse surrounding this change is full of accusations and misgivings. GamerGate was one thread of this, wherein there was a perception of how new and different kinds of games were somehow going to usurp the established industry landscape. And, to some extent, perhaps they have. A recent Pew study on American gaming and gamers reported that while 49 percent of all adults play video games, only 10 percent consider themselves "gamers."[1] This statistic was not surprising to those of us who have been studying the video game landscape for some time now, and it helps to reinforce arguments made by Adrienne Shaw which illustrate that the term "gamer" itself is packed with politics, wherein many people who play games have chosen to distance themselves from the label.[2]

But there is another potential reason for the results of this study. As different kinds of video games come on the market, and an increasing number of people play those games, terminology and identities (in relation to that terminology) are bound to shift. A person who plays *Candy Crush Saga* for three hours a day is not likely to label herself as a "gamer": not because she doesn't play video games but because those video games are not the ones commonly associated with that label. The rising popularity of casuals helps those audiences dominate a portion of the market. This shift means that we will increasingly need to find new labels to capture levels of enthusiasm toward the medium.

Or perhaps we don't. As video games continue to reach broader and more diverse audiences, the format itself will become formalized in such a way that this kind of polling will become increasingly irrelevant. After all, we don't see Pew polling Americans on the number of people that go to see films, and how many of those filmgoers consider themselves "film buffs." It is taken as an obvious point that many Americans go to see films at varying levels of frequency, and that the term "film buff" is meant to apply only to the very furthest of this extreme. Film viewership, as the medium progressed, has normalized its way into our lives and become, to a point, invisible. Perhaps as the video game medium becomes increasingly stabilized and invisible in our everyday lives, we will no longer have to ask large questions regarding the identity of those who play.

This was once a valley of men. But like all valleys, it is easy to get trapped in the monotony of geography. While some have been dismissive of the games discussed throughout this book, these very games are what have begun to push us beyond the valley and into the vast and lush landscape of what the future of digital play might look like.

"NOW ALL THAT REMAINS ARE OUR MONUMENTS, STRIPPED OF THEIR GLORIES."

Yet, for now, it is important to remember that the playful is political.[3] By using this phrase, I am drawing on the charge of second-wave feminism, which asserts that the "personal is political." In suggesting that the playful is political, I am furthering that conceit, as a reminder that when feminisms focus entirely on the business of work, the business of health activism, and other serious issues, something gets lost. The cultural focus on time, as discussed in chapter 2, seems to be a result on this marginalization of play for the sake of work. As women rose up corporate ladders due to second-wave activism, time for leisure increasingly fell into pockets. The cultural realization of this occurs now, in video games deliberately designed for female audiences. As I demonstrated throughout this book, these games help to promote segmented forms of leisure emulating productivity rather than fun, and emotional labor over the ecstasy of less complicated pleasures.

But this, too, is somewhat disingenuous. From an intersectional perspective, this representation of feminist discourse is not quite right because play and leisure are something permitted to *some* women: women of the "right" social class, ethnicity, family life, and sexuality. As with other limited modes of feminism, there has been an idealized woman at the center of it. In this sense, the playful is political because the playful (perhaps) might allow us to reach beyond stagnant representations of femininity. It pushes past biology, nurturing, and perhaps even learned consumptive practices. The playful is political because the playful is about the bending of boundaries in new ways, the remapping of identity, and the rethinking of traditional roles. In these ways, play can act as a catalyst for feminisms.

I began this book by insisting that "designed identity" was not about real identities. I argued that the designed identity of women players was a shadow of an identity and a ghost. I used "Jennifer" as an example of this, declaring that she was both real and not real. This was, perhaps, a bit misleading. In certain respects, the designed identity of Player Two is fictional and constructed. Yet the problem with designed identity is that it also maps to real, lived experiences. Time management games are designed for women audiences because the real lives of women often have complicated relationships with time. Emotional labor is part of video games because women and girls are taught to perform affect from a young age. Consumptive practices are designed in distinct ways for female audiences, replaying a long and complex history that trains us that women are expected to shop. And the body problem, for women, is part of the real and everyday burden of performing femininity. As such, designed identity is both a shadow of an identity but also a very real, lived experience.

In reality, it is impossible to fully disentangle the designed identity of women players from the lived experiences of actual women. The games I have discussed in detail throughout this book are effective not because they are convincing women to play into an entirely new identity, but because they remap old identities into new spaces. *Kim Kardashian: Hollywood* is not a good game because it is innovative in subject matter or form, but because it effectively turns the experiences of feminine style into a robust game world. *Diner Dash* did not inspire an entire genre of video games, the time management game, because it was extraordinary in the experiences it broadcast, but because those experiences are extremely ordinary. And the hidden object game, with its invisible player, resonates with its audience not despite that invisibility, but *because* of it. The games I have discussed throughout this book are remarkable because they effectively replay some of the primary issues in many women's lives, but also the issues that feminism has been struggling with for a very long time.

And, so, the playful is political. By continuing this thread of both studying and creating games that identify women audiences as important, my goal is to potentially find ways to advance a feminist agenda: one that not only includes leisure but hopefully also one that expands our understanding of who gets to be a woman within this process of identity production. As the video game industry continues to adjust to new audiences, there will need to be more women—of all kinds—writing games for women. This will continue to create rifts and disjunctures, as the Player One of the past reconfigures what the medium currently looks like, and what it might potentially become.

Now all that remains are our monuments, stripped of their glories. The old monuments of Player One might be run down, but they are certainly not stripped of their glories. They are being built again into new structures. As the monuments of gaming are torn down and remade, we have an opportunity to reboot both the existing industry and what the products of that industry might mean within larger cultural context. Additionally, we have an opportunity to rethink and replay with the identity of the game player.

"THIEVING PRINCESS, WHY HAVE YOU RETURNED?"

In chapter 4 of this book, I told a story about how when I first began researching women and video games, I badgered my mother about what kind of game she would like to play; she finally responded with an exhausted, "I don't know, Shira. How about a nice shopping game?" It has been almost ten years since she gave me this exasperated response. I have used it in dozens of PowerPoint presentations and referenced the moment hundreds of times.[4]

Now I can see a clear shift. Several months ago, while I was writing this book, my mother was visiting me. One evening, in between other things, I sat in my living room playing *Polar Pop Mania* on my iPhone. My mother leaned over and asked, "Oh! What are you playing? I always like to play new games!" At the time my response was a dismissive shrug. ("I don't know, Mom. I'm a mommy seal, popping bubbles to rescue her babies so they don't cry.") But after she left, I couldn't get that moment out of my head. Things have changed so dramatically in the last few years that my mother now is someone who now "always [likes] to play new games." I am not entirely sure when this change took place, although I suspect it was gradual.

Of course, I would like to think that this is a change in my mother and that she is a more playful person than she was a decade ago. But this is probably only one small part of the story. There are other, larger, factors as well. For one, the increased ubiquity of mobile devices and the power they wield has played a role in my mother's acceptance of digital games. While carrying a Nintendo DS around with her seemed far-fetched (although I did buy her one), her iPhone's constant presence makes snippets of play more regularly permissible than it once was. Additionally, the games available for iOS and Android have made that shift possible as well. Word games are particularly tempting to my mother (productive play), and it is far easier to find games with people and situations that seem more relatable to her than the games that were available a decade ago. Earlier in this book I quoted Sheri Graner Ray remarking that the video game industry treats women as a "genre" as opposed to a "market." But the diverse number of genres that have developed within this space illustrates a rapid shift. Increasingly, women *are* a market with multiple genres. Additionally, news media coverage about video games is not as negative as it was a decade ago: fewer and fewer articles and broadcasts focus entirely on "video game violence"; now in favor are topics that demonstrate the beneficial effects of playing video games. Finally, micro-purchasing and the free-to-play model have created more comfortable economic entry points for a diverse audience to engage with play. All of these factors have culminated in such a way that, it would seem, my mother, while not a "gamer," is a suddenly a woman who plays video games. But this should not be surprising—after all, mother (like me) is a white, heterosexual, cisgendered, abled, middle-class woman. In other words, she is the exact person for whom these games have been designed

However, as discussed in the preface, I have changed, too. A decade ago I spent hours playing *World of Warcraft* and other games that were not necessarily designed for an intended female audience. Because I was not the primary audience, I felt more entitled to experiment, to dip my toe into a variety of games. As I write this, I have been consistently playing a rotation of four games on my iPhone: *Kim Kardashian: Hollywood*, *Neko Atsume*, *Hungry Babies Mania*, and *Katy Perry: Pop*. Last year I tried to return to the *World of Warcraft*, but I learned that I no longer had the time nor patience for that kind of video game world.

So, while my mother is playing more diverse games than she was playing a decade ago, I am playing less diverse games. I have slipped into the feminized identity that has been designed specifically for me. Is this diversity?

Thieving princess, why have you returned?

I am not sure whether I am a thief. Like others who played video games at a time when the identity of the "gamer" was white and male, I once felt like an unauthorized intruder within someone else's culture. Today my play is more authorized, but my identity with and around that play feels fixed and stagnant. If feminism is going to appropriate that play, if we are to steal play for the sake of the political, then part of that thievery needs to be more expansive.

Player Two is ready. And so is everyone else.

ACKNOWLEDGMENTS

This book would not be possible were it not for the many wonderful people in my life, on both personal and professional levels.

Early ruminations of this book began as my dissertation, and I therefore I owe a great debt to my dissertation committee at Rensselaer Polytechnic Institute and, in particular, my dissertation chair, June Deery. Thanks to James P. Zappen, Nancy Campbell, Nathaniel Freier, and Katherine Isbister for all of their hard work and advice.

Jessica Maddox (née Hennenfent), my graduate assistant, was the first editor for most chapters of this book. She provided feedback on more things than I can possibly list. She will be on the job market soon and you should all give her jobs. All of you.

Jennifer Malson, my subsequent graduate assistant, was of immeasurable help in creating the index for this book and deserves enormous thanks.

Many thanks to Andy Kavoori, who gave me a great amount of advice at the proposal phase of this project. Additional thanks to my colleagues in the Department of Entertainment and Media Studies at the University of Georgia. In particular, thanks to James Biddle, Kate Fortmueller, James Hamilton, and Jeffrey P. Jones for their unwavering support.

A big thanks to Casey O'Donnell, who gave me feedback on an early version of the introductory chapter and proposal as well as much needed encouragement. T. L. Taylor offered a great deal of advice on my approaches and interviewing in chapter 1 and helped me to find the confidence to take the approach I did. Brooke Erin Duffy gave me substantial feedback on chapter 3. Allison Harvey gave me wonderful advice and helped to guide this book from early stages. Additionally, I would like to give extra thanks to Adrienne Shaw. At the fateful DiGRA 2014 conference in Snowbird, Utah, I had all but given up on writing this book; Adrienne reminded me why this book might still be relevant and important to write. An additional big thanks to Jennifer Jenson, Suzanne de Castell, and the rest of the ReFiG team.

Conferences have provided the conversations and advice necessary to continue to motivate this project. My academic friends on social media have helped in a variety of ways—both purposefully and accidentally, through conversations physical and virtual. Of these, I cannot thank Nina Huntemann enough for her support on this project when I needed it the most. Additional thanks to Roger Altizer, Jaime Banks, Kelly Bergstrom, Bridget Blodgett, Paul Jonathan Booth, Kelly Boudreau, Ashley ML Brown (sorry, re: Skea), Florence Chee, Mark Chen, Mia Consalvo, Lauren Cruikshank, Clara Fernandez, Emily Flynn-Jones, Lindsay Grace, Kishonna Gray-Denson, Cathy Hannabach, Todd Harper, Mikael Jakobsson (who let me have the title), Carly Kocurek, Nick LaLone, Angela Leone (who reluctantly delved back into *KK:H* on my behalf), Adrienne Massanari, Christopher A. Paul, Whitney Phillips, Anastasia Salter, Sarah Schoemann, Gillian Smith, Braxton Soderman, and Nicholas Taylor. I have likely left several important people off this list, for which I apologize.

I am deeply indebted to friends and colleagues who are knowledgeable of the video game industry and helped to guide my understanding of the processes and constraints of that world. Sheri Graner Ray's work was highly influential to chapter 1, and her interview was integral to my overall work. I owe her a tremendous thanks for her time and thoughtfulness. An enormous thanks as well to Lisa Brunette, Maria Cipollone, Manuel Correla, Megan Glaser, Brenda Laurel, Nicole Lazzaro, Stephen Marsh, Molly Proffitt, Nicolas Rounds, Tobi Saulnier, and Ian Schreiber, along with the wonderful anonymous interview subjects that informed this project.

Thanks to Erin Warholm-Wohlenhaus for her editorial assistance and guidance throughout my process with the University of Minnesota Press. I appreciate her patience and enthusiasm.

Amber Davisson and Hillary Ann Jones have long been a major part of my support system, as both colleagues and friends. Their friendship began in graduate school and has now spanned several states, jobs, and important life moments. Thank you.

Thanks to Eric Newsom for coauthoring my previous book with me. That project, in many ways, made me realize my desire to finish this one. I wonder if the Slender Man will read this fondly, pleased that he is no longer in my sights.

Rather unexpectedly, my life in Athens, Georgia, has provided me with a wonderful support network of friends, particularly women, over the past few years. While many of them were not directly involved in this book, their support has helped make this book possible. Thanks to Laura Alexander, Kate Fortmueller (who gets a second thank-you), Miriam Jacobson, Sabrina Orah Mark, Rielle Navitski, Emily Sahakian, Samara Sheckler, and Monika Sklar for all being lovely people. A large portion of this book was written at Walker's Pub and Coffee in Athens; thank you to the owners for making a perfect place to write.

An enormous thank-you to my family members for putting up with me throughout the process of writing this book. Thank you to my parents, Howard and Carol Chess, for their unwavering support. In particular, thanks to my mother for enduring my retellings of the "nice shopping game" story.

And, of course, thank you to Wes and Oliver. You are my magic, my inspiration, and my heart.

NOTES

PREFACE

1 One could, perhaps, argue that all textual-based game research is, in part, ethnographic since the study of those games is entirely dependent on the subject position of the player. But I do my best throughout this book to keep my personal experiences with games apart from my critical analysis.
2 Chess and Shaw, "A Conspiracy of Fishes."

INTRODUCTION

1 It is worth noting that none of the articles on the Nintendo Knitting Machine describes the specifics of how it functioned, how it might have been a game, or what the peripheral actually did. These aspects appear to remain a mystery.
2 Goldfarb, "Nintendo Almost Made a Knitting Add-On for NES."
3 Ibid.
4 Another final question, of course, is how it actually was intended to work.
5 It seems worth pointing out that combining fabric arts with computer games need not be essentializing. Feminist game designer and scholar Gillian Smith, for example, has worked with teams to create quilting games. One game, *Threadsteading*, combines the styles of territory games with quilting machines. These efforts envision a clever design that far exceeds what we know about the Nintendo Knitting Machine.
6 Kocurek, *Coin-Operated Americans*.
7 Modleski, *Loving with a Vengeance*.
8 Casti, "Women Play Video Games."
9 Or clone games like *Cow Clicker* meant to mock the format and game-play style.
10 Cline, *Ready Player One*, 53.
11 Walter, "Forget Iron Man–Child"; Roberts, "Why I'm Done With 'Geek Culture'"; Chu, "Your Princess Is in Another Castle."
12 Kocurek, *Coin-Operated Americans*; Bergstrom, Fisher, and Jenson, "Disavowing 'That Guy.'"

13 Consalvo, "Confronting Toxic Gamer Culture."

14 Kocurek, *Coin-Operated Americans*; Ray, *Gender Inclusive Game Design*.

15 Kent, *Ultimate History of Video Games*; Ray, *Gender Inclusive Game Design*.

16 Ibid.

17 Kocurek, *Coin-Operated Americans*, xvi.

18 Kent, *Ultimate History of Video Games*.

19 Cassell and Jenkins, "Chess for Girls?"

20 Glos and Goldin, "An Interview with Brenda Laurel."

21 Cassell and Jenkins, "Voices from the Combat Zone."

22 Gray, *Race, Gender, and Deviance in Xbox Live*.

23 Taylor, *Play between Worlds*, 123.

24 Marcotte, "Teen Girls Love Video Games, but They're Really Quiet about It."

25 Wirman, "Playing by Doing and Players' Localization of *The Sims 2*."

26 Pearce, *Communities of Play*.

27 Harvey, *Gender, Age, and Digital Games in the Domestic Context*.

28 Hardcore gaming will be described in more detail below.

29 Consalvo, "Crunched by Passion."

30 Makuch, "Percentage of Female Developers Has More Than Doubled since 2009."

31 Consalvo, "Crunched by Passion."

32 Fron et al., "Hegemony of Play," 1.

33 Gray, *Race, Gender, and Deviance in Xbox Live*.

34 Consalvo, "Confronting Toxic Gamer Culture."

35 Shaw, "Do You Identify as a Gamer?"; Shaw, "On Not Becoming Gamers"; Shaw, *Gaming at the Edge*.

36 Cote, "I Can Defend Myself."

37 Chess, "36-24-36 Cerebrum"; Fron et al., "Hegemony of Play."

38 Chess, "36-24-36 Cerebrum."

39 Harris, "Feminization of Gaming." Obviously, this predates our current moment where all these devices have been integrated into a single device, the smartphone.

40 Harvey, *Gender, Age, and Digital Games in the Domestic Context*, 135.

41 Juul, *Casual Revolution*, 8.

42 Ibid.

43 Consalvo, "Hardcore Casual."

44 Vanderhoef, "Casual Threats," para. 39.

45 In his book *A Casual Revolution*, Jesper Juul traces the roots of what he refers to as the "matching tile" game back to *Tetris*. However, it seems important within this book to focus on the feminized iterations of what has now become the match-3 genre of video games.

46 Kato, "Space Invaders," 40.

47 Chess, "How to Play a Feminist."

48 Kennedy, "Lara Croft"; Schleiner, "Does Lara Croft Wear Fake Polygons?"; Wirman, "Princess Peach Loves Your Enemies, Too."

49 Flanagan and Nissenbaum, *Values at Play in Digital Games*; Flanagan, *Critical Play*; Lazzaro, "Are Boy Games Even Necessary?"

50 Jenson and de Castell, "Theorizing Gender and Digital Gameplay"; Jenson and de Castell, "Ethnographic Study of Gender and Digital Gameplay"; Jenson, Fisher, and de Castell, "Disrupting the Gender Order"; Royse et al., "Women and Games"; Taylor, *Play between Worlds*; Downey, "Here and There of a Femme Cave."

51 Consalvo, "Confronting Toxic Gamer Culture"; Jenkins, "Complete Freedom of Movement"; Kocurek, *Coin-Operated Americans.*

52 Gray, "Collective Organizing, Individual Resistance, or Asshole Griefers?"; Gray, *Race, Gender, and Deviance in Xbox Live*; Nakamura, "Don't Hate the Player, Hate the Game."

53 Salter and Blodgett, "Hypermasculinity and Dickwolves"; Blodgett and Salter, "Hearing 'Lady Game Creators' Tweet."

54 Anable, "Casual Games, Time Management, and the Work of Affect"; Vanderhoef, "Casual Threats."

55 Cassell and Jenkins, "Chess for Girls?"

56 Subrahmanyam and Greenfield, "Computer Games for Girls."

57 Jenkins, "Complete Freedom of Movement"; Kafai, "Video Game Designs by Girls and Boys."

58 Laurel, *Utopian Entrepreneur.*

59 Flanagan, *Critical Play*; Kafai, "Video Game Designs by Girls and Boys."

60 Taylor, *Play between Worlds*, 99.

61 Royse et al., "Women and Games."

62 Consalvo, "Crunched by Passion"; Fullerton et al., "Getting Girls into the Game."

63 Shaw, "On Not Becoming Gamers"; Shaw, *Gaming at the Edge*; Taylor, *Play between Worlds.*

64 Downey, "Here and There of a Femme Cave."

65 Jenson and de Castell, "Theorizing Gender and Digital Gameplay," 64.

66 Consalvo, "Confronting Toxic Gamer Culture"; Shaw, "On Not Becoming Gamers."

67 Consalvo, "Confronting Toxic Gamer Culture," para. 13.

68 Shaw, "Do You Identify as a Gamer?"; Shaw, "On Not Becoming Gamers"; Shaw, *Gaming at the Edge.*

69 Cote, "I Can Defend Myself."

70 Huntemann, "Pixel Pinups," 254.

71 Schleiner, "Does Lara Croft Wear Fake Polygons?"

72 Kennedy, "Lara Croft," para. 1.

73 Richard, "Gender and Gameplay."

74 Gray, *Race, Gender, and Deviance in Xbox Live.*

75 Green, Hebron, and Woodward, *Women's Leisure, What Leisure?*

76 Ibid.

77 Deem, *All Work and No Play?* 81.

78 Hochschild, *Second Shift*, 4.

79 Ibid., 265–66.

80 Henderson, "One Size Doesn't Fit All," 150.

81 Ibid., 151.

82 Royse et al., "Women and Games."

83 Winn and Heeter, "Gaming, Gender, and Time," 11.

84 Or, more specifically, how *certain* women are expected to practice leisure.

85 Law, *After Method*, 2.

86 Latour, "On Technical Mediation," 64.

87 Taylor, "Assemblage of Play," 332.

88 O'Donnell, *Developer's Dilemma*.

89 Elias, *Civilizing Process*, 54.

90 Gill and Grint, "Gender–Technology Relation"; Millar, *Cracking the Gender Code*.

91 Gill and Grint, "Gender–Technology Relation," 3.

92 Cowan, *More Work for Mother*, 99.

93 Haraway, *Simians, Cyborgs, and Women*; Wajcman, *Feminism Confronts Technology*; Wajcman, *Technofeminism*; Wosk, *Women and the Machine*.

94 Wajcman, *Feminism Confronts Technology*, 13.

95 Ibid., 19.

96 Wajcman, *Technofeminism*, 107.

97 Green, "Technology, Leisure, and Everyday Practices," 185.

98 Lally, *At Home with Computers*.

1. PLAYING WITH IDENTITY

1   Sparks, "6 Tips on Captivating Players from Storm8's Chief Creative Officer."

2   While LeTourneau's interview does not specifically stipulate that Jennifer is white, middle class, or a mother, his description does not rule out that possibility. Several aspects of the game give the distinct impression that these descriptors (while not listed) are likely the case.

3   Kocurek, *Coin-Operated Americans*.

4   For example, I reveal Sheri Graner Ray, the author of *Gender Inclusive Game Design*, because she has previously published on this topic and her continued experience remains relevant in this context.

5   Flanagan and Nissenbaum, *Values at Play in Digital Games*, 9.

6   O'Donnell, "This Is Not a Software Industry."

7   Bogost, *Persuasive Games*, 3.

8   Paul, *Wordplay and the Discourse of Video Games*, 8.

9   Ibid., 161.

10 Ray, *Gender Inclusive Game Design*, xvii.

11 Ibid., 43.

12 Ibid., 74.

13 Sheri Graner Ray (author and game designer), in discussion with the author, August 19, 2015.

14 The publisher, Charles River Media, went out of business, making it difficult to know the exact number of copies sold. While *Gender Inclusive Game Design* is currently out of print, Ray is planning to offer a revised edition through a new publisher.

15 Taylor, "Review of Sheri Graner Ray's *Gender Inclusive Game Design*."

16 Sheri Graner Ray (author and game designer), in discussion with the author, August 19, 2015.

17 Ibid.

18 Adams, *Fundamentals of Game Design*, 619.

19 Ibid., 620.

20 In fact, some developers decided not to be part of this study, based on their belief that there is no such thing as games specifically *for* female audiences.

21 Sheri Graner Ray (author and game designer), in discussion with the author, August 19, 2015.

22 This reinforces work I have done elsewhere ("Strange Bedfellows"), where I discussed the incongruence between romance and video games.

23 I marked *Clash of Clans* as "low risk" although in reality it sits on the edge of a high/low–risk design. When players are not playing *CoC* their village can be attacked, depleting their resources for a short period of time when they return. This attribute, while higher risk than most of the other casual games I discuss, is lower risk than games where a player is more specifically set back. Other games (such as *World of Warcraft*) fall under the rubric of "depends how you play" when considering whether they are high or low risk. I would argue that that flexibility, unto itself, characterizes a lower-risk game.

24 Vanderhoef, "Casual Threats."

25 Rosewater, "Timmy, Johnny, and Spike."

26 The BBC briefly created radio listeners "Dave" and "Sue," although these were specifically marketing personas used in the promotion of the BBC Local Radio regional service. In other areas, marketing has created "persona templates" (Lee, "The Complete Beginner's Guide to Creating Marketing Personas"), although this practice is not meant for creative development as much as advertising to specific customer types.

2. PLAYING WITH TIME

1 Chess, "36-24-36 Cerebrum."

2 Ibid.

3 There are also, perhaps, Lacanian interpretations of "nothing" here, wherein "nothing" is potentially a phallus.

4 Hochschild, *Second Shift*.

5 Harvey, *Gender, Age, and Digital Games in the Domestic Context*.

6 Hochschild, *Time Bind*.

7 Booth, *Time on TV*, 5.

8 Ibid.

9 Zagal and Mateas, "Time in Video Games," 848.

10 Ibid.

11 Hochschild, *Time Bind*, 229–30.

12 Hochschild, *Second Shift*.

13 Deem, *All Work and No Play?*

14 Hochschild, *Time Bind*, 215.

15 Bolton, *Third Shift*.

16 Wyman, *Making Great Games*, 39.

17 Ibid.

18 Pitcher, "Glu Mobile Acquires *Diner Dash* Developer PlayFirst."

19 Schonfeld, "Zynga Raises $29 Million B Round."

20 *Kim Kardashian: Hollywood* will be discussed in greater detail in chapter 4, "Playing with Consumption."

21 Anecdotally, several people who play *Kim Kardashian: Hollywood* have admitted to me that they set timers on their phone so they are reminded to return and complete what they have started.

22 Birth, *Objects of Time*, 35.

23 Schüll, *Addiction by Design*, 206.

24 Chesler, *Women and Madness*; Friedan and Quindlen, *Feminine Mystique*; Maines, *Technology of Orgasm*.

25 Maines, *Technology of Orgasm*, 24.

26 Ibid., 20.

3. PLAYING WITH EMOTIONS

1 See http://www.mywiistory.com/. This website no longer contains the original "My Wii Story" submissions.

2 Freeman, "Creating Emotion in Games," 11.

3 Isbister, *Better Game Characters by Design*, 151.

4 Ibid., 193.

5 Baharom, Tan, and Idris, "Emotional Design for Games."

6 Ibid.

7 Shinkle, "Video Games, Emotion, and the Six Senses," 907.

8 Ibid., 910.

9 Apperley and Heber, "Capitalizing on Emotions," 158.

10 Ibid.

11 Wirman, "Princess Peach Loves Your Enemies, Too."

12 Hochschild, *Managed Heart*, 7.

13 Ibid., 113.

14 Ibid., 11.

15 Jarrett, "Relevance of 'Women's Work,'" 1.

16 Dalla Costa, "Development and Reproduction"; Fortunati, *Arcane of Reproduction*; Jarrett, "Relevance of 'Women's Work.'"

17 Jarrett, "Relevance of 'Women's Work,'" 117.

18 Ibid.; Jarrett, *Feminism, Labour and Digital Media*.

19 Tronto, "Women and Caring," 172.

20 Ibid., 174.

21 Graham, "Caring," 30.

22 Rich, *Of Woman Born*, 33.

23 Ibid., 34.

24 Lazzaro, "Are Boy Games Even Necessary?"

25 Ibid.

26 XEO Design, "*Diner Dash* and the People Factor," 4.

27 Anable, "Casual Games, Time Management, and the Work of Affect," para 4.

28 Ibid, para 5.

29 The customer "types" also neatly reinforce racial, sexual, ageist, and gendered stereotypes by the simplified equivalence of non-player character appearances and their overriding personality traits.

30 Birke, *Feminism and the Biological Body*, 113.

31 While there are iOS and Android versions of hidden object games as well, these tend to be considerably more difficult to play on smaller screens, and therefore a bit less popular.

32 I refer to this as a "cleaning" mechanic because the player is presented with such messy spaces. When the player clicks on specific items they disappear, virtually "cleaning" it from the larger landscape. The visual effect is that by the time you are done, the space feels (at least slightly) cleaner and less cluttered.

33 The relationship between cleaning and hidden object games occurred to me at a point when I was playing the games while neglecting cleaning my own home. I realized, in a way, that making objects disappear and return to their proper place would be more productive in the real world but was equally satisfying in the virtual world.

34 My comments on the game *Cooking Mama* primarily refer to the Nintendo DS and Nintendo Wii versions of the game. A version of *Cooking Mama* recently released for iOS and Android devices varies somewhat from the Nintendo iterations.

35 Chess, "Don't Worry, Mama Will Fix It!"

36 Turkle, "Whither Psychoanalysis in Computer Culture?" 26.

37 Cruikshank, "Taking Casual Seriously."

38 Apperley and Heber, "Capitalizing on Emotions," 159.

39 The player is always rewarded by repeat customer cats with "mementos" (such as a shiny acorn or a pair of mittens), which are small objects with no monetary game value but help to maintain an endearing relationship between the player and the cats.

40 Gee and Hayes, *Women and Gaming*; Jansz, Avis, and Vosmeer, "Playing *The Sims 2*."

41 Isbister, *Better Game Characters by Design*, 113.

42 Sample, "Virtual Torture."

43 I refer to this game a "bubble shooter" because bubbles are the most common things shot from the bottom of the screen. Occasionally things other than bubbles are shot, but the mechanic remains the same.

44 Additionally, the player is instructed to avoid gophers, which will pop up and steal food from the babies. While the gopher appears "cute" to me, the game mechanic does suggest that some animals are more worthy of nourishment than others.

45 "Two Players."

46 Often, social network games have an overlap with invest/express games, although not always. For example, *FarmVille* is both a social network game and an invest/express game. *Words with Friends*, however, is only a social network game. The primary distinction dividing point between the two is the ability to design a robust space within the game world.

47 Lee and Wohn, "Are There Cultural Differences in How We Play?"

48 Consalvo, "Using Your Friends," 188.

49 Contestabile, "What Are the Primary Demographics (Gender, Age, Ethnicity, Etc.) of the Average Social Game Enthusiast?"; Hepburn, "Infographic"; Thompson, "SponsorPay Reveals New Social/Mobile Demographics."

50 Thompson, "SponsorPay Reveals New Social/Mobile Demographics."

51 Not all SNGs necessarily *require* social behavior, although most reward it.

52 Terdiman, "Why Zynga Ticks Off the Games Industry."

53 Bogost, "Cow Clicker."

54 Pickles, my adopted baby in *KK:H*, requires a surprisingly low amount of maintenance, although it cost quite a few K-Coins to purchase her.

55 Chambers, "Wii Play as Family."

4. PLAYING WITH CONSUMPTION

1 Presumably the announcer is saying "phat," the slang word for something excellent, and not "fat," referring to the petite woman's weight.

2 "Today's Primary Shopper."

3 Horkheimer and Adorno, "Culture Industry," 43.

4 O'Donnell, "This Is Not a Software Industry," 43.

5 Holbrook and Chestnut, "Play as a Consumption Experience," 737.

6 Veblen, "Conspicuous Consumption," 187.

7 Spigel, "Designing the Smart House," 415.

8 My mother, for one, is tired of hearing me retell this story.

9 Marx, *Critique of Political Economy*, 195. Emphasis mine.

10 Turow and Draper, "Industry Conceptions of Audience in the Digital Space."

11 De Grazia, "Introduction"; Zukin and Maguire, "Consumers and Consumption."

12 Lury, *Consumer Culture*.

13 Firat, "Gender and Consumption," 210.

14 Juul, *Casual Revolution*, 101.

15 Sandlin and Maudlin, "Consuming Pedagogies."

16 Peiss, *Hope in a Jar*; McGee, *Self-Help, Inc.*

17 Ouellette, "Inventing the Cosmo Girl."

18 Wissinger, *This Year's Model*.

19 Subrahmanyam and Greenfield, "Computer Games for Girls," 66.

20 Milnes, "Move Over Kardashian."

21 Takahashi, "CrowdStar Is All-In on Mobile Gaming for Women with *Covet Fashion*."

22 Duffy, *Remake, Remodel*, 111.

23 Perhaps we can understand this desire to rebuild a mall as a kind of post-recession discourse.

24 Melby, "3 Game-Changing New Ways to Shop Online."

25 Technically, *World of Warcraft* combined these two models, costing money upfront and then charging a monthly fee for play.

26 To avoid confusion, I refer to these games as either free-to-play or F2P (not freemium) throughout this book. The term "freemium" has taken on a somewhat derogatory status within the video game industry.

27 Schneck, "Freemium."

28 Perez, "In-App Purchase Revenue Hits Record High."

29 Seppala, "Report."

30 Johnson, "Long Tail of Whales."

31 Nash, "Are Freemium Apps Killing Game Developers?"

32 Consalvo and Paul, "Welcome to the Discourse of the Real," 61.

33 Good, "Who Are the 'Whales' Driving Free-to-Play Gaming?"

34 McCabe, "Hit Kardashian Video Game Lifts Glu Mobile from E-List"; Seufert, "3 Reasons Why *Kim Kardashian: Hollywood* Has Exploded."

35 Morrissey, "Oh God, I Spent $494.04 Playing the Kim Kardashian Hollywood App."

36 *Lindsay Lohan's The Price of Fame* has been removed from the various app stores and appears to have been discontinued. According to reports about the game, it was actually created and designed by the lead guitarist of the band OK Go, perhaps accounting for its confounding play styles and game mechanics.

37 The Jason Statham title is a sniper game and not a celebrity fashion game, but it is often listed with the other celebrity games. Given its theme, style, and aesthetics it is very clearly not intended for Player Two.

38 Alejandro, "7 Celebrities Who Are Releasing Their Own Mobile App Games."

39 McCabe, "Hit Kardashian Video Game Lifts Glu Mobile from E-List."

40 Kuittinen, "Kim Kardashian Shocks the App Market"; Seufert, "3 Reasons Why *Kim Kardashian: Hollywood* Has Exploded."

41 Morrissey, "Oh God, I Spent $494.04 Playing the *Kim Kardashian: Hollywood* App."

42 As with all F2P games, time can be replaced with money.

43 At the time of this writing, I have spent eighty-five dollars on *KK:H*, though had I spent more I would have been able to play the game faster and more effectively. Real-world money also helped me purchase my baby, Pickles, and a personal jet that allows me to travel intercontinentally at no additional in-game cost.

44 For example, $105 worth of K-Coins equals $9.99 of real money. While on the surface this would mean that each K-Coin equals about one cent, but because K-Coins are also something the player gets for free through tasks, it becomes difficult to ascertain the actual monetary value of those coins. If not accounting for other means of gathering K-Coins, a wedding dress, then, that costs 120 K-Coins costs about $11, not considering the time spent working toward that purchase. When transferring K-Coins into energy points, the exchange rate then becomes roughly 1 energy point per K-Coin, but the rates shift when purchased in bulk or during occasional "sales."

45　Excepting, of course, that the only clothing available to the player is clothing selected, in the first place, as potential "celebrity fashion."

46　The less expensive wedding dresses are not attractive.

47　Duffy, "Romance of Work."

48　Upon reaching the No. 1 spot on the A-list, the player is giving the option to become a "comeback." Accepting this gives the player bonuses but reverts her status to the E-list, forcing her to work her way back up again.

49　Bordo, *Unbearable Weight*, 119.

50　Parkin, *Food Is Love*, 40.

5. PLAYING WITH BODIES

1　Liao, "Kegel Trainer Skea."

2　"Funny Old Sega Ads."

3　Tuana, "Speculum of Ignorance."

4　Birke, *Feminism and the Biological Body*.

5　Martin, "Egg and the Sperm."

6　Taylor, *Raising the Stakes*, 47.

7　Foucault, *Discipline and Punish*.

8　Ibid., 304.

9　Ibid., 138.

10　Ibid., 152–53.

11　Ibid., 141.

12　Chess, "Playing the Bad Guy."

13　Taylor, *Raising the Stakes*, 47.

14　Balsamo, *Technologies of the Gendered Body*, 5.

15　Bordo, *Unbearable Weight*, 205–6.

16　While most of these books talked about "girls'" and " women's" self-esteem, they were, of course, referring generally to the lives of white, middle-class, cis-gendered, heterosexual girls living in the United States or other Western nations.

17　Pipher and Ross, *Reviving Ophelia*.

18　Lazarus et al., *Killing Us Softly*.

19　Kilbourne, *Can't Buy My Love*, 132.

20　Jamieson, *Beyond the Double Bind*, 16.

21　Thurer, *Myths of Motherhood*, 229.

22　Raymond, *Transsexual Empire*.

23　Riddell, "Divided Sisterhood"; Sullivan, "Transvestite Answers a Feminist."

24　Birke, *Feminism and the Biological Body*, 43.

25　Manovich, *Language of New Media*, 111–12.

26　Harvey, *Gender, Age, and Digital Games in the Domestic Context*.

27　Jones and Thiruvathukal, *Codename Revolution*, 32.

28　Ibid., 91.

29　Kennedy, "Lara Croft"; Schleiner, "Does Lara Croft Wear Fake Polygons?"

30 Baker-Whitelaw, "Gamers Angry over Lack of Women in the New 'Assassin's Creed' Game."

31 As an experiment, I went through a period where I changed my skin color every time I changed my outfit in the game. Non-player characters within the game world never noted this.

32 One clone game of *KK:H*, *Love and Hip Hop* (produced by 345 Games) only allows players to select non-white skin tones. This game gives the players two body options: a curvy body or a very curvy body. While the selections offered in *L&HH* certainly recognize the need for diversity in the genre, the push toward necessarily pairing brown bodies with larger hips is troubling.

33 Birke, *Feminism and the Biological Body*, 44.

CONCLUSION

1 Duggan, "Gaming and Gamers."

2 Shaw, "Do You Identify as a Gamer?"; Shaw, *Gaming at the Edge.*

3 This phrase, itself, has baggage. I used it originally in a 2010 essay titled "How to Play a Feminist," which I am constantly wishing I could rewrite with the perspective afforded by time. I later appropriated the phrase into the title of a "fishbowl" session at DiGRA 2014, organized with Adrienne Shaw. This fishbowl was later centralized as part of vast conspiracy theory which Adrienne and I have discussed in detail elsewhere. However, I still feel that the phrase is pertinent and worth repeating, for the reasons described throughout this chapter.

4 Again, my mother would really like me to stop relaying this anecdote.

BIBLIOGRAPHY

Adams, Ernest. *Fundamentals of Game Design*. 2nd ed. Berkeley, Calif.: New Riders Press, 2010.

Alejandro, Alba. "7 Celebrities Who Are Releasing Their Own Mobile App Games." *New York Daily News*, August 5, 2015. http://www.nydailynews.com/entertainment/music/7-celebrities-releasing-mobile-app-games-article-1.2315790.

Anable, Aubrey. "Casual Games, Time Management, and the Work of Affect." *Ada: A Journal of Gender, New Media, and Technology* 2 (June 2013). http://adanewmedia.org/2013/06/issue2-anable/.

Apperley, Tom, and Nicole Heber. "Capitalizing on Emotions: Digital Pets and Natural User Interface." In *Game Love: Essays on Play and Affection*, edited by Jessica Enevold and Esther MacCallum-Stewart, 149–61. Jefferson, N.C.: McFarland, 2015.

Baharom, Shahrel Nizar, Wee Hoe Tan, and Mohammad Zaffwan Idris. "Emotional Design for Games: A Framework for Player-Centric Approach in the Game Design Process." *International Journal of Multimedia and Ubiquitous Engineering* 9, no. 10 (2014): 387–98.

Baker-Whitelaw, Gavia. "Gamers Angry over Lack of Women in the New 'Assassin's Creed' Game." *Daily Dot*, June 11, 2014. http://www.dailydot.com/gaming/lack-of-women-assassins-creed/.

Balsamo, Anne. *Technologies of the Gendered Body*. Durham, N.C.: Duke University Press, 1999.

Bergstrom, Kelly, Stephanie Fisher, and Jennifer Jenson. "Disavowing 'That Guy': Identity Construction and Massively Multiplayer Online Game Players." *Convergence* 22, no. 3 (2016): 233–49.

Birke, Lynda. *Feminism and the Biological Body*. New Brunswick, N.J.: Rutgers University Press, 2000.

Birth, Kevin K. *Objects of Time: How Things Shape Temporality*. New York: Palgrave Macmillan, 2012.

Blodgett, Bridget Marie, and Anastasia Salter. "Hearing 'Lady Game Creators' Tweet: #1ReasonWhy, Women and Online Discourse in the Game Development Commu-

nity." *Selected Papers of Internet Research* 14, no. 0 (2013). http://spir.aoir.org/index
.php/spir/article/view/694.

Bogost, Ian. "Cow Clicker: The Making of Obsession." *Ian Bogost,* July 21, 2010. http://
bogost.com/writing/blog/cow_clicker_1/.

———. *Persuasive Games: The Expressive Power of Videogames.* Cambridge, Mass.: MIT
Press, 2007.

Bolton, Michele Kremen. *The Third Shift: Managing Hard Choices in Our Careers, Homes,
and Lives as Women.* San Francisco: Jossey-Bass, 2000.

Booth, Paul. *Time on TV: Temporal Displacement and Mashup Television.* New York:
Peter Lang, 2012.

Bordo, Susan. *Unbearable Weight: Feminism, Western Culture, and the Body.* Berkeley:
University of California Press, 1993.

Cassell, Justine, and Henry Jenkins. "Chess for Girls? Feminism and Computer Games."
In *From Barbie to Mortal Kombat: Gender and Computer Games,* edited by Justine
Cassell and Henry Jenkins, 2–45. Cambridge, Mass.: MIT Press, 1998.

———. "Voices from the Combat Zone: Game Grrlz Talk Back." In *From Barbie to Mortal
Kombat: Gender and Computer Games,* edited by Justine Cassell and Henry Jenkins,
328–41. Cambridge, Mass.: MIT Press, 1998.

Casti, Taylor. "Women Play Video Games: Can We Cut the Sexist Crap Now?" *Huffington
Post,* April 24, 2014. http://www.huffingtonpost.com/2014/04/24/female-gamers
_n_5207137.html.

Chambers, Deborah. "'Wii Play as Family': The Rise in Family-Centred Video Gaming."
Leisure Studies 31, no. 1 (2012): 69–82.

Chesler, Phyllis. *Women and Madness.* Rev. ed. New York: Palgrave Macmillan, 2005.

Chess, Shira. "A 36-24-36 Cerebrum: Productivity, Gender, and Video Game Advertising."
Critical Studies in Media Communication 28, no. 3 (2011): 230–52.

———. "'Don't Worry, Mama Will Fix It!': Playing with the Mama Myth in Video Games."
In *The Motherhood Business: Consumption, Communication, and Privilege,* edited
by Anne Teresa Demo, Jennifer L. Borda, and Charlotte Kroløkke, 197–215. Tusca-
loosa: University of Alabama Press, 2015.

———. "How to Play a Feminist." *Thirdspace: A Journal of Feminist Theory & Culture*
9, no. 1 (2010): http://journals.sfu.ca/thirdspace/index.php/journal/article/view
Article/273.

———. "Playing the Bad Guy: *Grand Theft Auto* in the Panopticon." In *Digital Gameplay:
Essays on the Nexus of Game and Gamer,* edited by Nate Garrelts, 80–90. Jefferson,
N.C.: McFarland, 2005.

———. "Strange Bedfellows: Subjectivity, Romance, and Hidden Object Video Games."
Games and Culture 9, no. 6 (2014): 417–28.

Chess, Shira, and Adrienne Shaw. "A Conspiracy of Fishes, or, How We Learned to Stop
Worrying about GamerGate and Embrace Hegemonic Masculinity." *Journal of
Broadcasting & Electronic Media* 59, no. 1 (2015): 208–20.

Chu, Arthur. "Your Princess Is in Another Castle: Misogyny, Entitlement, and Nerds."
Daily Beast, May 27, 2014. http://www.thedailybeast.com/articles/2014/05/27/
your-princess-is-in-another-castle-misogyny-entitlement-and-nerds.html.

Cline, Earnest. *Ready Player One*. New York: Broadway Books, 2012.

Consalvo, Mia. "Confronting Toxic Gamer Culture: A Challenge for Feminist Game Studies Scholars." *Ada: A Journal of Gender and New Media Technology* 1 (November 2012). http://adanewmedia.org/2012/11/issue1-consalvo/.

———. "Crunched by Passion: Women Game Developers and Workplace Challenges." In *Beyond Barbie and Mortal Kombat: New Perspectives on Gender and Gaming*, edited by Yasmin B. Kafai, Carrie Heeter, Jill Denner, and Jennifer Y. Sun, 177–91. Cambridge, Mass.: MIT Press, 2008.

———. "Hardcore Casual: Game Culture Return(s) to Ravenhearst," 50–54. Foundations of Digital Games Conference, Orlando, Fla., April 26–30, 2009.

———. "Using Your Friends: Social Mechanics in Social Games." In *Proceedings of the 6th International Conference on Foundations of Digital Games*, 188–95 (New York: ACM, 2011).

Consalvo, Mia, and Christopher A. Paul. "Welcome to the Discourse of the Real: Constituting the Boundaries of Games and Players," Foundations of Digital Games Conference, Crete, Greece, May 13–17, 2013.

Contestabile, Giordano Bruno. "What Are the Primary Demographics (Gender, Age, Ethnicity, Etc.) of the Average Social Game Enthusiast?" *Quora*, October 28, 2010. http://www.quora.com/What-are-the-primary-demographics-gender-age-ethnicity-etc-of-the-average-social-game-enthusiast.

Cote, Amanda. "'I Can Defend Myself': Women's Strategies for Coping with Harassment while Gaming Online." *Games and Culture* (May 2015): http://journals.sagepub.com/doi/abs/10.1177/1555412015587603.

Cowan, Ruth. *More Work for Mother: The Ironies of Household Technology from the Open Hearth to the Microwave*. New York: Basic Books, 1983.

Cruikshank, Lauren. "Taking Casual Seriously: Game Studies and Nurturing/Neglecting Games." Paper presented at the International Conference on Meaningful Play, East Lansing, Mich., 2014.

Dalla Costa, Mariarosa. "Development and Reproduction." In *Women, Development, and Labor of Reproduction*, edited by Mariarosa Dalla Costa and Giovanna Dalla Costa, 11–46. Trenton, N.J.: Africa World Press, 1999.

Deem, Rosemary. *All Work and No Play? A Study of Women and Leisure*. Philadelphia: Open University Press, 1986.

De Grazia, Victoria. "Introduction." In *The Sex of Things: Gender and Consumption in Historical Perspective*, edited by Ellen Furlough, 1–10. Berkeley: University of California Press, 1996.

Downey, Genesis. "The Here and There of a Femme Cave: An Autoethnographic Snapshot of a Contextualized Girl Gamer Space." *Cultural Studies, Critical Methodologies* 12, no. 3 (2012): 235–41.

Duffy, Brooke Erin. *Remake, Remodel: Women's Magazines in the Digital Age*. Urbana: University of Illinois Press, 2013.

———. "The Romance of Work: Gender and Aspirational Labour in the Digital Culture Industries." *International Journal of Cultural Studies* 19, no. 4 (2016): 441–57.

Duggan, Maeve. "Gaming and Gamers." *Pew Research Center: Internet, Science &*

Tech, December 15, 2015. http://www.pewinternet.org/2015/12/15/gaming-and
-gamers/.

Elias, Norbert. *The Civilizing Process: Sociogenetic and Psychogenetic Investigations.*
Oxford, U.K.: Blackwell, 1939.

Firat, A. Fuat. "Gender and Consumption: Transcending the Feminine?" In *Gender Issues
and Consumer Behavior,* edited by J. A. Costa. London: Sage, 1994.

Flanagan, Mary. *Critical Play: Radical Game Design.* Cambridge, Mass.: MIT Press, 2009.

Flanagan, Mary, and Helen Nissenbaum. *Values at Play in Digital Games.* Cambridge,
Mass.: MIT Press, 2014.

Fortunati, Leopoldina. *The Arcane of Reproduction: Housework, Prostitution, Labor and
Capital.* Translated by Hilary Creek. New York: Autonomedia, 1995.

Foucault, Michel. *Discipline and Punish: The Birth of the Prison.* Translated by Alan
Sheridan. New York: Random House, 1977.

Freeman, David. "Creating Emotion in Games: The Craft and Art of Emotioneering." *ACM
Computers in Entertainment* 2, no. 3 (2004): 1–11.

Friedan, Betty, and Anna Quindlen. *The Feminine Mystique.* New York: Norton, 2001.

Fron, Janine, Tracy Fullerton, Jacquelyn Ford Morie, and Celia Pearce. "The Hegemony
of Play." DiGRA International Conference: Situated Play, Tokyo, September 24–27,
2007.

Fullerton, Tracy, Janine Fron, Celia Pearce, and Jacquelyn Ford Morie. "Getting Girls into
the Game: Toward a 'Virtuous Cycle.'" In *Beyond Barbie and Mortal Kombat: New
Perspectives on Gender and Gaming,* edited by Yasmin B. Kafai, Carrie Heeter, Jill
Denner, and Jennifer Y. Sun, 161–76. Cambridge, Mass.: MIT Press, 2008.

"Funny Old Sega Ads." *ZippyGamer,* July 18, 2010. http://www.zippygamer.com/2010/07
/funny-old-sega-ads-adults-only/.

Gee, James Paul, and Elisabeth R. Hayes. *Women and Gaming: The Sims and 21st Cen-
tury Learning.* New York: Palgrave Macmillan, 2010.

Gill, R., and K. Grint. "The Gender–Technology Relation: Contemporary Theory and Research." In *The Gender–Technology Relation,* edited by R. Gill and K. Grint, 1–28.
London: Taylor & Francis, 1995.

Glos, Jennifer, and Shari Goldin. "An Interview with Brenda Laurel (Purple Moon)." In
From Barbie to Mortal Kombat: Gender and Computer Games, edited by Justine
Cassell and Henry Jenkins, 118–35. Cambridge, Mass.: MIT Press, 1998.

Goldfarb, Andrew. "Nintendo Almost Made a Knitting Add-On for NES." *IGN,* August 30,
2012. http://www.ign.com/articles/2012/08/31/nintendo-almost-made-a-knitting
-add-on-for-nes.

Good, Owen. "Who Are the 'Whales' Driving Free-to-Play Gaming? You'd Be Surprised."
Kotaku, August 25, 2013. http://kotaku.com/who-are-the-whales-driving-free-to
-play-gaming-youd-1197333118.

Graham, Hillary. "Caring: A Labour of Love." In *A Labour of Love: Women, Work and
Caring,* edited by Janet Finch and Dulcie Groves, 13–30. London: Routledge, 1983.

Gray, Kishonna. "Collective Organizing, Individual Resistance, or Asshole Griefers? An
Ethnographic Analysis of Women of Color in Xbox Live." *Ada: A Journal of Gen-*

der and New Media Technology 2 (June 2013). http://adanewmedia.org/2013/06 /issue2-gray/.

———. Race, Gender, and Deviance in Xbox Live: Theoretical Perspectives from the Virtual Margins. New York: Routledge, 2014.

Green, Eileen. "Technology, Leisure, and Everyday Practices." In Virtual Gender, edited by Eileen Green and Alison Adam, 173–88. New York: Routledge, 2001.

Green, Eileen, Sandra Hebron, and Diana Woodward. Women's Leisure, What Leisure? New York: New York University Press, 1990.

Haraway, Donna. Simians, Cyborgs, and Women. New York: Routledge, 1991.

Harris, M. "Feminization of Gaming: Nintendo Makes a Move on Underserved Female Consumer." Edmonton Journal, October 6, 2006.

Harvey, Alison. Gender, Age, and Digital Games in the Domestic Context. New York: Routledge, 2015.

Henderson, Karla A. "One Size Doesn't Fit All: The Meanings of Women's Leisure." Journal of Leisure Research 28, no. 3 (1996): 139–54.

Hepburn, Aden. "Infographic: Social Gaming Demographics 2012." Digital Buzz Blog, July 15, 2012. http://www.digitalbuzzblog.com/infographic-social-gaming-demographics-statistics-2012/.

Hochschild, Arlie Russell. The Managed Heart: Commercialization of Human Feeling. 2nd ed. Berkeley: University of California Press, 1983.

———. The Second Shift. New ed. New York: Penguin Books, 2003.

———. The Time Bind: When Work Becomes Home and Home Becomes Work. New York: Owl Books, 2001.

Holbrook, Morris B., and Robert W. Chestnut. "Play as a Consumption Experience: The Roles of Emotions, Performance, and Personality in the Enjoyment of Games." Journal of Consumer Research 11, no. 2 (1984): 728–39.

Horkheimer, Max, and Theodor Adorno. "The Culture Industry: Enlightenment as Mass Deception." In Media and Cultural Studies: Keyworks, edited by Durham Meenakshi Gigi and Douglas M. Kellner, 41–72. Malden, Mass.: Blackwell, 2002.

Huntemann, Nina B. "Pixel Pinups: Images of Women in Video Games." In Race/Gender/Media, edited by Rebecca Ann Lind, 251–65. Boston: Allyn & Bacon, 2010.

Isbister, Katherine. Better Game Characters by Design: A Psychological Approach. Boston: CRC Press, 2006.

———. How Games Move Us: Emotion by Design. Cambridge, Mass.: MIT Press, 2016.

Jamieson, Kathleen Hall. Beyond the Double Bind: Women and Leadership. New York: Oxford University Press, 1995.

Jansz, Jeroen, Corinne Avis, and Mirjam Vosmeer. "Playing The Sims 2: An Exploration of Gender Differences in Players' Motivations and Patterns of Play." New Media & Society 12, no. 2 (2010): 1–26.

Jarrett, Kylie. Feminism, Labour and Digital Media: The Digital Housewife. New York: Routledge, 2015.

———. "The Relevance of 'Women's Work': Social Reproduction and Immaterial Labor in Digital Media." Television & New Media 15, no. 1 (2013): 14–29.

Jenkins, Henry. "'Complete Freedom of Movement': Video Games as Gendered Play Spaces." In *From Barbie to Mortal Kombat: Gender and Computer Games*, edited by Justine Cassell and Henry Jenkins, 262–47. Cambridge, Mass.: MIT Press, 1998.

Jenson, Jennifer, and Suzanne de Castell. "An Ethnographic Study of Gender and Digital Gameplay." *Feminist Media Studies* 11, no. 2 (2011): 167–79.

———. "Theorizing Gender and Digital Gameplay: Oversights, Accidents and Surprises." *Eludamos: Journal for Computer Game Culture* 2, no. 1 (2008): 15–25.

Jenson, Jennifer, Stephanie Fisher, and Suzanne de Castell. "Disrupting the Gender Order: Leveling Up and Claiming Space in an After-School Video Game Club." *International Journal of Gender, Science and Technology* 3, no. 1 (2011): 148–69.

Johnson, Eric. "A Long Tail of Whales: Half of Mobile Games Money Comes from 0.15 Percent of Players." *Recode*, February 26, 2014. http://recode.net/2014/02/26/a-long-tail-of-whales-half-of-mobile-games-money-comes-from-0-15-percent-of-players/.

Jones, Steven E., and George K. Thiruvathukal. *Codename Revolution: The Nintendo Wii Platform*. Cambridge, Mass.: MIT Press, 2012.

Juul, Jesper. *A Casual Revolution: Reinventing Video Games and Their Players*. Cambridge, Mass.: MIT Press, 2010.

Kafai, Yasmin B. "Video Game Designs by Girls and Boys: Variability and Consistency of Gender Differences." In *From Barbie to Mortal Kombat: Gender and Computer Games*, edited by Justine Cassell and Henry Jenkins, 90–118. Cambridge, Mass.: MIT Press, 1998.

Kato, Michael. "Space Invaders." *Game Informer*, April 2007.

Kennedy, Helen W. "Lara Croft: Feminist Icon or Cyberbimbo? On the Limits of Textual Analysis." *Game Studies: The International Journal of Computer Games Research* 2, no. 2 (2002). http://www.gamestudies.org/0202/kennedy/.

Kent, Steven L. *The Ultimate History of Video Games*. New York: Prima Publishing, 2001.

Kilbourne, Jean. *Can't Buy My Love: How Advertising Changes the Way We Think and Feel*. New York: Touchstone, 1999.

Kocurek, Carly A. *Coin-Operated Americans: Rebooting Boyhood at the Video Game Arcade*. Minneapolis: University of Minnesota Press, 2015.

Kuittinen, Tero. "Kim Kardashian Shocks the App Market." *BGR*, July 11, 2014. http://bgr.com/2014/07/11/kim-kardashian-hollywood-ios-app/.

Lally, Elaine. *At Home with Computers*. New York: Bloomsbury Academic, 2002.

Latour, Bruno. "On Technical Mediation: Philosophy, Sociology, Genealogy." *Common Knowledge* 3, no. 2 (1994): 29–64.

Laurel, Brenda. *Utopian Entrepreneur*. Cambridge, Mass.: MIT Press, 2001.

Law, John. *After Method: Mess in Social Science Research*. New York: Routledge, 2004.

Lazarus, Margaret, Renner Wunderlich, Patricia Stallone, and Joseph Vitagliano. *Killing Us Softly: Advertising's Images of Women*. Cambridge, Mass.: Cambridge Documentary Films, 1979.

Lazzaro, Nicole. "Are Boy Games Even Necessary?" In *Beyond Barbie and Mortal Kombat: New Perspectives on Gender and Gaming*, edited by Yasmin B. Kafai, Carrie Heeter, Jill Denner, and Jennifer Y. Sun, 199–230. Cambridge, Mass.: MIT Press, 2008.

Lee, Kevan. "The Complete Beginner's Guide to Creating Marketing Personas." *Social,*
March 27, 2014. https://blog.bufferapp.com/marketing-personas-beginners-guide.

Lee, Yu-Hao, and Donghee Yvette Wohn. "Are There Cultural Differences in How We Play?
Examining Cultural Effects on Playing Social Network Games." *Computers in Human Behavior* 28, no. 4 (2012): 1307–14.

Liao, Rita. "Kegel Trainer Skea: Play *Temple Run* with Pelvic Floor Muscles." *TechNode,*
July 15, 2014. http://technode.com/2014/07/15/kegel-training-fitbit-skea-imagine
-playing-temple-run-pelvic-floor-muscles/.

Lury, Celia. *Consumer Culture.* Brunswick, N.J.: Rutgers University Press, 1996.

Maines, Rachel P. *The Technology of Orgasm: "Hysteria," the Vibrator, and Women's Sexual Satisfaction.* Baltimore: Johns Hopkins University Press, 2001.

Makuch, E. "Percentage of Female Developers Has More Than Doubled since 2009."
GameSpot, June 24, 2014. http://www.gamespot.com/articles/percentage-of-female
-developers-has-more-than-doubled-since-2009/1100-6420680.

Manovich, Lev. *The Language of New Media.* Cambridge, Mass.: MIT Press, 2002.

Marcotte, Amanda. "Teen Girls Love Video Games, but They're Really Quiet about It." *Slate,*
August 18, 2015. http://www.slate.com/blogs/xx_factor/2015/08/18/teen_girls_play
_video_games_but_they_minimize_their_contact_with_other_players.html.

Martin, Emily. "The Egg and the Sperm: How Science Has Constructed a Romance Based
on Stereotypical Male–Female Roles." *Signs* 16, no. 3 (1991): 485–501.

Marx, Karl. *Critique of Political Economy.* Translated by Maurice Dobbs. New York: International Publishers, 1999.

McCabe, Caitlin. "Hit Kardashian Video Game Lifts Glu Mobile from E-List." *Bloomberg Technology,* July 10, 2004. http://www.bloomberg.com/news/articles/2014-07-10
/hit-kardashian-video-game-lifts-publisher-glu-mobile-from-e-list.

McGee, Micki. *Self-Help, Inc.: Makeover Culture in American Life.* Oxford, U.K.: Oxford
University Press, 2005.

Melby, Leah. "3 Game-Changing New Ways to Shop Online." *Glamour,* April 14, 2015.
http://www.glamour.com/fashion/blogs/dressed/2015/04/best-new-shopping
-apps-sites.

Millar, M. S. *Cracking the Gender Code: Who Rules the Wired World.* Toronto: Second
Story Press, 1998.

Milnes, Hilary. "Move Over Kardashian, This Mobile Game Is Striking a Chord with
Women and Retailers." *Digiday,* April 3, 2015. http://digiday.com/brands/move
-kardashian-mobile-game-striking-chord-women-retailers/.

Modleski, Tania. *Loving with a Vengeance: Mass-Produced Fantasies for Women.* New
York: Routledge, 1982.

Morrissey, Tracie Egan. "Oh God, I Spent $494.04 Playing the *Kim Kardashian: Hollywood*
App." *Jezebel,* July 1, 2014. http://jezebel.com/oh-god-i-spent-494-04-playing-the
-kim-kardashian-holl-1597154346.

Nakamura, Lisa. "Don't Hate the Player, Hate the Game: The Racialization of Labor in
World of Warcraft." *Critical Studies in Media Communication* 26, no. 2 (2009):
128–44.

Nash, Ted. "Are Freemium Apps Killing Game Developers?" *Developer Economics,* Decem-

ber 2, 2014. http://www.developereconomics.com/freemium-apps-killing-game
-developers/.

Norman, Don. *Emotional Design: Why We Love (or Hate) Everyday Things.* New York: Basic Books, 2005.

O'Donnell, Casey. *Developer's Dilemma: The Secret World of Videogame Creators.* Cambridge, Mass.: MIT Press, 2014.

———. "This Is Not a Software Industry." In *The Video Game Industry: Formation, Present State, and Future,* edited by Peter Zackariasson and Timothy L. Wilson, 17–33. New York: Routledge, 2012.

Ouellette, Laurie. "Inventing the Cosmo Girl: Class Identity and Girl-Style American Studies." *Media, Culture & Society* 21, no. 3 (1998): 359–83.

Parkin, Kathleen. *Food Is Love: Advertising and Gender Roles in Modern America.* Philadelphia: University of Pennsylvania Press, 2006.

Paul, Christopher A. *Wordplay and the Discourse of Video Games: Analyzing Words, Design, and Play.* New York: Routledge, 2012.

Pearce, Celia. *Communities of Play: Emergent Cultures in Multiplayer Games and Virtual Worlds.* Cambridge, Mass.: MIT Press, 2009.

Peiss, Kathy Lee. *Hope in a Jar: The Making of America's Beauty Culture.* Philadelphia: University of Pennsylvania Press, 2011.

Perez, Sarah. "In-App Purchase Revenue Hits Record High: Accounts For 76% of U.S. iPhone App Revenue, 90% In Asian Markets." *TechCrunch,* March 28, 2013. http://social.techcrunch.com/2013/03/28/in-app-purchase-revenue-hits-record-high-accounts-for-76-of-u-s-iphone-app-revenue-90-in-asian-markets/.

Pipher, Mary, and Ruth Ross. *Reviving Ophelia: Saving the Selves of Adolescent Girls.* New York: Riverhead Books, 2005.

Pitcher, Jenna. "Glu Mobile Acquires *Diner Dash* Developer PlayFirst." *Polygon,* May 1, 2014. http://www.polygon.com/2014/5/1/5670576/glu-mobile-acquires-diner-dash-developer-playfirst.

Raymond, Janice G. *The Transsexual Empire: The Making of the She-Male.* New York: Teachers College Press, 1994.

Ray, Sheri Graner. *Gender Inclusive Game Design: Expanding the Market.* Hingham, Mass.: Charles River Media, 2004.

Rich, Adrienne. *Of Woman Born: Motherhood as Experience and Institution.* New York: Norton, 1995.

Richard, G. T. "Gender and Gameplay: Research and Future Directions." In *Playing with Virtuality: Theories and Methods of Computer Game Studies,* edited by B. Bigl and S. Stoppe, 269–84. Frankfurt: Peter Lang Academic, 2013.

Riddell, Carol. "Divided Sisterhood: A Critical Review of Janice Raymond's *The Transsexual Empire.*" In *The Transgender Studies Reader,* edited by Susan Stryker and Stephen Whittle, 144–58. New York: Routledge, 2006.

Roberts, Bobby. "Why I'm Done With 'Geek Culture.'" *Portland Mercury,* August 21, 2014. http://www.portlandmercury.com/BlogtownPDX/archives/2014/08/21/why-im-done-with-geek-culture.

Rosewater, Mark. "Timmy, Johnny, and Spike." *Wizards of the Coast,* March 8, 2002.

http://archive.wizards.com/Magic/magazine/article.aspx?x=mtgcom/daily/mr11b.

Royse, Pam, Joon Lee, Baasanjav Undrahbuyan, Mark Hopson, and Mia Consalvo. "Women and Games: Technologies of the Gendered Self." *New Media & Society* 9, no. 4 (2007): 555–76.

Salter, Anastasia, and Bridget Blodgett. "Hypermasculinity and Dickwolves: The Contentious Role of Women in the New Gaming Public." *Journal of Broadcasting & Electronic Media* 56, no. 3 (2012): 401–16.

Sample, Mark. "Virtual Torture: Videogames and the War on Terror." *Game Studies: The International Journal of Computer Games Research* 8, no. 2 (2008). http://www.gamestudies.org/0802/articles/sample.

Sandlin, Jennifer A., and Julie G. Maudlin. "Consuming Pedagogies: Controlling Images of Women as Consumers in Popular Culture." *Journal of Consumer Culture* 12, no. 2 (2012): 175–94.

Sarkeesian, Anita. *Tropes vs. Women in Video Games*. https://feministfrequency.com/tag/tropes-vs-women-in-video-games/.

Schleiner, Anne-Marie. "Does Lara Croft Wear Fake Polygons? Gender and Gender-Role Subversion in Computer Adventure Games." *Leonardo* 34, no. 3 (2001): 221–26.

Schneck, Barbara Findlay. "Freemium: Is the Price Right for Your Company?" *Entrepreneur*, February 6, 2011. http://www.entrepreneur.com/article/218107.

Schonfeld, Erick. "Zynga Raises $29 Million B Round (Led by Kleiner Perkins) and Buys Virtual-World Facebook App *YoVille*." *TechCrunch*, July 22, 2008. http://social.tech crunch.com/2008/07/22/zynga-raises-29-million-b-round-led-by-kleiner-per kins-and-buys-virtual-world-facebook-app-yoville/.

Schüll, Natasha Dow. *Addiction by Design: Machine Gambling in Las Vegas*. Princeton, NJ: Princeton University Press, 2014.

Seppala, Timothy J. "Report: Less Than 1 Percent of Mobile Gamers Responsible for Half of All in-App Purchases." *Engadget*, February 27, 2014. http://www.engadget.com/2014/02/27/swrve-freemium-game-revenue/.

Seufert, Eric Benjamin. "3 Reasons Why *Kim Kardashian: Hollywood* Has Exploded." *Mobile Dev Memo*, July 14, 2014. http://mobiledevmemo.com/3-reasons-kim-kardashian-hollywood-exploded/.

Shaw, Adrienne. "Do You Identify as a Gamer? Gender, Race, Sexuality, and Gamer Identity." *New Media & Society* 14, no. 1 (2012): 28–44.

———. *Gaming at the Edge: Sexuality and Gender at the Margins of Gamer Culture*. Minneapolis: University of Minnesota Press, 2015.

———. "On Not Becoming Gamers: Moving Beyond the Constructed Audience." *Ada: A Journal of Gender, New Media, and Technology* 2 (2013). http://adanewmedia.org/2013/06/issue2-shaw/.

Shinkle, Eugénie. "Video Games, Emotion, and the Six Senses." *Media, Culture & Society* 30, no. 6 (2008): 907–15.

Simon, Bart, Kelly Boudreau, and Mark Silverman. "Two Players: Biography and 'Played Sociality' in *EverQuest*." *Game Studies: The International Journal of Computer*

Games Research 9, no. 1 (2009). http://gamestudies.org/0901/articles/simon_boud reau_silverman.

Sparks, Kira. "6 Tips on Captivating Players from Storm8's Chief Creative Officer." *Vungle*, March 6, 2015. http://vungle.com/blog/2015/03/06/6-tips-on-captivating-players-from-storm8s-chief-creative-officer/.

Spigel, Lynn. "Designing the Smart House: Posthuman Domesticity and Conspicuous Production." *European Journal of Cultural Studies* 8, no. 4 (2005): 403–26.

Subrahmanyam, Kaveri, and Patricia Greenfield. "Computer Games for Girls: What Makes Them Play?" In *From Barbie to Mortal Kombat: Gender and Computer Games*, edited by Justine Cassell and Henry Jenkins, 46–71. Cambridge, Mass.: MIT Press, 1998.

Sullivan, Lou. "A Transvestite Answers a Feminist." In *The Transgender Studies Reader*, edited by Susan Stryker and Stephen Whittle, 159–64. New York: Routledge, 2006.

Takahashi, Dean. "CrowdStar Is All-In on Mobile Gaming for Women with *Covet Fashion*." *VentureBeat*, February 26, 2015. http://venturebeat.com/2015/02/26/crowdstar-is-all-in-on-mobile-gaming-for-women-with-covet-fashion/.

Taylor, T. L. *Play between Worlds: Exploring Online Game Culture*. Cambridge, Mass.: MIT Press, 2006.

———. *Raising the Stakes: e-Sports and the Professionalization of Computer Gaming*. Cambridge, Mass.: MIT Press, 2015.

———. "Review of Sheri Graner Ray's *Gender Inclusive Game Design*." *Game Research: The Art, Business, and Science of Video Games*, May 11, 2006. http://game-research.com/index.php/book-reviews/review-of-shery-graner-rays-gender-inclusive-game-design/.

———. "The Assemblage of Play." *Games and Culture* 4, no. 4 (2009): 331–39.

Terdiman, Daniel. "Why Zynga Ticks Off the Games Industry." *CNET*, April 12, 2010. http://www.cnet.com/news/why-zynga-ticks-off-the-games-industry.

Thompson, Mike. "SponsorPay Reveals New Social/Mobile Demographics." *SocialTimes*, February 12, 2013. http://www.adweek.com/socialtimes/sponsorpay-reveals-socialmobile-demographics/604632.

Thurer, Shari. *The Myths of Motherhood: How Culture Reinvents the Good Mother*. New York: Penguin Books, 2004.

"Today's Primary Shopper." PLMA Consumer Research Study, 2013. http://plma.com/2013PLMA_GfK_Study.pdf?utm_source=GfK+Report+to+Press&utm_campaign=GfK+PR&utm_medium=email.

Tronto, Joan C. "Women and Caring: What Can Feminists Learn about Morality from Caring." In *Gender/Body/Knowledge: Feminist Reconstructions of Being and Knowing*, edited by Alison M. Jaggar and Susan R. Bordo, 172–87. New Brunswick, N.J.: Rutgers University Press, 1992.

Tuana, Nancy. "The Speculum of Ignorance: The Women's Health Movement and the Epistemologies of Ignorance." *Hypatia* 21, no. 3 (2006): 1–19.

Turkle, Sherry. "Whither Psychoanalysis in Computer Culture?" *Psychoanalytic Psychology* 21, no. 1 (2004): 16–30.

Turow, Joseph, and Nora Draper. "Industry Conceptions of Audience in the Digital Space: A Research Agenda." *Cultural Studies* 28, no. 4 (2014): 643–56.

Vanderhoef, John. "Casual Threats: The Feminization of Casual Video Games." *Ada: A Journal of Gender, New Media, and Technology* 2 (June 2013). http://adanewmedia.org/2013/06/issue2-vanderhoef/.

Veblen, Thorstein. "Conspicuous Consumption." In *The Consumer Society Reader*, edited by Juliet Schor and Douglas B. Holt. New York: New Press, 2000.

Wajcman, Judy. *Feminism Confronts Technology*. University Park: Penn State University Press, 1991.

———. *Technofeminism*. Malden, Mass.: Polity Press, 2004.

Walter, Damien. "Forget Iron Man–Child: Let's Fight the White Maleness of Geek Culture." *The Guardian*, January 31, 2014. http://www.theguardian.com/books/booksblog/2014/jan/31/iron-man-white-male-geek-culture-fantasy-science-fiction.

Winn, Jillian, and Carrie Heeter. "Gaming, Gender, and Time: Who Makes Time to Play?" *Sex Roles* 61, nos. 1–2 (2009): 1–13.

Wirman, Hanna. "Playing by Doing and Players' Localization of *The Sims 2*." *Television & New Media* 15, no. 1 (2014): 58–67.

———. "Princess Peach Loves Your Enemies, Too." In *Game Love: Essays on Play and Affection*, edited by Jessica Enevold and Esther MacCallum-Stewart, 131–48. Jefferson, N.C.: McFarland, 2015.

Wissinger, Elizabeth. *This Year's Model: Fashion, the Media, and the Making of Glamour*. New York: New York University Press, 2015.

Wolf, Naomi. *The Beauty Myth: How Images of Beauty Are Used against Women*. New York: Harper Perennial, 1991.

Wosk, Julie. *Women and the Machine: Representations from the Spinning Wheel to the Electronic Age*. Baltimore: Johns Hopkins University Press, 2003.

Wyman, Michael Thornton. *Making Great Games: An Insider's Guide to Designing and Developing the World's Greatest Video Games*. Boston: Focal Press, 2010.

XEO Design. "*Diner Dash* and the People Factor." 2005. http://www.xeodesign.com/diner-dash-and-the-people-factor/.

Zagal, Jose, and Michael Mateas. "Time in Video Games: A Survey and Analysis." *Simulation & Gaming* 41, no. 6 (2010): 844–68.

Zukin, Sharon, and Jennifer Smith Maguire. "Consumers and Consumption." *Annual Review of Sociology* 30, no. 1 (2004): 173–97.

GAMEOGRAPHY

Many of the games listed in this gameography are older games in the "casual" category. Unfortunately, many of the developers and publishers involved in these games have since gone out of business, making it occasionally difficult to obtain precise information for all of the games. I have, however, gone to great lengths to make sure that the information below is as current and accurate as possible. The publication dates listed reflect the year a game first came to market, not any subsequent updates, eschewing different entries for future platforms. For example, *Sally's Salon* was first developed as a computer game in 2007, and later developed as an iOS game. The date listed for the entry is 2007, which is only the initial release of that game. Obviously, it was not developed as an iOS game until later, although the gameography does not reflect that.

America's Test Kitchen: Let's Get Cooking. Nintendo DS. Developed by indieszero. Nintendo of America, 2010.

Angry Birds. Android, iOS. Developed by Rovio Mobile. Clickgamer Technologies, 2009. Numerous other versions have been developed for a variety of mobile, console, web-based, and other platforms.

Animal Crossing. GameCube. Developed by Nintendo EAD. Nintendo, 2001. Subsequent versions of this game have appeared on the Nintendo DS and Nintendo Wii.

Assassin's Creed: Unity. PlayStation 4, Windows, Xbox One. Developed and published by Ubisoft, 2014.

Avenue Flo. OS X, Windows. Developed and published by PlayFirst, 2009.

Baby Pals. Nintendo DS. Developed and published by THQ, 2008.

Babysitting Mania. Nintendo DS, OS X, Windows. Developed by Gogii Games. Majesco, 2008.

Barbie Fashion Designer. OS X, Windows. Developed by Digital Domain. Mattel Media, 1996.

Bejeweled. J2ME (mobile), OS X, Palm OS, Web, Windows, Windows Mobile. Developed and published by PopCap, 2000. Various versions and sequels have subsequently appeared on many platforms.

Black & White. OS X, Windows. Developed by Lionhead Studios. Electronic Arts, 2001.

Bubble Mania. Android, iOS. Developed and published by Storm8 Studios, 2012.

Burger Bustle. iOS, OS X, Windows. Developed and published by Sulus, 2010.

Burger Shop. Android, iOS, OS X, Windows. Developed by GoBit. Big Fish Games, 2007.

BurgerTime. Coin-op. Developed by Data East. Mattel Electronics, 1982. Numerous versions have appeared on several different platforms over several decades.

Busy Bea's Halftime Hustle. OS X, Windows. Developed by Gold Sun Games. Big Fish Games, 2011.

Cake Mania. BREW, J2ME, OS X, Nintendo DS, Palm OS, Windows. Developed and published by Sandlot Games, 2006.

Cake Shop. OS X. Windows. Published by EleFun Games, 2009.

Call of Duty. OS X, PlayStation, Windows, Xbox. Developed by Infinity Ward. Activision, 2003. Sequels to this game have appeared for numerous platforms.

Campus Life. iOS. Developed and published by Pocket Gems, 2012.

Candy Crush Saga. Android, iOS, Web, Windows Phone. Developed by Midasplayer AB. King.com, 2012.

Candy Crush Soda Saga. Android, iOS, Web, Windows Phone. Developed and published by King.com, 2014.

Castle Story. Android, iOS. Developed and published by Storm8 Studios, 2012.

CastleVille. Android, iOS, Web. Developed and published by Zynga, 2011.

Celebrity Girl. iOS. Published by Dreamheart, 2013.

Celebrity Mommy's Newborn Baby Doctor. iOS. Published by App Whisperer, 2015.

Centipede. Coin-op. Developed and published by Atari, 1981. Multiple versions of this game have appeared on several subsequent platforms.

CityVille. Web. Developed and published by Zynga, 2010.

Clash of Clans. Android, iOS. Developed and published by Supercell Oy, 2012.

Cooking Academy. iOS, OS X, Windows. Developed and published by Fugazo, 2008.

Cooking Dash. iOS, OS X, Windows. Developed by Aliasworlds Entertainment. PlayFirst, 2008. Subsequent versions have been developed for several platforms. In 2014 Glu Mobile acquired PlayFirst and subsequently released new versions of this game.

Cooking Mama. Nintendo DS. Developed by Office Create. Taito, 2006. Sequels have been developed for iOS, Nintendo DS, and Wii platforms.

Cosmopolitan Virtual Makeover. Linux, Macintosh, Windows. Published by Mindscape, 1999.

Costume Chaos. OS X, Windows. Developed and published by Reflexive Entertainment, 2008.

Covet Fashion. iOS. Developed and published by CrowdStar, 2014.

Cow Clicker. Web. Developed and published by Ian Bogost, 2010.

Dairy Dash. OS X, Windows. Developed and published by PlayFirst, 2008. In 2014 Glu Mobile acquired PlayFirst and subsequently released new versions of this game.

Dance Dance Revolution. Coin-op, PlayStation. Developed by KCE Tokyo. Konami, 1999. Sequels have been made for both home consoles and coin-ops.

Deco Fever. OS X, Windows. Developed and published by BlooBuzz Studios, 2014.

Delicious Emily's Home Sweet Home. Android, iOS, OS X, Windows. Developed by Blue Giraffe. GameHouse, 2015.

Delicious Emily's Hopes and Fears. Android, iOS, OS X, Windows. Developed by Blue Giraffe. GameHouse, 2015.

Delicious Emily's New Beginnings. Android, iOS, OS X, Windows. Developed by Blue Giraffe. GameHouse, 2014.

Delicious Emily's True Love. Android, iOS, OS X, Windows. Developed and published by GameHouse, 2012.

Delicious Emily's Wonder Wedding. Android, iOS, OS X, Windows. Developed and published by GameHouse, 2013.

Depression Quest. Linux, OS X, Web, Windows. Developed and published by Zoë Quinn, 2013.

Diamond Quest! iOS. Developed and published by Storm8 Studios, 2014.

Diaper Dash. OS X, Windows. Developed by Zemnott, PlayFirst, 2009.

Diner Dash. OS X, Windows. Developed by GameLab. PlayFirst, 2003. The original game has also appeared on various other mobile and web-based platforms. In 2014 Glu Mobile acquired PlayFirst and subsequently released new versions of this game.

Diner Dash 2: Restaurant Rescue. Android, Blackberry, OS X, Windows, Windows Mobile. Developed and published by PlayFirst, 2006.

Diner Dash: boom! OS X, Windows. Developed and published by PlayFirst, 2010.

Diner Dash: Flo on the Go. Blackberry, BREW, J2ME, OS X, Windows. Developed and published by PlayFirst, 2006.

Diner Dash: Flo through Time. OS X, Windows. Developed and published by PlayFirst, 2007.

Diner Dash: Hometown Hero. OS X, Windows. Developed and published by PlayFirst, 2007.

DinerTown Detective Agency. OS X, Windows. Developed by Absolutist. PlayFirst, 2009.

DinerTown Tycoon. OS X, Windows. Developed and published by PlayFirst, 2009.

Doggie Dash. OS X, Windows. Developed and published by PlayFirst, 2008. In 2014, Glu Mobile acquired PlayFirst and subsequently released new versions of this game.

Doom. PlayStation, Sega Saturn. Developed and published by Williams Entertainment, 1995.

Dream Day Honeymoon. OS X, Windows. Developed by Oberon Media. iWin.com, 2007.

Dream Day Wedding. Blackberry, J2ME, OS X, Windows. Developed by Oberon Media. Pogo.com, 2007.

Egg Baby. Android. iOS. Developed and published by Nix Hydra, 2014.

EnchantU. Android, iOS. Developed and published by Glu Mobile, 2012.

Episode: Choose Your Story. Android, iOS. Developed and published by Pocket Gems, 2013.

EverQuest. OS X, Windows. Developed by Verant Interactive. 989 Studios, 1999.

Fallout. OS X, Windows. Developed and published by Black Isle Studios, 1997. Subsequent versions of this game have appeared in several iterations, with new narratives and scenarios on a variety of platforms via Interplay Entertainment.

Farm Frenzy. Android, BlackBerry, iOS, PlayStation 3, PSP, Symbian, Windows. Developed by Melesta. Alawar Entertainment, 2007. Subsequent versions of the game have been developed for several platforms.

FarmVille. Web. Developed and published by Zynga, 2009. Also ported to iOS.

FarmVille 2: Country Escape. Android, iOS, OS X, Web, Windows Phone. Developed and published by Zynga, 2014.

Fashion Craze. Windows. Developed by Five-BN. Alawar Entertainment, 2007.

Fashion Dash. OS X, Windows. Developed by Funlime. PlayFirst, 2008.

Fashion Rush. OS X, Windows. Developed by Ovogame. Big Fish Games, 2006.

Fearful Tales: Hansel and Gretel. Android, iOS, OS X, Windows. Developed by Eipix Entertainment. Big Fish Games, 2013.

Fever Frenzy. OS X, Windows. Developed by Legacy Interactive and Rainbow Creatures. Published by Legacy Interactive, 2009.

Fitness Bustle: Energy Boost. OS X, Windows. Developed and published by Big Fish Games, 2013.

Fitness Dash. OS X, Windows. Developed by Sarbakan. PlayFirst, 2008.

Fitness Frenzy. OS X, Windows. Developed by Goggi Games. Big Fish Games, 2008.

FooPets. Web. Developed and published by FooMojo, 2008.

FrontierVille. Web. Developed and published by Zynga, 2010. The name of this game was changed to *The Pioneer Trail* in 2011.

Gone Home. Linux, OS X, PlayStation 4, Windows, Xbox One. Developed and published by The Fullbright Company, 2013.

GoPets: Vacation Island. Nintendo DS. Developed by 1st Playable Productions and Engine Software. Konami, 2008.

Gourmania. Android, iOS, Windows. Developed by Butterfly iSoft. Alawar Entertainment, 2008.

Grand Theft Auto III. Android, iOS, OS X, PlayStation 2, Windows, Xbox. Developed by DMA Design. Rockstar Games, 2001.

Grand Theft Auto IV. PlayStation 3, Windows, Xbox 360. Developed by Rockstar North. Rockstar Games, 2008.

Grim Legends: The Forsaken Bride. Android, OS X, Windows, Windows Phone. Developed by Artifex Mundi. Big Fish Games, 2014.

Grim Tales: The Bride. OS X, Windows. Developed by Elephant Games. Big Fish Games, 2011.

Grim Tales: The Stone Queen. OS X, Windows. Developed by Elephant Games. Big Fish Games, 2012.

Halo: Combat Evolved. Windows, Xbox. Developed by Bungie. Microsoft Studios, 2001.

Hamsterz Life. Nintendo DS. Developed by MTO, Digital Kids. Ubisoft, 2006.

Harlequin Presents: Hidden Objects of Desire. Macintosh, OS X. Developed by GameMill Entertainment. Big Fish Games, 2009.

Horsez. Nintendo DS. Developed by Lexis Numerique, SA, Virtual Toys, SL. Ubisoft, 2006.

Hospital Haste. Macintosh, OS X. Developed by Artifex Mundi. Big Fish Games, 2008.

Hospital Hustle. Macintosh, OS X. Developed and published by GameInvest, SA, 2008.

Hotel Dash: Suite Success. iOS, OS X, Windows. Developed by Kef Sensei. PlayFirst, 2009.

Hungry Babies Mania. Android, iOS. Developed and published by Storm8 Studios, 2015.

Ice Cream Craze: Natural Hero. OS X, Windows. Developed by Game Fools. Big Fish Games, 2011.

iLive. Android, iOS. Developed and published by LGD Studio, 2015.

Iron Chef America: Supreme Cuisine. Nintendo DS, Wii. Developed by Black Lantern Studios. Destineer, 2008.

Island Tribe 4. OS X, Windows. Developed by Realore Studios. Big Fish Games, 2012.

Jane's Hotel. Android, iOS, OS X, PlayStation 3, PSP, Windows. Developed and published by Realore Studios, 2007.

JoJo's Fashion Show. Windows. Developed by GameLab. GSP, 2008.

Katy Perry: Pop. Android, iOS. Developed and published by Glu Mobile, 2015.

Kim Kardashian: Hollywood. Android, iOS, OS X, Web. Developed by Blammo Games. Glu Mobile, 2014.

Kinectimals. Xbox 360. Developed by Frontier Developments. Microsoft Game Studios, 2010.

Kitchen Scramble. Android, iOS. Developed and published by RockYou, 2014.

Legend of Zelda: The Windwalker. GameCube, Wii U. Developed by Nintendo EAD. Nintendo, 2002.

Life Quest 2: Metropoville. iOS, OS X, Windows. Developed and published by Big Fish Games, 2012.

Lindsay Lohan's The Price of Fame. Android, iOS. Developed and published by Space Inch, 2014.

Love and Death: Bitten. OS X, Windows. Developed and published by PlayFirst, 2010.

Love and Hip Hop. iOS, Android. Developed and published by Behaviour Interactive, 2016.

Love Rocks Shakira. Android, iOS. Developed and published by Rovio Entertainment, 2015.

Lunch Food Maker. Android, iOS. Developed and published by Crazy Cats Media, 2012.

Magic Life. OS X, Windows. Developed by Meridian 93. Big Fish Games, 2010.

Metal Gear Solid. PlayStation. Developed by Konami Computer Entertainment Japan. Konami, 1998.

Milkshake Maker. Android, iOS. Developed and published by Crazy Cats Media, 2015.

Monument Valley. Android, iOS, Windows Phone. Developed and published by Ustwo Studio, 2014.

Mortal Kombat. Coin-op. Developed and published by Midway Games, 1992.

Ms. Pac Man. Coin-op. Developed and published by Bally/Midway Manufacturing, 1982. Subsequent versions of the game have been developed for several platforms.

My Baby (Virtual Pet). iOS. Developed and published by Anton Tonev, 2014.

My Boo. Android, iOS. Developed and published by Tapps Tecnologia da Informacao LTDA, 2015.

Myst. Windows. Developed by Cyan. Broderbund Software, 1993. Versions of the game were later made for a variety of platforms.

Mysteries of the Ancients: Deadly Cold. OS X, Windows. Developed by Mariaglorum. Big Fish Games, 2015.

Mystery Case Files: Ravenhearst. OS X, Nintendo 3DS, Windows. Developed and published by Big Fish Games, 2006.

Mystery Case Files: Return to Ravenhearst. Android, iOS, OS X, Nintendo 3DS, Windows. Developed and published by Big Fish Games, 2008.

Mystery Chronicles: Betrayals of Love. OS X, Windows. Developed by Lazy Turtle Studios. Big Fish Games, 2011.

Mystery Tales: The Lost Hope. iOS, OS X, Windows. Developed by Domini Games. Big Fish Games, 2013.

Nanny Mania. iOS, OS X. Developed by Toybox Games. Gogii Games, 2007.

Neko Atsume. Android, iOS. Developed and published by HitPoint, 2014.

Nintendogs. Nintendo DS. Developed by Nintendo EAD. Nintendo of America, 2005.

Panda Pop. Android, iOS, Web, Windows. Developed by Jam City. SGN, 2015.

Parking Dash. OS X, Windows. Developed by Kef Sensei. PlayFirst, 2008.

Personal Trainer: Cooking. Nintendo DS. Developed by indieszero. Nintendo, 2008.

Polar Pop Mania. Android, iOS. Developed and published by Storm8 Studios, 2015.

Pong. Coin-op. Developed and published by Atari, 1972. Versions of this game have been remade for several platforms.

PuppetShow: Destiny Undone. OS X, Windows. Developed by ERS Game Studios. Big Fish Games, 2013.

PuppetShow: The Mystery of Joyville. Android, iOS, OS X, Windows. Developed by ERS Game Studios. Big Fish Games, 2009.

Purr Pals. Nintendo DS. Developed by Crave Entertainment and Brain Toys. Crave Entertainment, 2007.

Quake. Amiga, DOS, Linux, Nintendo 64, OS X, Sega Saturn, Windows, Zeebo. Developed by id Software. GT Interactive, 1996.

Ranch Rush. iOS, OS X, Web, Windows. Developed by Aliaswords Entertainment. Fresh-Games, 2008.

Redemption Cemetery: The Island of the Lost. iOS, OS X, Windows. Developed by ERS Game Studios. Big Fish Games, 2013.

Rescue Frenzy. OS X, Windows. Developed by Melesta. Alawar Games, 2011.

Restaurant Story 2. Android, iOS. Developed and published by Storm8 Studios, 2014.

Riddles of Fate: Into Oblivion. iOS, OS X, Windows. Developed by Elephant Games. Big Fish Games, 2013.

Rockett's New School. OS X, Windows. Developed and published by Purple Moon, 1997.

Roller Rush. Windows. Developed and published by Toybox Games, 2005.

Sally's Salon. BlackBerry, iOS, OS X, Nintendo DS, Windows. Developed and published by GamesCafe.com, 2007.

Second Life. Linux, OS X, Windows. Developed and published by Linden Research, 2003.

Secret Paths in the Forest. OS X, Windows. Developed and published by Purple Moon, 1997.

Shopaholic World. Android, iOS. Developed by Spil Games. Mobile Pie, 2015.

Shopmania. Windows. Developed by Brighter Minds. iWin, 2008.

Shopping Mall. Android, iOS, Windows Phone. Developed by Stark Apps GmbH. Modern Stark Games, 2013.

Sid Meier's Civilization. Amiga, Atari ST, DOS, Macintosh, PC-98, PlayStation, SNES, Windows. Developed by MPS Labs. MicroProse Software, 1991. Several subsequent versions of the game have appeared on many platforms.

SimCity 2000. DOS, OS X, Windows. Developed and published by Maxis Software, 1996.

The Sims. OS X, Windows. Developed by Maxis Software. Electronic Arts, 2000. Several sequels and bonus packs have been developed for this game.

Stardom: The A-List. Android, iOS. Developed and published by Glu Mobile, 2011.

Style Quest. Windows. Developed and published by Dare to Dream, 2015.

Super Mario Bros. Coin-op. Developed and published by Nintendo Co., 1985. Several versions of the game and sequels have appeared on many Nintendo platforms.

Supermarket Management 2. Android, iOS, OS X, Windows. Developed by Playful Age. G5 Games, 2013.

Super Monkey Ball 2. GameCube. Developed by Amusement Vision. Sega Corporation, 2002.

Super Princess Peach. Nintendo DS. Developed and published by Nintendo Australia, 2005.

Surface: The Noise She Couldn't Make. OS X, Windows. Developed by Elephant Games. Big Fish Games, 2012.

Temple Run. Android, iOS. Developed and published by Imangi Studios, 2011.

Tetris. PC. Developed by Alexey Pajitnov / AcademySoft. Spectrum Holobyte, 1986. Various versions have been developed and popularized on many other platforms.

Texas Holdem Poker. Android, iOS, Web. Developed and published by Zynga Games, 2008.

Threadsteading. Singer CE-400 Futura. Developed by Disney Research Pittsburgh, 2016.

Tomb Raider. Game Boy Color. Developed by Core Design. Eidos Interactive, 2000.

Turbo Subs. OS X, Windows. Developed by Aliasworlds Entertainment. Oberon Media, 2008.

Uru: Ages Beyond Myst. Windows. Developed by Cyan Worlds. Ubisoft, 2003.

Wedding Dash. Android, BlackBerry, iOS, Nintendo DS, OS X, Windows. Developed by ImaginEngine. PlayFirst, 2007. Subsequent versions have been developed for several platforms. In 2014 Glu Mobile acquired PlayFirst and subsequently released new versions of this game.

What's Cooking: Jamie Oliver. Nintendo DS. Developed and published by Atari, 2008.

Wii Fit. Wii. Developed by Nintendo EAD. Nintendo of America, 2008.

Words with Friends. Android, iOS, Web, Windows. Developed and published by Newtoy, 2009.

World of Warcraft. OS X, Windows. Developed and published by Blizzard Entertainment, 2004. Several updates and expansions continue to be developed for this game.

Youda Jewel Shop 2. OS X, Windows. Developed and published by Youda Games, 2012.

YoVille (later *YoWorld*). Web. Developed and published by Tall Tree Games (later Zynga), 2008.

INDEX

Episode: Choose Your Story, 140
ethnicity, 30, 37, 40, 130, 157, 166, 168, 176. *See also* whiteness
EverQuest, 10–11, 116
exergaming, 29, 56, 162, 164
EyeToy, 161, 162

Facebook, 1, 14, 45, 79, 96, 117
fairy tales. *See* game thematic elements
Fallout, 6
families, x, xi, 7, 9, 11, 13, 20, 21, 44, 50, 61, 64, 74, 89, 90, 91, 96, 97, 98, 101, 108, 112, 117, 119, 122, 123, 133, 140, 162–63
Farmville. See Ville games
fashion. *See* game thematic elements
Fearful Tales: Hansel and Gretel, 106
feminine style, 5, 12, 15, 43, 176
femininity, 2, 4, 5, 12, 14, 15, 16, 24, 26, 32, 38, 40, 41, 42, 43, 44, 48, 54, 55, 62, 82, 86, 87, 94, 96, 97, 98, 99, 101, 110, 112, 115, 122, 129, 130, 138, 147, 148, 158, 159, 164, 166, 176
feminism, xii, 17, 22, 101, 158, 159, 160, 176, 177, 179; feminist game studies, 16–19, 27; feminist leisure studies, 19–22; intersectional, xi, 16, 19, 28, 37, 147, 160, 167, 171–72, 176; Marxist, 96; popular, 141, 159; second-wave, 58, 61, 175; techno-, 26–27
fitness. *See* game thematic elements
Flanagan, Mary, 34–35, 36
food, 29, 54, 68, 74, 76, 77, 111–12, 113, 126, 144, 145–48, 161
Frag Dolls, 10
Freeman, David, 92
freemium/free-to-play (F2P), 7, 29, 54, 84, 123, 125, 127, 132, 138–40, 143, 147, 178. *See also* consumerism; currency
frenzy, 86, 100
FooPets, 109
Foucault, Michel, 152–57, 158

Furbies, 109–10

game: consoles, xii, 1, 2, 8, 9, 12, 18, 39, 46, 47, 125, 155, 162, 163, 165
game controllers, 44, 70, 93, 119, 121, 149, 150–51, 155, 161–65
game design, 5, 6, 10, 16, 17, 20, 23, 24, 28, 29, 30, 32, 33, 36, 37–40, 41–56, 92, 93, 94, 96, 139, 161; categories, 42–56; designers, xii, 17, 18, 24, 31, 33, 34, 35, 36, 40, 41–56, 57, 66, 80, 92, 99, 118, 131, 133, 149, 155, 185n5; gender inclusivity in, 17, 37–40
GamerGate, xii–xiii, 12–13, 16, 173, 174
gamer identity, ix, xi, 12, 57, 81, 119, 138, 155, 163; feminine, xii, 5, 6, 10, 15, 17–18, 42, 117, 133, 139, 141, 157, 162, 166, 171, 172; masculine, xii, 5, 8, 11, 12, 16, 18, 32, 42, 148; non-identifying, xii, 18, 174, 178; and toxic gamer culture, 18. *See also* GamerGate
GameStop (store), 121–22
game thematic elements, 43–44, 51; animals, 50, 51, 111–12, 113–15, 166; baby, 86, 109, 113, 119, 192n54; bucolic, 7, 14, 39, 43, 45, 56, 62, 64, 79, 80, 81, 82, 83, 92, 117, 118, 170; caregiving, 29, 90, 91, 92, 98, 107–12, 115, 117, 119; cooking, 43, 66–72, 73, 76, 92, 108–9, 126, 145–48, 165, 167; dance, 44, 151, 162; fairy tales, 43, 68, 106; fashion, 10, 39–40, 43, 47, 50, 54, 56, 68, 77, 123, 126, 127, 130, 132–38, 139, 140, 141, 143–45, 148, 161, 166–67; fitness, 13, 44, 56, 68, 73, 162, 164; mystery, 7, 14, 43, 44, 56, 103–7, 171; shopping, 15, 29, 39, 40, 77, 123, 128, 129, 132–38, 139, 140, 145; supernatural, 43, 44, 72, 77–78, 103–7
gamification, 74, 77, 150
geeks, 7–8
gender: cis-, xi, 6, 8, 30, 58, 148, 150, 167, 171, 172, 178; diversity, 2, 37, 56, 147;

and game design, ix, x, 5, 9–13, 18, 32, 33, 37–40, 41, 42, 45, 46, 47, 48, 50, 53–56, 60, 84, 92, 101, 110, 112, 127, 128, 130, 148, 157, 163, 168, 171; inclusivity, 19, 37–40, 41, 50, 132, 140, 162; leisure, 4, 5, 19–22, 46, 48, 56; stereotypes, 23, 25, 29, 65, 83, 86, 90, 96, 97, 99, 100, 101, 110, 126, 131, 132, 133, 149, 157, 162; technology, 25–27; transgender, 159–60
genres, 4, 5, 14, 15, 23, 29, 32, 33, 34, 39, 43, 56, 61, 62, 66, 67, 72–79, 85, 86, 92, 103, 104, 106, 113, 146, 147, 161, 176, 178
Glu Mobile, 65, 67, 68, 79, 138, 140, 141, 142, 168, 169, 170. *See also Kim Kardashian: Hollywood*
Gone Home, xiii
Gourmania, 86
Graham, Hillary, 97
Grand Theft Auto: III, 154; *IV*, 51, 53, 71
Gray, Kishonna, 10, 19
Greenfield, Patricia, 133
Grim Legends, 104
Grim Tales, 104, 106

Hamsterz Life, 109
hardcore games, xii, xiii, 11, 12, 13–16, 19, 39, 42, 46, 165. *See also* casual games
Harlequin Presents: Hidden Objects of Desire, 107
Harvey, Alison, 11, 13, 61, 120, 162
Heber, Nicole, 94, 110–11
Henderson, Karla A., 21–22
hidden object games, 7, 14, 29, 43, 46, 48, 50, 56, 92, 103–7, 113, 123, 131, 132, 171, 176
Hochschild, Arlie Russell, 20, 61, 64, 66, 95, 100
Horsez, 109
human computer interaction, 93
Hungry Babies Mania, 7, 113, 115, 166, 178
Huntemann, Nina, 18

hysteria, 29, 85–87, 90, 161

indie games, xii, xiii, 13, 35
intersectionality. *See* feminism: intersectional
invest/express games, ix, 14, 29, 43, 56, 57, 62, 64, 65, 67, 72, 78, 79–83, 85, 86, 111, 118, 166, 192n46
invisibility, 103, 107, 148, 171–72, 175, 176
iOS games, 79, 109, 136, 137, 178
Isbister, Katherine, 92–93, 94, 112
Island Tribe, 62, 65, 77

Jamieson, Kathleen Hall, 159, 161
Jarrett, Kylie, 95–96
Jennifer (imaginary player), 31, 57–58, 171–72, 176
Jenson, Jennifer, 18
Jones, Steven E., 162, 163

Katy Perry: Pop, 65, 140, 168, 169, 170, 178
kegels, 149
Kennedy, Helen, W., 19
Kilbourne, Jean, 158
Kim Kardashian: Hollywood, 7, 14, 29, 32, 42, 45, 46, 47, 50, 54, 56, 62, 64, 65, 67, 80, 81, 83, 118, 119, 124, 132, 138, 140–45, 146, 155, 166, 168–69, 170, 171, 172, 176, 178, 190n21, 192n54, 193n43, 193n44, 195n32
Kinect, 152, 155, 161, 162, 163. *See also* Xbox
Kinectimals, 110–11
Kocurek, Carly, 5, 9, 32

labor: affective, 29, 74, 95, 96, 115, 116, 117, 118, 119, 136, 147; aspirational, 145; domestic, xi, 2, 20, 90, 96, 98, 103, 107; emotional, ix–x, 29, 74, 90, 91, 92, 94–99, 100, 101, 102, 103, 104, 106, 107, 109, 110, 111, 112, 115, 116, 117, 118, 119, 136, 175, 176; glamour, 133, 136; immaterial, 95–96, 117, 136;

productive consumption, 128, 129, 130, 133, 140

PuppetShow, 104, 106

purchasing mechanics, 29, 123. *See also* freemium/free-to-play (F2P)

Purple Moon, 10

Purr Pals, 109

puzzle games, 14, 29, 46, 56, 70, 80, 81, 103, 104, 105, 107, 112–16, 131, 137, 140, 166, 173

Quinn, Zoë, xii, xiii, 13

Ray, Sheri Graner, 37–40, 41, 44, 46, 48, 50, 51, 56, 178

Ready Player One, 7–8

resource management games, 77–78. *See also* time management games

Rich, Adrienne, 97–98

Rockett's New School, 10

romance, 4, 15, 44, 102, 104, 106, 107, 119

Sarkeesian, Anita, xii, 13, 19

Schleiner, Anne-Marie, 18

Second Life, 168, 170

second shift, 20, 61, 64, 66. *See also* third shift

Secret Paths in the Forest, 10

sexuality, xiii, 19, 30, 37, 157, 165, 168, 170, 176

Schüll, Natasha Dow, 84

Sega, 9, 149–50

Shaw, Adrienne, 12, 18, 174, 195n3

Shinkle, Eugénie, 93–94

Shopmania, 77, 86, 136–37

shopping. *See* game thematic elements

Shopping Mall, 136–37

Sid Meier's Civilization, 77, 78

Sims, The, 11, 92, 112, 136

Skea, 149–52, 164

slenderness, 158, 166, 167

social networking games, 14, 29, 92, 112, 116–19, 192n46. *See also* Facebook; *Ville* games

speed. *See* time

Stardom: The A-List, 140

Steam, xii

STEM, 10, 17, 27

stereotypes, 2, 3, 5, 6, 13, 16, 22, 23, 25, 26, 29, 30, 42, 44, 47, 48, 90, 95, 96, 97, 98, 130, 133, 134, 140. *See also* gender

Storm8 Studios, 31, 79, 114, 115, 171

Style Quest, 134

Subrahmanyam, Kaveri, 133

Super Mario Bros., 9

Supermarket Management 2, 74

Super Monkey Ball 2, 93

supernatural. *See* game thematic elements

Super Princess Peach, 94

Surface: The Noise She Couldn't Make, 92, 103, 104–5, 106

Tamagotchi, 109, 112

Taylor, T. L., 11, 17, 23–24, 38, 152, 155–56

Texas Holdem Poker, 117

themes. *See* game thematic elements

third shift, 66, 84. *See also* second shift

Thiruvathukal, George K., 162, 163

Threadsteading, 185n5

Thurer, Shari, 159

time: anxiety, 20, 85–87; clock, 83–85; elasticity, 67, 84–85, 156; game-world time, 63–64, 66, 79, 85; monotony, 40, 61, 72, 74, 78, 154, 156; real-world time, 22, 63–64, 66, 79, 80, 83, 84, 85; speed, 65, 68, 73, 80, 85–87; temporal frames, 64, 66, 85; temporality, 62, 63, 80, 85. *See also* leisure

time management games, ix, 14, 28, 29, 43, 56, 61, 62, 63, 64–66, 67–70, 72–79, 81, 82, 83–85, 87, 92, 99–103, 104, 112, 118, 136, 146, 156, 161, 166, 176; time–people management games, 72–79; time–product management games, 72–79; time-resource management games, 72–79. *See also Dash* games time management products, 64–65, 70, 72, 73, 156

transgender. *See* gender

Tronto, Joan C., 96–97, 109

Tuana, Nancy, 151

Turbo Subs, 65, 76, 85

Vanderhoef, John, 14, 55

Veblen, Thorstein, 127, 130

video game industry, ix, xi, xii, xiii, 1, 2, 4, 5, 6, 7, 8, 9–13, 14, 15, 16–17, 19, 22, 23, 24, 27, 30, 31–34, 35, 36, 37, 39, 40, 41, 42, 48, 50, 56, 57–58, 62, 65, 67, 73, 78, 80, 86, 94, 118, 123, 124, 138, 139, 152, 163, 172, 173, 174, 177, 178

Ville games, 46, 62, 79, 171; *CastleVille*, 79; *CityVille*, 65, 79; *FarmVille*, 7, 14, 39, 45, 46, 56, 62, 64, 65, 79, 81, 83, 92, 118, 170, 192n46; *FarmVille 2*, 81, 82, 117, 118; *FrontierVille*, 79; *YoVille*, 79. *See also* Facebook; social networking games; Zynga

virtual pets, 109–11

virtual reality, 161

Wajcman, Judy, 26–27

Wedding Dash. See Dash games

Whiteness, xi, xii, xiii, 6, 7, 8, 12, 28, 30, 31, 57, 58, 121–22, 123, 127, 139, 148, 165, 166, 167, 170, 171, 172, 178, 179, 188n2, 194n16

Wirman, Hanna, 11, 94

Wissinger, Elizabeth, 133, 136

Wolf, Naomi, 158

Words with Friends, 14, 39, 45, 46, 56, 92, 117

work. *See* labor

World of Warcraft, 10, 136, 138, 168, 178, 189n23

Xbox, 10, 12, 119, 121, 162

Youda Jewel Shop 2, 77

Zagal, Jose, 63, 66

Zynga, 14, 46, 62, 65, 78, 79, 81, 82. *See also Ville* games

Shira Chess is assistant professor of entertainment and media studies at the University of Georgia in the Grady College of Journalism and Mass Communication. Her research has been published in many journals, including *Critical Studies in Media Communication, New Media and Society, Games and Culture,* and *Feminist Media Studies.*